HALIFAX
Special

HALIFAX Special

Bruce Robertson

LONDON

IAN ALLAN LTD

Contents

First published 1990

ISBN 0 7110 1920 7

Published by Ian Allan Ltd, Shepperton, Surrey; and printed by Ian Allan Printing Ltd at their works at Coombelands in Runnymede, England

Front cover:
The BIII was both numerically and operationally the most important version of the Halifax and introduced the change from in-line Rolls-Royce Merlin engines to the Bristol Hercules radial engines. MZ454 flew successively with Nos 424, 431 and, as shown, 425 Canadian Squadrons of No 6 Group. It was lost in a crash due to excessive icing in March 1945.
Cover artwork, Peter G. Cooksley

Rear cover, top to bottom:
The original contract for two prototype Handley Page HP56 bombers specified two Rolls-Royce Vulture engines, changed to four Merlins as type HP57. Completed at Cricklewood the month war was declared, the first, L7244, was dismantled and re-erected at Bicester for its first flight, 25 October 1939 in the form shown; it ended its days as instructional airframe 3299M.

Production Halifaxes were finished in the Temperate Land Scheme for night bombers with anti-searchlight black undersurfaces and a disruptive pattern of dark earth and dark green uppersurfaces, with mainplane and tailplane leading and trailing edges dictating the demarcation line. L9619 depicted, an early production BII serving with No 10 Squadron, was abandoned by its crew who were lost and it fell at Keld in Yorkshire after only 10 flying hours.

The BVI, a more powerful version of the BIII, is represented by NP763 of No 346 *Guyenne* Squadron, one of two Free French squadrons operating Halifaxes in No 4 Group. This aircraft survived the war, being sold as scrap in 1949, but many of the BVIs operated by the Free French went to the re-constituted French Air Force.

The Royal Egyptian Air Force acquired 14 Halifax Mk IXs which it numbered 1150-1163. Deliveries were made in standard Bomber Command finish, but the green-brown uppersurfaces were replaced later with brown and mid-stone. For ferrying to Egypt the aircraft were temporarily marked with British civil registrations, 1163 shown being G-ALVH.

1941: Into Service **5**

1942: The Slow Build-up **11**

1943: Expansion and Attrition **18**

The Nightly Hazard **27**

1944: The Peak Year **31**

Coastal Commitment **39**

Airborne Operations **44**

Halifax Nose Art **50**

1945: Re-equipment and Disbandment **56**

Postwar Phaseout **62**

Technical Treatise **69**

Basic Data **76**

Variants **77**

Production and Disposal 1939-52 **78**

Bomber Command Halifax Sortie Statistics **79**

ACKNOWLEDGEMENTS

The author gratefully acknowledges the assistance given directly or indirectly by the following individuals: A. Andrews, Chris Ashworth, G. Bailey, Chaz Bowyer, M. J. F. Bowyer, Tony Cartwright, E. F. Cheesman, W. R. (Bill) Chorley, Peter G. Cooksley, H. C. Coverley, T. E. Eagleton, Jonathan Falconer, J. O. Friend, L. Greenham, B. Gurr, J. J. Halley, R. A. Hobbs, M. Levy, Ken A. Merrick, Ray Punnett, K. M. Robertson, W. Russel, Alison Scadeng, D. C. Smith, J. Stanley, D. Sutton, H. S. T. Usher, G. Zwanenburg; and the following organisations: Australian War Memorial, Imperial War Museum, Ministry of Defence, Public Archives of Canada, Royal Air Force Museum and Short Bros & Harland Ltd.

1941: Into Service

The role of the Handley Page Halifax, one of the mainstays of RAF Bomber Command's strategic air offensive, was eclipsed by the Avro Lancaster and understandably so. It was inferior in performance to the Lancaster and in the late war years inferior in numbers, as well as having a higher proportional loss rate. AVM D. C. T. Bennett, who commanded the Pathfinder Force, summed it up as 'not as good as the Lancaster, but nevertheless did a sound job of work' and he revealed that his Commander-in-Chief, Air Marshal Harris, heartily disliked it, which may go some way to explaining why wartime publicity rarely

gave the type its due. Bomber Command was in the process of phasing out the Halifax when Germany collapsed.

The criteria for assessing the operational worth of a bomber is by the weight of bombs that it drops. Operational research statistics show the Halifax to have made less than half the Lancaster's contribution in this respect, for in the final analysis of Bomber Command's offensive, only 23.5% of the total bomb tonnage was dropped by Halifaxes to 63.7% by Lancasters. However, these percentages resound to the Halifax's credit if viewed another way. They mean

Left:
The first prototype Halifax L7244 when undergoing basic handling and performance trials with Rolls-Royce Merlin X engines fitted with duralumin-bladed de Havilland variable pitch propellers. *AM10234 D&G*

5

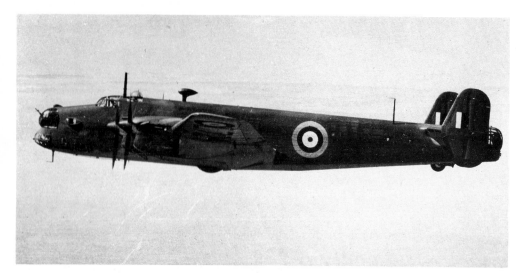

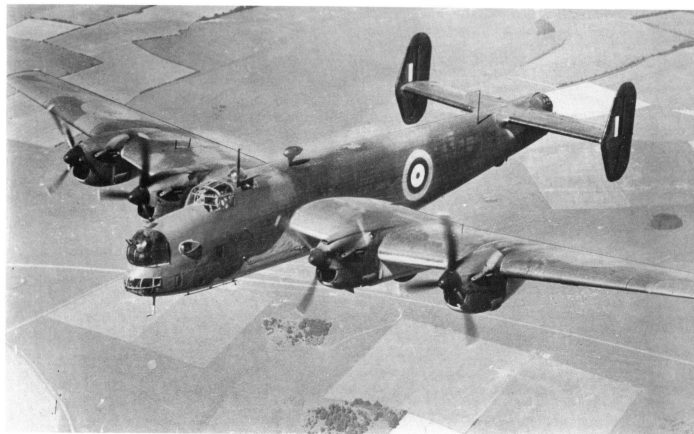

that the Halifax's contribution in Bomber Command's offensive was, excepting the Lancaster, greater than all the other types of aircraft in the Command put together – and that included Battles, Blenheims, Bostons, Fortresses, Hampdens, Manchesters, Mitchells, Mosquitos, Stirlings, Venturas, Wellingtons and Whitleys. This makes the Halifax a very important aircraft in the history of World War 2. Also, unlike the Lancaster, which was almost exclusive to Bomber Command, the Halifax served in Bomber, Coastal and Transport Commands at home, and overseas in Commands in the Near, Middle and Far East.

The Halifax had evolved from Air Staff plans for two bombers defined by Air Ministry Specifications B12/36 and P13/36 for respective four- and twin-engined bombers with 45000 and 55000lb bomb load capacity, Handley Page, tendering design HP56 for a twin-engined Rolls-Royce Vulture-powered bomber, received a contract for two prototypes on 30 April 1937. Due to a delay in the development of the Vulture engine, an alternative of a four-engined Rolls-Royce Merlin version was proposed later in that year.

Before the prototypes had evolved, a production order for 100 of the Merlin-engined version, designated HP57, was placed by the Air Ministry on 7 January 1938 to their Specification 32/37. The name Halifax was agreed, but not immediately divulged, at

Right:
L9485, the first production Halifax, additionally featured dorsal and ventral armament for trials, in this case Boulton Paul 'C' & 'K' turrets which were omitted or removed from many production aircraft.
Ken Merrick

Below:
L9515, an early Mk I, was retained at the Aeroplane and Armament Experimental Establishment (A&AEE), Boscombe Down, as trials aircraft for a series of improvements until late in 1943 when it became an instructional airframe.
RAF Museum (RAFM) P6829

that time. While the firm tooled up for bulk production the first hand-crafted prototype, L7244, was completed at the firm's Cricklewood works in late August 1939.

For trials of the heaviest bomber so far produced by Handley Page, their own airfield at Radlett, with a maximum of 750yd runway, was considered inadequate. The Air Ministry allotted RAF Bicester in Oxfordshire for its tests to where the prototype was taken by road in a dismantled state. After re-assembly and taxying trials the first Halifax took to the air on 25 October 1939. Following intensive trials at the Aeroplane and Armament Experimental Establishment at Boscombe Down, L7244 went to Radlett,

which had been expanded, for modifications. The second prototype, L7245, the first fully armed Halifax, flew from Radlett on its initial flight on 17 August 1940, and from 11 October that year the production Halifaxes were also taking the air from Radlett.

It is not always appreciated that the Halifax commenced operations a year before the Lancaster. The Stirling, which had preceded the Halifax into operational use by a month, received all the publicity for the introduction of four-engined bombers by the RAF; in any case the introduction of the Halifax into No 35 Squadron was not auspicious. Aircraft trickled in from production early in 1941 with a series of teething problems resulting in temporary groundings.

FINKENWARDER AERODROME.
HAMBURG.

On the night of 10/11 March 1941 the squadron was ordered to put up seven aircraft, to join eight Blenheims, in an attack on shipping at Le Havre. As it was, only six aircraft could be readied. Of these only four found the primary target but after crossing the British coast on the return there was stark tragedy. A British nightfighter pilot, knowing well enough that the new four-engined Stirling had a large single fin, was not apprised of the twin-finned Halifax and so shot L9489 down near Aldershot.

Just two nights later three Halifaxes made a token appearance over Germany, joining 85 aircraft which included four Manchesters also making their debut over German territory. These two aircraft types were in the same category for although the Manchester was twin-engined by configuration, it was deemed four-engined by power since its Rolls-Royce Vulture engines were each of 24 cylinders; in fact the Vulture had been specified in the original P13/36 Air Ministry Specification for the Halifax. But, with its four 12-cylinder Merlins, and in spite of its many problems, the Halifax was already showing potential superior to the Manchester, and to the Stirling which at that time had yet to attack a target inside Germany.

So much then depended on the success of the Halifax that Bomber Command, after sending another two Halifaxes to the same target the following night, decided first to eliminate the operating snags and at

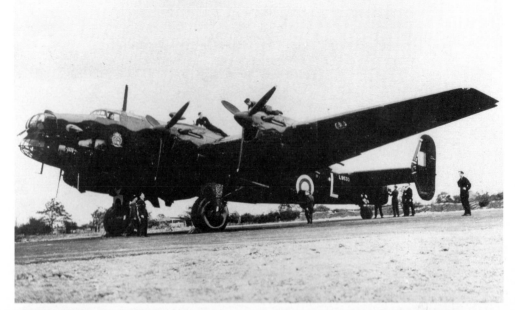

Left:
Halifaxes first attacked Germany on the night of 12/13 March 1941 following it up the next night, in both cases joining other bomber types in attacking Hamburg. This is one of a series of photographs sent to No 35 Squadron, taken by a photographic reconnaissance Spitfire on 14 March following the second raid to show damage and cratering.
K. M. Robertson Collection

Above right:
Delivered to No 35 Squadron, the first Halifax unit, L9530 later became MP-L of No 76 Squadron, the second Halifax unit where it was flown by Plt Off C. Cheshire, brother of the famous Leonard Cheshire VC, who became a prisoner-of-war when the aircraft was lost over Germany on 12/13 August 1941. *RP6200*

Right:
Two of the force of 18 Halifaxes over Brest on 18 December 1941. It was persistent attacks such as this that finally caused the Germans to risk the dash through the Channel to take the warships named to the relative safety of German ports. *Mol*

9

The great bulk of a Halifax, towering over a civilian Piper Cub Coupé impressed for RAF liaison duties. Propeller blades, it will be seen, were yellow-tipped as a safety measure to make the extent of the arc more visible when they were revolving.

the same time use the squadron to train personnel for No 76 Squadron re-forming with the Halifax. Apart from five of No 35's aircraft attacking Kiel on 15/16 April, the Halifax was not again operational until the night of 11 June when nine attacked Duisburg.

The first exclusive four-engined bomber raid to a single target, the chemical works at Huls, followed the next night involving 11 Halifaxes with seven Stirlings. In general, less than a dozen Halifaxes operated at a time for the rest of June. At the end of the month six were sent out in daylight to attack Kiel, to use cloud cover which proved to be non-existent. They reached their target safely but after encountering heavy flak at Kiel and persistent attacks by Messerschmitt Bf110s causing one loss and damage to others, Halifaxes reverted to night attacks.

Until the end of 1941 the two squadrons operated on average once a week, sending out from one to 14 bombers to join in night attacks on German cities including Berlin and once to Turin. While further daylight sorties over Germany were not considered practicable, Bomber Command's support for the war at sea necessitated attacks on the French ports. With the *Scharnhorst* at La Pallice on 24 July an unescorted Halifax force of 15 attacked the port in daylight encountering flak and fierce fighter opposition. Direct hits damaged the German battle cruiser for the loss of five shot down and the rest sustaining damage in varying degrees. Another Halifax was lost on 18 December attacking Brest in concert with Stirlings and Manchesters which fared worse. Finally on 30 December, 16 Halifaxes in an exclusive raid on Brest lost three of their number and sustained damage in most of the others.

Experience in these daylight attacks brought out the poor view to the rear from the astrodome, so that the rear gunners were appointed crew fighter controllers for the future.

1942: The Slow Build-up

At the beginning of 1942 less than half the 84 Mk I Halifaxes built had survived operations and crashes, but the Mk II with more powerful Merlins was in production and replaced the Mk Is in Nos 35 and 76 Squadrons. The build-up of the Halifax force started with three (Nos 10, 78 & 102) Whitley V and two Wellington II (Nos 158 & 405) squadrons converting to Halifax IIs in the first half of the year. This was all within No 4 Group, which for logistical purposes was a Merlin-engined aircraft group, with a planned policy to convert completely to the Halifax by the end of the year.

With the Lancaster then unproven, it fell to the Halifax and Stirling to carry out special raids. To bomb the *Tirpitz*, then reported in Trondheim fjord, nine Halifaxes and seven Stirlings went out the night

Above left:
The year 1942 brought the Halifax Mk II into general service, re-equipping existing squadrons. R9441 shown was delivered to No 35 Squadron and later served in No 102 Squadron. *Via M. J. F. Bowyer*

Left:
W7676 came from a later batch of Mk IIs and was delivered to No 35 Squadron; it differed slightly in finish with regard to the demarcation between upper and lower surface painting.
Via J. J. Halley

Left:
No 405 Squadron was the first Canadian unit to receive Halifaxes, represented here by W7710 LQ-R.

Right:
Lost in the attempt to bomb the *Tirpitz* on the night of 27/28 April 1942, W1018, abandoned by its crew after crash landing on a frozen lake in Norway, sank and remained underwater for 31 years until a UK expedition had it floated to the surface by attached air drums and towed ashore for eventual display at the RAF Museum, Hendon. The missing mid-upper turret was found to be in a nearby house.
H. S. T. Usher & MoD

of 29/30 January to find the battleship, but only two reached its area. The dash of the German battle cruisers *Scharnhorst* and *Gneisenau* with the cruiser *Prinz Eugen* through the Channel to Northern ports on 12 February brought Bomber Command's largest daylight operation up to that time. Although only 13 Halifaxes participated in this abortive attempt to stop the ships, the aircraft had already played their part in forcing the Germans to remove them from the French ports.

At night only small numbers of Halifaxes were called out at intervals, but unusual was an attack by six on the night of 21/22 February on airfields in Norway as a diversion for a fleet aircraft strike. Most attacks were to German targets, but 20 joined in bombing the Renault factory at Billancourt, west of Paris.

On the last night in March an all-Halifax force of 34, the largest to date, sought once again to disable the *Tirpitz* that, in the event, could not be located. These special Halifax operations were coming to an end, for that March the Lancaster, evolved from the failure of the Manchester, commenced operations and on 17 April made their famous daylight raid across the heart of Germany to strike at Augsburg.

When 31 Halifaxes set out on 27/28 April to bomb the *Tirpitz* and other warships in Trondheim fjord, they were accompanied by Lancasters. It was on this attack that Wg Cdr D. C. T. Bennett was shot down, but managed to escape back to Britain via Sweden; W1048, one of the four Halifaxes lost, is now the sole surviving example of its type, and can be seen at the Bomber Command Museum, Hendon.

Air Chief Marshal Sir Arthur Harris having taken over Bomber Command on 22 February, made the grand gesture of a 1,000-bomber raid on the night of 30/31 May. Calling for a maximum effort and by bringing in training groups and other commands, 1,092 sorties were flown, 131 of them by Halifaxes to

the main target – the city of Cologne. Many of the Halifax crews participating were operating for the first time. Two nights later, while the '1,000 Force' was still alerted, and to convey the impression to the enemy that such raids could be sustained, 127 Halifaxes joined 827 other bombers in an attack on Essen. But after an attack of similar magnitude involving 124 Halifaxes on the night of 25/26 June, attacking Bremen, the Halifax force was spent for a period.

Losses, damage and a series of engineering snags affecting serviceability had reduced Halifax availability for operations. During July the numbers of Lancasters operating exceeded those of Halifaxes. Then, with the formation of the Pathfinder Force, No 4 Group lost its prime squadron, No 35, to the new Force on 1 August.

Overseas, the reliability of the Merlin engines was in question. While the Lancaster remained home-based throughout the war years, in July the Halifax became the only British-built four-engined bomber to operate from overseas bases. Nos 10 and 76 Squadrons provided detachments, totalling 32 Halifax IIs, staging through Malta to Aqir in Palestine, from where they bombed Tobruk and other North African ports. In September the two detachments were amalgamated to form No 462 (RAAF) Squadron, but there was no surplus of Halifaxes on strength as the majority had to be sent to servicing units with engine troubles.

Back in the UK during September the Halifax returned in force on operations to a variety of targets. On the first night of October, Bomber Command tried sending each of the three types of four-engined bombers to different targets. While 27 Lancasters went to Wismar to attack the Dornier works and 27 Stirlings raided the submarine pens at Lübeck, 27 Halifaxes attempted to bomb similar pens at Flensburg which proved an absolute disaster. The flak

KÖLN

defences had been greatly strengthened and the Halifaxes, coming down to 2,000ft, flew through a hail of shrapnel. Twelve of the force failed to return.

For the rest of 1942 only on two occasions did the Halifax force go out in numbers exceeding 50. The build-up in production was not being carried forward into operations. One reason was the call of other Commands on bomber aircraft types and Harris, realising the virtues of the Lancaster, was willing to sacrifice Halifaxes when forced to forgo some of his promised bomber aircraft.

With the possibility of the H_2S radar navigational and bombing aid becoming a production fitment, Handley Page had been asked in mid-March 1942 to prepare the prototype installation in a Halifax. V9977 made the first H_2S experimental flight from Hurn on 16 April, but power supply problems thwarted the test. However, next day the possibilities of the new instrument were revealed when towns were indicated from 8,000ft. The Telecommunications Flying Unit, taking over the aircraft, had testing in hand when on 7 June it caught fire at 500ft, and crashed at Welsh

Bickner killing six scientists, the crew and an RAF liaison officer.

Frantic efforts were made to prepare a further prototype set for installation in W7711 that July. Several months elapsed before sets were ready for service trials on Halifax W7808 by the Bomber Development Unit at Gransden Lodge and again there was a set-back. On H_2S high level trials over Liverpool Bay on 15 November an internal coolant leak caused an engine fire. The pilot instructed the crew to prepare to abandon the aircraft, bringing the plaintive response from one crew member that he had not got his parachute, engendering an unsympathetic 'Hard Luck' from another member.

Mindful of the valuable equipment, as well as the unfortunate crew member, the pilot prepared for an emergency landing. The two navigators and the flight engineer dismantled the H_2S components, bringing them to the rear escape door. RAF Kimbolton had been alerted and with flames playing around the port wing the Halifax was brought safely down while the crew brought out the equipment.

Left:
The centre of Cologne in wartime shortly before the 1,000-bomber raid that started the destruction of the city. The famous cathedral, which suffered only minor damage, can be seen by its plan view in the shape of a cross to the right of the Hohenzollern bridge over the Rhine (centre) by the railway station that was later devastated.
K. M. Robertson Collection

Right:
Following the Cologne attack, a heavy raid was made on Bremen. While the Focke Wulf factory was the aiming point for the Lancasters, Halifaxes were given the docks and shipyards as their main target.
K. M. Robertson Collection

Above left:
To improve performance by reducing weight and drag, nose turrets on many Halifaxes were removed. The first 'Z' fairing fitted by Tollerton Aircraft Services was made on W7776 shown, ex-NF-L of No 138 Squadron, making it the first Mk II Srs I (Special).
Via J. J. Halley

Left:
By late 1942 Halifaxes were operating in the Middle East. These in the main had the faired noses.
Australian War Memorial (AWM) ME701

Above:
Seemingly a motley crew – as indeed No 462 (RAAF) Squadron's personnel were at first – with British and Australian detachments, using a mixture of tropical and temperate wear including service and side caps and bush hats. *W. Russel*

Right:
H₂S was pioneered in Halifaxes. Its value depended much on the skill of the operator interpreting the indications on his plan position indicator (PPI) which might look something like this photograph of an H₂S PPI indication during H₂S trials.
K. M. Robertson Collection

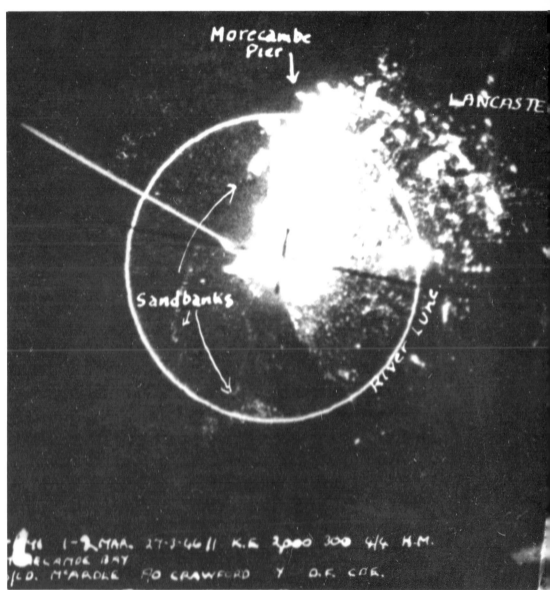

1943: Expansion and Attrition

From early 1943, Halifaxes were frequently out mining, usually a relatively safe operation, but it was their misfortune to lose four of a force of 78 on this task on 9/10 January. On the 14th, six were sent in daylight to Leer, using cloud cover, but their target could not be located.

Canadian bomber squadrons were being transferred to a new No 6 (Canadian) Group. While most of their squadrons operated Wellingtons, three had been equipped with Halifaxes by the beginning of the year when the new group officially formed. Their Halifaxes first operated on the night of 14/15 against Lorient, starting an attempt to render French ports untenable to German warships, particularly U-boats. There were a series of nine attacks on Lorient in five weeks, involving 527 Halifax sorties. In the docks the torpedo and ship's stores buildings were destroyed and hulks used for work on U-boats were sunk.

H_2S was first used operationally on the night of 30 January when six of the 13 H_2S-equipped aircraft participating were Halifax BIIs of No 35 Squadron. The target, Hamburg, was shrouded in cloud. Although the sets were plagued with snags, two Halifax crews marked the target by their new instrumentation. The system was proven, improved and ordered in quantity, but there were delays before its fitting was extended to the Main Force where Lancasters had priority. On the last night of February attacks switched to St Nazaire, interspersed with Halifaxes operating against targets in Germany with over 100 sorties per night at times.

It was not only the RAF that flew Halifaxes — and not only men. The Air Transport Auxiliary made 9,326 ferry flights with Halifaxes from factories and maintenance units. A Halifax was loaned to the organisation for instructional use of Class V ATA pilots, the men and women authorised to fly four-engined aircraft. On 10 April, Flt Capt R. H. Henderson was about to land his Halifax when the 'up' lock of the undercarriage leg broke off, locking the leg up. Breaking off his approach, the pilot put a pupil on the controls while he armed himself with the crash axe to force the wheel down. First he chipped away the back of the rest bunk to make a hole in the fuselage wall above the leg and then succeeded in coupling up the emergency manually operated undercarriage lowering system, to make a safe landing.

The period March to July was known as the Battle of the Ruhr, but Halifaxes at times ranged further afield, sometimes with drastic results. When the

Left:
DT497, 'E' of No 462 (RAAF) Squadron, operating in the Near East from 1942 onwards, seen at Fayid, Egypt. *J. Stanley*

Above right:
Queenie, Mk V LK640 SE-Q of No 431 Squadron at Tholthorpe, Yorks, 1943 was lost later that year on 19 November, attacking Ludwigshafen.
Jonathan Falconer Collection

Right:
Early in 1943 the Mk V entered service, differing from the Mk II only by change of undercarriage from a Messier to a Dowty unit. One of the first Mk Vs, DG235 shown, served in No 408 (RCAF) Squadron.
AM 10962/RAFM P6833

26140

Skoda armament factory at Pilsen was targeted on the night of 16/17 April, not only was the wrong factory attacked, but 18 of the 130 Halifaxes participating were lost.

In the first half of 1943 there were nine Halifax ditchings. For this eventuality the Halifax carried "Q" Type dinghy stowed in the port mainplane with normal capacity for seven crew. From a total of 64 aircrew involved in the Halifax ditchings, 41 were saved by the air/sea rescue services. The rescue of the crew of a No 102 Squadron Halifax early on 5 May, returning from Dortmund, made history by entailing the first use of the airborne lifeboat. This, dropped from a Hudson, landed about 200ft downwind of the crew's dinghy.

That June, for the first time, over 200 Halifaxes set out some nights. The next month was notable for its heavy attacks on Hamburg, but additionally Bomber Command allotted the destruction of some smaller towns to the Halifax force. Over half the 374 aircraft detailed to attack the German border town of Aachen on 13/14 July were Halifaxes. The town, an important railway junction with some factories had some 3,000 buildings destroyed causing a massive exodus; it cost 20 aircraft, 15 of them Halifaxes.

Two nights later the Peugeot Works at Montbéliard were the designated target for an all-Halifax attack. With No 35 Squadron of the Pathfinders joining the Main Force from No 4 Group, the force totalled 165. Although conditions were favourable, the target was mis-identified. Photographic cover later showed only seven buildings in the extensive works were hit — but the nearby Montluçon Dunlop factory, an important tyre-producing plant, was severely hit and stores were set on fire. Later it was learnt through the French Resistance that seven million tyres, ready for transporting to Germany, had been burnt.

For the raid on Remscheid, visited for the first time on the night of 30/31 July, Halifaxes again led in numbers with 95, to 87 Stirlings and 82 Lancasters. Over three-quarters of the town was devastated, its price for having a steel industry specialising in forgings, particularly aero engine crankshafts.

In the final attack by bombers from Britain on Italian cities, conducted on the night of 16/17 August mainly by Stirlings, the target marking of Turin, home of the Fiat works, was an exclusive Halifax affair by No 35 Squadron. In the ground marking plan, the blind markers, whose crews relied on instruments, were to drop red indicators, while those marking visually would use yellow, and backing up crews green. Because of a haze over the target all six visual markers were scattered over five miles apart. By taking the centre of the reds as the aiming point the centre of this industrial town was assumed, but it was outlying districts that suffered.

The need for Bomber Command to bomb Italian targets had passed as, with the North African campaign over, bombers in the Middle East could concentrate on Italian and Balkan targets. These included the Halifaxes of No 462 (RAAF) Squadron and for six months of the year the Halifax IIs of No 178 Squadron.

The night of 17/18 August brought the first of Bomber Command's raids against the V-weapon menace when the experimental establishment of Peenemünde was heavily attacked, in which 218 of the 596 sorties were by Halifaxes. Among the six Pathfinder squadrons were two Halifax units. No 35 Squadron supplied two aiming-point shifters and two

Above left:
Production by Halifax contractors was well underway in 1943. Here the BIIs of No 10 Squadron are from production by the London Passenger Transport Group and the English Electric Company; they were still delivering Mk IIs with front turrets mounted.
Imperial War Museum (IWM) CH7900

Left:
L9613 an early BII with No 138 (Special Duties) Squadron based in the UK on detachment at Fayid, Egypt, during 1943.
H. Levy

Right:
Serving with No 462 (RAAF) Squadron in the Middle East, W7971 ended up crash-landing on Malta after sustaining battle damage on 7 November 1943.
Via Chaz Bowyer

Left:
A photoflash shot taken during a heavy night raid showing scattered incendiary bombs burning and flashes from the explosions of HE bombs.
K. M. Robertson Collection

Below:
A scene at Dalton, Yorkshire, in mid-1943 with a BV of No 428 (RCAF) Squadron in the foreground. *Via M. J. F. Bowyer*

Below right:
Battle damage sustained by a Halifax after an encounter with a Messerschmitt Bf110 over Berlin on the night of 23/24 August 1943. *Via Chaz Bowyer*

backers-up, plus two non-markers which meant that they operated purely as bombers; No 405 (RCAF) Squadron supplied the Deputy Master of Ceremonies, two aiming-point shifters, four backers-up and five non-markers.

A series of heavy attacks on the German capital started on the night 23/24 August with 727 bombers being detailed, 251 of them Halifaxes from which 23 failed to return. It was not a promising start for the Battle of Berlin as the main weight of bombs fell several miles from the aiming point. The official PFF narrative of operations ruefully stated that useful damage was done, but the main credit for that was due to the Germans for building their capital so large! Four nights later, of the 221 Halifaxes participating, 11 were lost attacking Nuremburg in another off-target attack; indeed, the official report stated that the Main Force followed the PFF and exaggerated the errors in marking to an appalling extent.

For München Gladbach, the target for 30/31 August, 185 Halifaxes took the air, including those with the PFF. No 405 Squadron, converting to Lancasters, operated for several weeks both Lancasters and Halifaxes for target marking, but their activity was thwarted that night. An expected westerly wind was in fact a strong NNW wind that blew many crews, less experienced than the Pathfinders, off course. The very next night it was a Berlin raid which the Pathfinders officially expressed as a complete failure; the cost in Halifaxes alone was 20.

Such were the losses being sustained by Halifaxes and Stirlings that the next Berlin raid was an all-Lancaster operation, but 195 Halifaxes sent to Mannheim on the night of 5/6 September proved a textbook attack for the Pathfinders.

Ten nights later over 200 Halifaxes were the Main Force for a return to Montluçon. The initial bombing was so accurate that the target became obscured by thick black smoke from burning rubber. Halifaxes were also predominant the following night on Mondane where marshalling yards and the main line on the France to Italy rail route were damaged in the bright moonlight conditions.

Throughout the rest of September, all October and into November a major target was attacked every few days involving Halifaxes averaging around 200 sorties per raid. The period was also the peak of the Battle of Berlin with eight separate attacks up to the end of the year. While the first was a Lancaster only raid, 248 Halifaxes with a lesser number of Stirlings went to Mannheim. The next Berlin attack on 22/23 November, involving 234 Halifaxes, was the last raid in which Stirlings were sent to bomb German targets, leaving the Lancaster and the Halifax as the main heavy bombers. From then on Berlin was the main target for the Lancasters while Leverkusen, Frankfurt, Stuttgart and Leipzig were among the towns raided by Halifaxes.

Above left:
In the quest for the carriage of heavier bombs by the Halifax, V9985 was retained on trials with bulged bomb doors.
Via Ken Merrick

Left:
By the end of 1943, after a year of operating in the Mediterranean area, some veteran Halifaxes were notching up sizeable sortie records – 44 as evinced by the one nearest the camera. *Via Chaz Bowyer*

Above:
Late production BIIs introduced a perspex nose, rectangular fins and revised radio equipment which dispensed with fuselage masts; also many were delivered with H₂S installed as seen by the ventral bulge scanner housing on JP228, destined for service overseas. *MAP 12586C*

Right:
In World War 1, caterpillar tractors were introduced for towing Handley Page 0/400 bombers. The four-engined bombers of World War 2 were moved by John Brown or Fordson tractors. Here a towing is viewed through the perspex nose of an early Halifax.
IWM C14457

26

The Nightly Hazard

Over 2,000 Halifaxes succumbed to the German defences and failed to return, while many others that did return received damage putting them out of commission permanently or temporarily. But in addition to the havoc they wrought – in company in the main with Lancasters – upon German industry and morale, the immense diversion of manpower, armament and equipment that they caused to be diverted to defence, that might have been used for offence, should be appreciated.

Below:
Along the enemy coast from Norway to Biscay there was a chain of radar watching stations to give an early warning of an incursion of German-controlled airspace. This, the nearest enemy radar station to Britain at Cap Blanc Nez, is shown as photographed by a No 168 Squadron Mustang, on 31 July 1943. An earlier attempt to bomb the station is seen to have caused a cliff fall.
K. M. Robertson Collection

Observatory

Site of the most Easterly TARGET (Giant Wuerzburg)

View looking South East

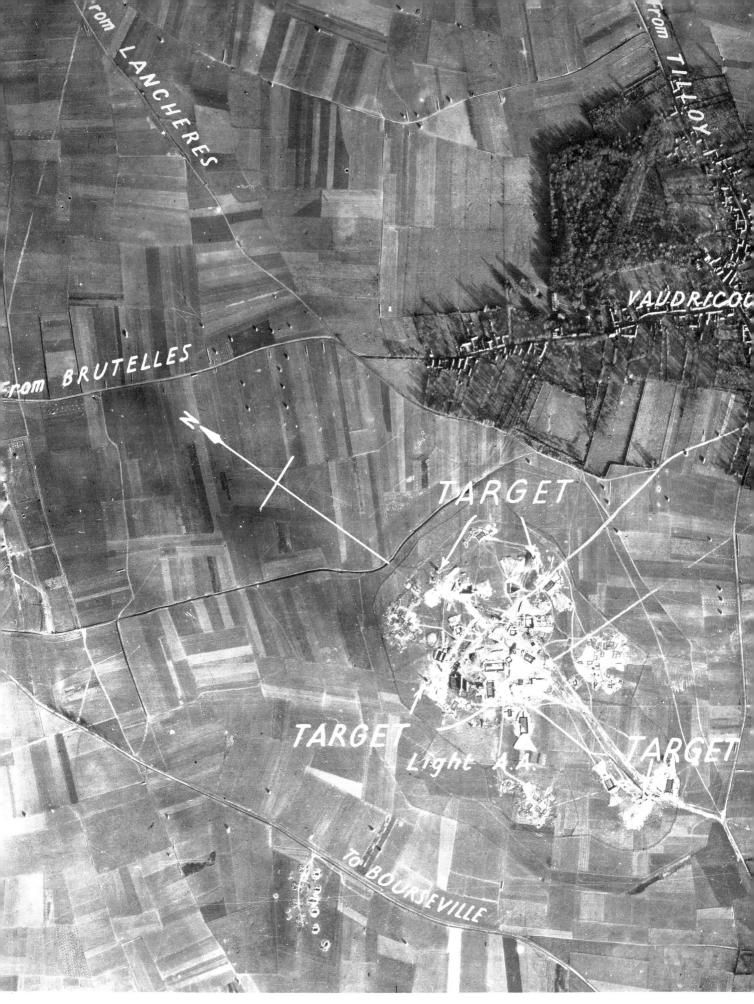

Facing page and Bottom left: Inland from the enemy coast were aircraft reporting stations with a series of radars to track the bomber streams. The Abbeville/Vaudricourt aircraft reporting station is shown as it appeared from the air in 1943, and drawn in plan view. Marking on both were made at the time when it was deemed an important RAF target. The village of Vaudricourt was a few hundred yards east of the station.
K. M. Robertson Collection

Left: Also along the enemy coast were belts of heavy and light anti-aircraft guns.
K. M. Robertson Collection

Below: At the coast and inland, with concentrations near centres of industry, searchlights were located. Many of these were radar-directed and acted as markers for other lights to cone the bombers to enable the fighters to close in for the kill.
K. M. Robertson Collection

Bottom: Luftwaffe officers at a fighter control desk of a reporting centre.

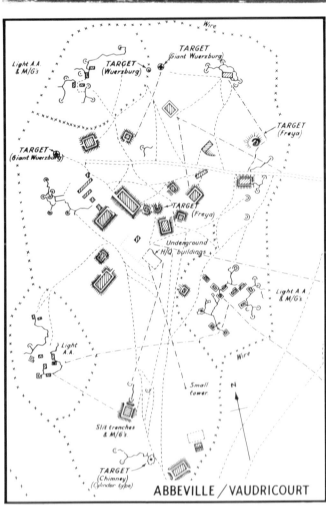

ABBEVILLE / VAUDRICOURT

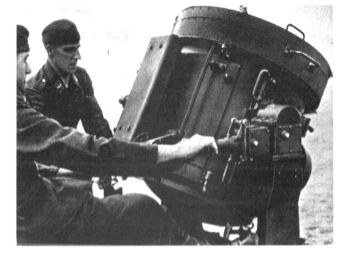

29

Above:
Once ground control alerted their fighters to the direction and height of the bombers, it was up to the fighter crew to fly to the area and make an interception aided by their airborne radar, evinced by the nose antenna on this captured Heinkel He219A-5 *Uhu* (Owl).   *ATP*

Right:
In moonlight conditions, non-radar equipped aircraft such as this Messerschmitt Bf109G-3 nightfighter could be directed through its FuG 16z radio from a controlling centre.
Messerschmitt AG Foto: 045

Below right:
The tragic result of the co-ordinated enemy defences, a Merlin engine with its large shrouded exhausts from one of seven Halifaxes lost raiding Stettin on the night of 20/21 April 1943.   *Museet for Deinmarks Frihedskamp*

1944: The Peak Year

The new year opened with a stand-down for Halifaxes in general, a break helping the introduction of the new Halifax III. First deliveries had been made the previous year bringing production difficulties in the change from Merlin to Hercules engines, involving modification to engine nacelles, instruments, installations and systems.

Halifaxes returned to the fray in force on the night of 20/21 January with Berlin the target, but whereas 13 of the 495 Lancasters participating were lost, 22 of the 264 Halifaxes failed to return. Flak was reported as remarkably light for this important target, so it was assumed the losses were mainly due to fighters. Next night was even more disastrous with 35 Halifaxes failing to return from Magdeburg. Thus the next Berlin attack on 27/28 was left to Lancasters and Mosquitos with just 21 pathfinding Halifaxes attacking Heligoland as a diversion. But next night 241 Halifaxes were committed to Berlin where flak was heavier than usual and, judging by the flares put up by the defences, fighters were also active resulting in 26 Halifax losses. For the following attack on the capital, two nights later, only 82 Halifaxes were detailed.

For a fortnight the heavy bombers were given a break, apart from small numbers out mining, in preparation for the final large onslaught on Berlin in which the largest force to date of Halifaxes participated, a total of 314 of which 17 were lost. Four nights later, 19/20 February, one of the highest loss rates was experienced by Halifax crews when 34 of the 255 despatched to Leipzig failed to return. Winds, much lighter than forecast, had resulted in Main Force crews arriving before Pathfinders marked the target, necessitating orbiting over a heavily defended area.

Bomber Command, analysing the losses, concluded that the deficiencies of the defence and performance of the Merlin-engined Halifax, the Mks II and V, made them unsuited to long-haul heavily defended targets and they were not called upon again to venture over Germany.

Harris, having brought his Command up to its peak strength, sought to improve its quality. But while all Halifax manufacturing plants were changing over to the Mk III, it had to fit in with the Ministry of Aircraft Production scheduling. Up to mid-1944 there was still an output of the Merlin-engined versions, although these were mostly delivered direct to Heavy Conversion Units (HCU) or off-set to meet the demands of other Commands. At this time Bomber Command operated 10 HCUs with an average establishment of 32 Halifaxes and some five other HCUs had previously operated Halifaxes.

For the rest of February's operations Halifax numbers were down; 126 to Stuttgart, 169 to Schweinfurt and 123 to Augsburg in raids that were predominantly by Lancasters. After an attack on Stuttgart on 1/2 March, Halifaxes were made the lead aircraft for attacking targets in France. Typical was the attack on Meulan les Mureaux factory and airfield where Messerschmitt Bf109 components were made and Bf108 communications aircraft assembled and tested. The 117 Halifaxes seriously damaged the factory. By the end of March, in attacks on major targets such as Berlin and Essen, Halifaxes were once more operating at 200-plus strength, rising to over 250 in April.

During May the Halifax force went over from area bombing to specific targetting in attacks on marshalling yards, locomotive depots and coastal gun positions in France as a prelude to the invasion of the Continent. With short-haul targets including railway yards as close as Boulogne, the original Merlin-engined Halifaxes could be fully committed. Losses on these attacks were relatively light, but there were exceptions. When a force of 105 Halifax IIIs from No 4 Group attacked the marshalling yards at Trappes on the night of of 2/3 June, 15 were lost.

The night preceding D-Day, 5/6 June, Halifaxes were allotted coastal gun battery destruction at Houlgate, Mont Fleury, Maisy and Sallennelles. From the 412 sorties, there were two lost and three damaged.

Harris soon switched back to strategic bombing. Attacking Sterkrade in the Ruhr, 22 of the 162 Halifaxes were lost and others sustained damage from flak and fighters. Again the night of 28/29 June, a force of 183 Mk IIIs, with 19 of the increased span Mk VIIs just coming into service, lost 18 mainly from fighters in the Paris area as they returned from attacking railway yards at Metz and Blainville.

During July rail centres in France were still an occasional target for Halifaxes interspersed with mining and supply dropping to Resistance parties. The Halifax IIs and Vs of No 138 and 161 Squadrons had been carrying out these Special Duty tasks since 1942. A major change mid-month was a switch to V-weapon targets, where hardly any flak was experienced and enemy fighters were foxed by a 50-plus Halifax force providing a diversionary flight over the North Sea. On one of these attacks, when Nos 4 and 6 Group Halifaxes were allotted different launching sites, reconnaissance next day revealed that No 4 Group had missed its target by a mile at least, while No 6 Group's bombing was practically all on target.

Armament and gunnery problems persisted. As the Halifax Force prepared to return to long-haul targets, training was intensified at HCUs with ciné gyro gunnery and night fighter affiliation exercises. These facilities evidently paid off for No 4 Group had a Command record for July of 34 enemy aircraft claimed destroyed of which all but one was confirmed. Ventral defence continued to be a problem with a .5in mid-under turret proving unsatisfactory until No 77 Squadron at Full Sutton took the matter in hand and produced a better balanced gun mounting and improved comfort for the gunner. At Driffield a rear turret was modified to permit the gunner to wear a pilot type parachute to facilitate quicker evacuation in an emergency.

A challenging task came on the night of 23/24 July when No 4 Group Halifaxes represented a sixth of the 600-strong force attacking Kiel, a surprising target for the short summer night, chosen as the bulk of the Luftwaffe's night fighters in the west had moved to the Low Countries. The enemy was further confused by another 100 Halifaxes crossing the Brittany coast to bomb an oil refinery at Donges where 10 large storage tanks were destroyed. Yet another 52 Halifaxes went to Les Catelliers to attack a lanching site and still the Command could put up 69 Halifaxes to join Wellingtons from OTUs in creating a diversion over the sea. The following night again involved Halifaxes in over 300 sorties.

Flying bomb sites continued to be attacked with Harris's decision during August that flying bomb targets would be in the province of Nos 1, 4 and 6 Groups only. But the night of 7/8 August attacks were made in the land battle area to smooth the way for the advance of the 1st Canadian Army, that later overran the V-weapon sites freeing the Halifax force for attacks on oil targets.

As an experiment, for the 379 strong attack on Brunswick, the night of 12/13 August, the 137 Halifaxes involved were all H2S equipped, with the object of bombing by instruments without involving the Pathfinder Force. While the majority bombed by H2S, others with unserviceable equipment bombed by estimated time of arrival or like many, by the glow created by the first arrivals. As a result the effectiveness of the H2S could not be properly assessed.

As prelude to the renewed night offensive; 1,004 aircraft — 385 of them Halifaxes — attacked enemy fighter airfields in the Low Countries by day on 15 August. Once more Halifaxes provided about a third of the forces operating almost every night over Germany with the occasional diversion by day to attack strong points holding out along the French coast. In a maximum effort to swamp the Le Havre defences, 426 Halifaxes were directed in a single day to bomb strong points, later the Calais area received attention on five different occasions.

In the final quarter of 1944, it was an almost complete return to the hard slog of systematically destroying German towns to cripple their industries. But it was notable for the Halifax force in that on many nights more Halifaxes participated than Lancasters; on peak nights up to 425 Halifax sorties were flown. Also, as evidence of the weakening of the German defences, 338 bombers — 248 of them Halifaxes — attacked German airfields in daylight on Christmas Eve.

Overseas, at Celone in Italy, No 462 (RAAF) Squadron had been renumbered No 614 Squadron (its original number was given to a new squadron in Bomber Command) to take on a pathfinding role, lighting the way by flares, among other things, for the mining of the Danube. In the Special Duties role, No 624 Squadron with Mk IIs and Vs covered from Italy a wide orbit of supply dropping from Southern France to the Balkans, being joined in this work by Halifaxes that partially equipped No 148 Squadron.

Left:
Taken on D-Day, 6 June 1944, a Halifax is pictured over a heavily cratered part of the Pas de Calais area. *MoI*

Centre left:
Halifaxes of No 425 (RCAF) Squadron at Tholthorpe where, late in 1943, the unit had exchanged its Wellington Xs for Halifax BIIIs.
Via M. J. F. Bowyer

Below:
A lucky escape for the crew of BIII MZ307 HD-B of No 466 (RAAF) Squadron: the aircraft swung on take-off at Driffield, 17 September 1944, causing the undercarriage to collapse, crushing the bomb-bay and scattering its bombs. *RAAF*

Right:
Overseas BIIs were still operating long-haul bombing and supply missions, such as JP246 of No 148 Squadron shown which crashed at Brindisi, Italy, on 8 October 1944. *RAFM P9947*

Above:
In 1944 Halifax BIIs of No 148 Squadron became part of the Balkan Air Force flying supply missions to partisans in Yugoslavia and the beleaguered resistance fighters in Warsaw. Personnel of the squadron are here seen with officers of the Russian element of the Force. *IWM CH18442*

Left:
After a Hercules failed on MZ987 of No 578 Squadron returning from attacking Essen, 12 December 1944, the pilot was forced to crash-land at Wormingford, a USAAF fighter base near Colchester, with this result. *Ken Kemp via Jonathan Falconer Collection*

Right, top to bottom:
An all-round look at a BIII on the ground and in the air. MZ359 of No 77 Squadron survived the war and was scrapped in 1947. *ATP151, 154, 155, 159 & 368*

Below:
Although LV776 and LV838 –
BIIIs re-engined with Hercules
100 engines to become BVI
prototypes – flew from late 1943,
production output did not start
until August 1944 when airframe
deliveries from Handley Page
went to store to await engines,
60 of them never to be flown.
MAP 11702B

Bottom:
LL599 of No 462 (RAAF)
Squadron was fated to be lost in
collision with Lancaster LM691
during return from a raid on
Essen, 23 October 1944.   *RAAF*

HALIFAX B. MK
HERCULES.
MAY 1944.

Coastal Commitment

Within the scope of Bomber Command operations the Halifax had played a notable part in the war at sea, both by bombing enemy ports and mining enemy waters. They played their part in the 'Mining Blitz' of 27-29 April 1943 when, within 48hr, 1,051 mines were laid from the Gulf of Danzig down to the Spanish frontier. Overall, in Bomber Command, Halifaxes made 3,716 mining sorties laying 9,572 sea mines. During the critical stage of the Battle of the Atlantic in 1942 a Lancaster squadron had been transferred temporarily to Coastal Command for anti-submarine patrolling. After return to its own command, further squadron transfers were requested resulting in the Halifaxes of No 405 (RCAF) Squadron moving from Topcliffe in Yorkshire to Beaulieu in Hampshire from 25 October 1942 to 1 March the following year, and No 158 Squadron providing detachments. During that time, in 365 sorties of arduous patrol work, 11 U-boat sightings were made and on three occasions attacks resulted.

It also appeared that Halifax crews could look after themselves. During an anti-submarine patrol in the Bay of Biscay on 9 December, Halifax 'N' of No 405 Squadron was attacked by a formation of three Ju88s that fortunately attacked piecemeal. The rear gunner got the first to attack, sending it down with smoke pouring from an engine. The second, going in from the port quarter and persisting in side attack, gave the mid-upper gunner three chances to get in bursts before it broke away with smoke billowing to make a controlled ditching. At this the third Ju88 gave up the fight and flew off.

Coastal Command pressed for an allocation of Halifaxes from production to replace their ageing Whitleys. By March 1943 Nos 58 and 502 Squadrons were fully operational on Halifax GRIIs with a programme for installing Mk III ASV search radar. Based on Holmsley South and St Eval for operations over the Biscay area, they faced attack by Luftwaffe aircraft. On one occasion BB276 'F' of No 58

Above left:
A number of BIIs were converted to GRII standard. JD376 shown served as a bomber in No 78 Squadron and No 1663 HCU before conversion for general reconnaissance work.
MAP 1366 1D

Left:
When Halifax Mk III production was well underway, numbers were allotted for coastal work. NR187 shown, after service as a BIII in No 102 Squadron, went to No 111 OTU at Nassau, demonstrating the use of H_2S as a navigational aid in showing coastlines in bad visibility.
Via J. J. Halley

Squadron was under attack for 47min by seven Ju88s, yet reached base with only minor damage. In fact later coastal Halifaxes were generally better armed than bomber versions. Browning .5in nose guns were carried to reply to surfaced U-boat fire and as a ventral H$_2$S dome was not applicable, an FN64 underturret could be fitted.

Up to October 1943 the two squadrons made 115 U-boat sightings and No 58 Squadron in May 1943 recorded 15 sightings and 13 attacks with Torpex depth charges. Shipping attacks were mainly in the province of the Beaufighter and Mosquito squadrons, but on Christmas morning 1943, a strike force of eight Halifaxes from No 502 Squadron was sent out to prevent a blockade runner, escorted by destroyers, from reaching its French port destination. Tactics changed during 1944 to night patrols, dropping flares on receipt of ASV contact, and attacking with 600lb anti-submarine bombs using the Mk XIV bombsight.

Halifaxes of No 58 Squadron were credited with the destruction of three German U-boats and an Italian submarine during 1943, and No 502 Squadron sunk one U-boat in 1943 and another in 1944. This was by no means their total contribution to anti-submarine warfare, for on many other occasions they made sightings leading to U-boat destruction by other aircraft or surface ships. Their very presence on patrol restricted enemy submarine activity to a degree that it would not be possible to compute.

In the late summer of 1944 Nos 58 and 502 Squadrons moved to Stornaway with the particular task of distrupting enemy shipping in the Skagerrak and Kattegat between Denmark and Norway. These forays continued until the end of the war in Europe, 99 attacks by night being made in March 1945 alone, including two direct hits on the SS *Isar* of 9,000 tons carrying 1,500 German service personnel.

Weather forecasting had become a vital factor in planning operations. The Hampdens performing this task had been vulnerable to French-based enemy aircraft and those in No 517 Squadron were replaced by Halifax Mk Vs in mid-1943; also, a new meteorological squadron, No 518, formed that summer with Halifax Mk IIIs. These Halifaxes had a specially equipped meteorological observer's station, radio altimeters to enable more accurate measurement of pressures, Gee or Loran for accurate positioning in measuring high level winds, and Mk II ASV for bad weather homing assistance. One Halifax Met Squadron flew sorties on all but two days in a year.

These Met Squadrons had a vital part to play on 4 June 1944 in the weather predictions for D-Day. While the initial landings on the Continent of Europe were being made on the morning of 6 June, a Halifax was ditching some 700 miles off Land's End with a drama taking place to effect the saving of its crew. The Met Squadrons were disbanded in 1946, but the Cold War in the late 1940s brought them back into operation.

Above left:
Many sighting attacks were made on a suspected periscope wake or oil slick.

Left:
On rare occasions a U-boat might be caught on the surface and attacked before it could dive as in this Halifax attack.
AMPR C3575

Above:
Delivered from production via No 44 Maintenance Unit (MU) as a METII to No 518 Squadron, where it is seen in Northern Ireland in 1944, LK966 was ditched off Portugal after an engine failure on 24 November 1944 when serving with No 520 Squadron.   *J. O. Friend*

Right:
A No 517 Squadron Halifax ditched in the Atlantic where it remained afloat for some seven hours.   *IWM C5462*

41

Left:
JP328, a GRII, served with both Halifax Coastal Command squadrons, Nos 502 and 58 in turn, and is seen here in 1944 with the former. *M. J. F. Bowyer*

Below left:
The Halifax carried a self-inflating 'Q' type dinghy for its crew.

Bottom left:
Several Halifax aircrew were rescued by airborne lifeboats dropped by Hudsons or Warwicks and courses were arranged for aircrew to train in their handling, as seen here on the Norfolk Broads. *ATP 834*

Right:
The U-boat menace over: surrendered U-boats in Kristiansand Sound photographed by an aircrew member in Halifax V9-H of No 502 Squadron, 19 May 1945.
K. M. Robertson Collection

Below:
Serving postwar in No 202 Squadron on meteorological duties, Halifax METVI RT923 hit a BABS (Blind Approach Beam System) vehicle causing the undercarriage to collapse, 6 September 1949.
RAFM P1742

Bottom right:
The Mk XIV Bombsight system fitted in many Bomber and Coastal Command Halifaxes:
1 Suction pipe, **2** Air supply, **3** Sight cock, **4** Exhaust, **5** Static, **6** Pitot, **7** Pipe stowage, **8** Distribution box, **9** DR Compass connection, **10** Switchbox, **11** Suppressor, **12** Fusebox, **13** as 7, **14** Flexible drives, **15** Air drier, **16** Computer, **17** Sighting head.

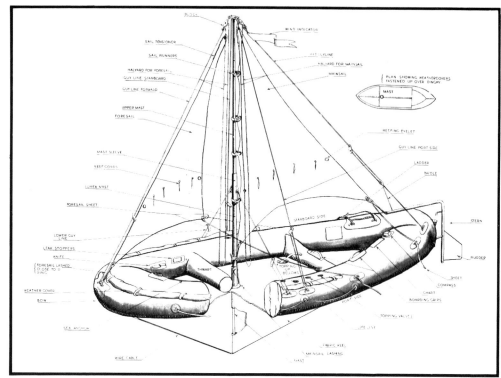

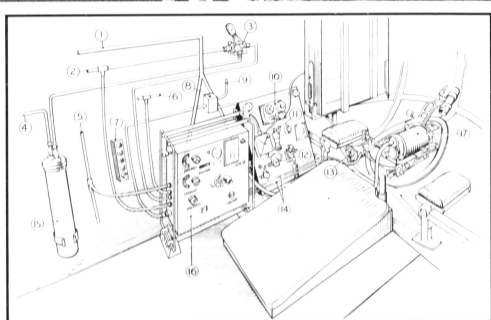

Airborne Operations

As part of the preparations to provide an airborne force of 5,000 paratroops and 5,000 gliderborne troops a training centre, the Central Landing School (later Establishment), was opened at Ringway, 19 June 1940. The aircraft were such Whitleys as could be spared from their main requirement as bombers, the policy being that Bomber Command would supply the aircraft for any assault by airborne troops. With the Whitley as the standard paratrooper and glider tug, it was No 4 Group of Bomber Command that had this airborne secondary task, and by the replacement of its Whitley by Halifaxes the latter was brought into the airborne role.

The first Halifaxes allotted to the Air Landing Establishment arrived in mid-October 1941 for parachute dropping trials, as a result of which crew escape hatches were modified for paratrooping on production lines to comply with the No 4 Group airborne commitment. Other Halifaxes were involved in glider towing with up to three Hotspurs on tow by a single Halifax. While the twin-engined Whitley was capable of a short-haul Horsa tow, a Halifax, or similar four-engined aircraft, was essential for any long-haul. With the Lancaster showing promise as the prime bomber and the Stirling's fuselage lending itself more conveniently to paratrooping, this left the Halifax as the obvious choice for glider towing.

Moreover, for the new Hamilcar light tank carrying glider, only a four-engined aircraft could tackle its short-haul.

First of the airborne operations involving the Halifaxes, ended in stark tragedy. Warned of Germany's quest for an atomic bomb for which 'heavy water' was being produced at the Norsk Hydro Plant in Norway, plans were in hand to land two sabotage parties in Norway to wreck the plant. Contact had been made with Norwegian resistance groups who were supplied with Eureka beacons to place at two landing spots. Three Halifaxes, one a spare, were fitted with Rebecca transmitters to home on to the Eureka sets. Towing two Horsas the Halifaxes moved to Skitten, a satellite of Wick airfield, as the jumping off point. The two Halifax/Horsa combinations, each carrying a party of 16 Royal Engineer officers and men, took-off on the evening of 19 November 1942. After crossing the Norwegian coast the tow of one combination broke and the Halifax tug crashed into hills killing the crew. The glider too, crash-landed killing three of the occupants while the rest were captured and shot within hours. The other combination suffering severe icing, had the tow break under the weight and the Halifax returned to Skitten with little fuel to spare. Meanwhile the glider had crashed on top of a snow-covered mountain killing the officer

Left:
The first of the operational gliders for the airborne forces, this Horsa I, is shown with towline to the Halifax connected to attachment points under the wings. *MoI CH7785-WK*

Top right:
A group of three Horsa Is under tow. In the later Mk II, the towline from the Halifax was changed to a single line attached to the Horsa's nosewheel.
K. M. Robertson Collection

in charge and two senior NCOs. Of the remainder, four severely injured were sent to hospital by the Germans and subsequently poisoned by the Gestapo; the rest were shot.

The build-up in Bomber Command during 1942 from four to 11 squadrons equipped with Halifaxes, mainly by rearming Whitley squadrons, had meant that the Whitley, still in production, could equip the new squadrons forming in No 38 Group to support the airborne forces without call upon No 4 Group. But an increase in the small Halifax element was also required. For while the training of the force centred in the UK, the hub of actual land operations in the midwar years was in North Africa and the Middle East. The 1st Airborne Division and the 1st Airlanding Brigade arrived by sea in North Africa during the spring of 1943. While they were being supplied with Waco Hadrian gliders from the USA, there was a requirement to move Horsas to the Force by air; a task that only the Halifax could perform.

No 295 Squadron was given the task to arrange the ferrying of 36 Horsas to Salé in French Morocco. There were delays in modifying the Halifaxes for towing and training crews. As good navigation was essential, navigators were supplied by Coastal Command. To reduce glider drag to the minimum, in view of the maximum fuel load carried, the undercarriages were jettisoned after take-off and a spare undercarriage was carried for fitting after arrival.

In the invasion of Sicily seven Halifaxes drawn from Nos 296 and 297 Squadrons participated in Operation 'Ladbrook' to capture Syracuse and again in Operation 'Fustian' to secure a bridge over the River Simeto. In both cases they towed Horsas. No 295 Squadron then returned to England to ferry back more gliders.

For the invasion of the Continent the No 38 Group requirement was for four Stirling, four Albemarle and two Halifax squadrons. The Halifax element was met by Nos 298 and 640 Squadrons with 18 plus 2 tug aircraft and 70 Hamilcar and 50 Horsa respectively glider establishment. An added complication was that for Hamilcar towing the Merlin 20s of the Halifax

Mks II & V had to be replaced by Merlin 22s. The Halifax then represented an eighth of the air element of the Airborne Force on D-Day and this proportion was maintained for the Arnhem operations of 17-22 September that year.

With the tide of battle in Europe nearing Germany, the Airborne Forces bases were relocated in East Anglia to reduce their length of haul in future operations. Nos 298 and 644 Squadrons were moved to Woodbridge and Nos 296 and 297 Squadrons at Earls Colne had their Albemarles replaced by Halifaxes. It was planned to increase Halifax squadron establishment in the force to 35 aircraft and an allocation of 50 Mk IIIs was requested. These were being delivered to the squadrons when Operation 'Varsity', the airborne assault element in the Rhine crossing of 24 March 1945, was launched with Halifaxes providing a quarter of the British airlifting aircraft.

There were a series of small operations involving supplies and reinforcements to special forces behind enemy lines. The final wartime operations of the force involved the reoccupation of Denmark and Norway. Nine Halifaxes joined 43 other aircraft in Operation 'Schnapps', the conveyance of personnel and equipment of the 1st Airborne Division to Copenhagen starting on 8 May with following re-supply flights. This was followed by Operation 'Doomsday', the conveyance of troops and supplies for the takeover of Norway from the Germans. The Halifax element was limited to Mk IIIs and the few Mk IIs in use. They proved unsuitable for the task as being basically bombers, they had not been designed to land with heavy freight and fuel loads. As sufficient fuel had to be carried for the flight back, some of the freight was carried in parachute containers stowed in the bomb bays and dropped before landing.

In the Far East, the ubiquitous Dakota was the main aircraft for airborne operations, but a Halifax AVII element was planned. No 298 Squadron was in the process of flying out to India when the Japanese surrender came in August 1945 and No 644 Squadron, scheduled to follow, stayed in the UK.

Left:
Largest of the operational gliders was the General Aircraft Hamilcar which only the Halifax could tow. Here one of the two prototypes is under tow.
RP2727

Below:
A line-up of Hamilcars marked up with 'Invasion Stripes' and on the left the Merlin 22s of a Halifax II that supplied the power to tow them.
CEB 293-25 for GAL

Right:
A Hamilcar exhibiting its large hold in which a Tetrarch light tank could be airlifted by a Halifax. *ATP*

Below right:
On the eve of D-Day, two lines of Hamilcar gliders, each headed by a Horsa, are sandwiched between the Halifax II tugs of Nos 298 and 644 Squadrons at Tarrant Rushton. *MoI CL26-XP*

27.

Left:
A shot taken from a Halifax Mk II while on a supply mission to Arnhem. This gives a good idea of the length of tow between a Halifax and a Horsa.
Sqn Ldr R. A. Hobbs

Below:
A Halifax, with a well decorated nose, taking off with a Horsa in tow.   *CEB 6028-3*

Right:
Halifax AVII NA414 of No 298 Squadron demonstrating a supply drop in 1946.

Below right:
Halifax AIX RT841 of No 1 Parachute Training School exercising paratroops postwar.

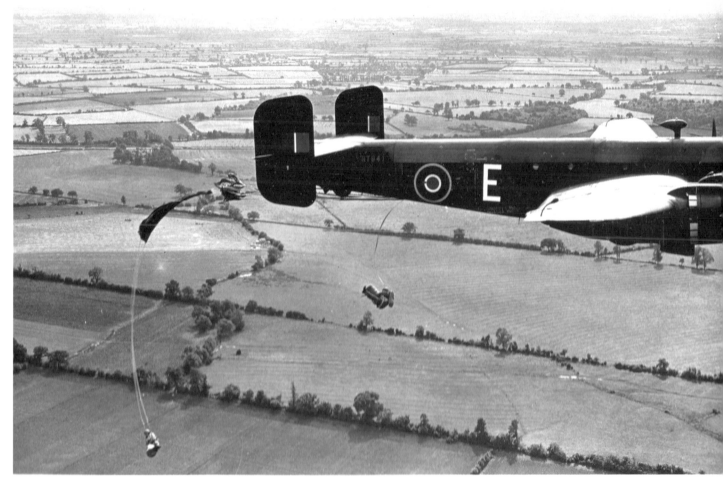

Halifax Nose Art

Many aircraft were given unofficial names and insignia by their crews. In the case of the Halifax, only one was officially individually named as Halifax. This was L9608, the last production Mk I, named by Lady Halifax at Radlett on 12 September 1941. In Bomber Command it became usual to denote each bombing sortie by a bomb silhouette on the nose.

Below left:
This insignia of the ugly duckling
speaks for itself on the gaunt
faired nose of a BII.

Right:
Named after the notorious Ned
Kelly this insignia on BIII NA169
HD-E of No 466 (RAAF)
Squadron was painted by the
crew's wireless operator who
took account of his captain's
name, Flt Lt S. P. Kelly.
via Ken Merrick

Below:
Vera the Virgin showing
evidence of 49 conquests for BIII
MZ516 MP-V of No 76
Squadron, from which only three
of its crew escaped by baling out
when it crashed at Tibenham,
Norfolk. *G. Bailey/D. Sutton
via Bill Chorley*

Left:
The most bomb-decorated Halifax, BIII LV907 *Friday the 13th*, was so-named from its delivery to No 158 Squadron on Friday 13 March 1944, and is seen exhibited in London during 1945. *ATP*

Far left:
A whimsical wish expressed on a BIII of No 467 (RAAF) Squadron. The swastika above the display of bomb silhouettes denotes an enemy fighter shot down.
Ken Merrick

Below left:
Classical comedy on this BIII of No 466 (RAAF) Squadron implying deeds not words, exemplified by this pyramid of bomb silhouettes which was compiled from the bottom upwards. *Ken Merrick*

Above right:
A macabre insignia on this Halifax named *Intuition* which, with 41 sorties, had operated more than the normal crew's operational tour set at 31 operations. *RAFM P8377*

Right:
A proud crew of their BIII, a veteran of 91 operations. LW172 HD-F of No 466 Squadron has, between Popeye and Olive Oyl, its name of 'Guts' reading down with 'Get Up Them Stairs' reading across. *T. E. Eagleton*

Left and Below left:
Jean, MZ335 a BIII of No 77
Squadron, shown from port and
starboard sides. *ATP*

Bottom left:
O-de-O, being 'O' of No 76
Squadron, has a neat display of
60 operations, but its serial
number cannot be confirmed.
*B. Gurr/L. Greenham
via Bill Chorley*

Below:
Roger de Coverley cannot be
traced, but it is known that Flt Lt
H. D. Coverley was taken
prisoner-of-war after operating
against Nuremburg on the night
of 30/31 March 1944.
H. D. Coverley via Bill Chorley

Right:
LW648 *The Black Prince*,
so-named in honour of its
Nigerian wireless operator.
Being 'A' of No 76 Squadron it
also carried the name *Achtung*.
The penultimate bomb symbol of
the top row is capped by a 'D' for
its D-Day coastal battery
bombing.
A. R. Andrews via Bill Chorley

Below right:
Unit insignia was strictly
forbidden on RAF aircraft, but
this BVI in French Air Force
service en route for Indo-China
(now Vietnam) in the late 1940s,
bears the insignia of the *1re
Escadrille* of the French bomber
group GBI/25. *M. J. F. Bowyer*

1945: Re-equipment and Disbandment

In the first two months of 1945 Halifaxes were committed to support Lancasters in the night bombing offensive. For the operations on the night of 2/3 January, while 521 Lancasters went to Nuremburg, 309 BIII and 42 BVII Halifaxes set out for Ludwigshafen. But with the start of the scale-down of the Halifax force they never exceeded that number on night operations again. However, the quality of the force was improving with the more powerful BVI replacing earlier marks.

From late February onwards there was an increasing number of day raids. In the final attack on Cologne, 303 Halifaxes dropped 963.5 tons of bombs on the city. But while losses by day were relatively small, there were occasional high losses in night raids.

As far back as August 1943, early marks of Halifax had been used on bomber support operations with No 192 Squadron and on 23 November that year a No 100 (Special Duties) Group had been formed to embrace squadrons on such special duties employing various electronic counter-measures. Among its 13 squadrons in 1945 it operated four (Nos 171, 192, 199 and 462 RAAF) using specially equipped Halifax IIIs.

It had long been feared that the Luftwaffe would attempt large-scale intruder operations over Britain as bombers returned to their bases in the early hours. This happened the night of 3/4 March, as 200 Halifaxes of No 4 Group returned from a successful attack on an oil refinery near Kamen without loss over the target. As the bombers neared their bases the intruding Ju88s, Me210s and Me410s struck. Halifaxes fell at Sledmore, Hibaldstow and Woodbridge and near Elvington, Skellingthorpe, Cranwell, Sutton Derwent and Knaresborough. Additionally a No 1664 HCU Halifax returning from a diversionary sweep fell at Boroughbridge and two further Halifaxes of No 100 Group fell near East Dereham and Little Snoring.

Two nights later, it was No 6 (RCAF) Group who were out of luck with icing conditions causing laden aircraft to crash on take-off; a Lancaster and seven Halifaxes being lost in this way, three of them from No 462 (RAAF) Squadron. One Halifax, apart from having six of its crew killed, caused civilian casualties when it fell at York.

With German defences weakening, the night raids were having a devastating effect. Halifaxes operated by day and night with force strengths up to around 300. As many as 332 Halifaxes were put up for the pounding by day of the naval base, airfield and town of the island of Heligoland. The final Halifax operation in force was a day attack on coastal batteries on the Frisian island of Wangerooge during 25 April. But the very last operation for Halifaxes was by No 100 Group aircraft over Kiel the night of 2/3 May

Left:
In the Far East Halifaxes of No 1341 Flight had a radio countermeasures role using specially modified BIIIs with an additional direction finding loop, seen housed aft of the H_2S blister; PN369 is shown.
IWM C5458

Right:
During the second half of 1945, Bomber Command flew 'Post Mortem' exercises to show ground crews and staff the devastation caused by the bombing campaign, and of which many photographs were taken. Cologne cathedral is seen standing virtually unharmed amid the destruction around; other views show wrecked areas of Coblenz (*Centre*) and Frankfurt (*Right*).
K. M. Robertson Collection

Frankfurt

in which two Halifaxes from No 199 Squadron were the last Bomber Command casualties of the war in Europe.

The run-down of Halifax bomber squadrons was dramatic. Of the No 4 Group squadrons, No 578 was disbanded before hostilities ceased and was followed within weeks by No 640. Eight, the bulk of the squadrons, were transferred in May to Transport Command to fly Dakotas, Liberators and Stirlings. Later the two Free French squadrons were transferred to the French Air Force and the group disbanded at the end of the year, by which time all four of the Halifax bomber support units had also disbanded. In No 6 (RCAF) Group, 12 of the original Halifax squadrons had converted to Lancasters by mid-1945, two others had disbanded and another had been transferred to Transport Command.

The Halifax still had a part to play in roles other than bombing and plans were for 20 as long-range transports, an equal number as medium-range transports and 50 for duty as meteorological aircraft with Coastal Command. However, at the beginning of 1946 only two Halifax transports were on strength and although 44 meteorological aircraft were held in Coastal Command, less than 20 were serviceable.

At the end of 1945 the Halifax as a bomber existed only in long-term storage to meet contingency plans. The actual holdings at the end of 1945 were:

Standard	Total	For storage	Remarks
BI	Nil	Nil	Declared obsolete June 1944
BII	114	Nil	All but two for scrapping
AIII	29	16	Ten held deficient of equipment
BIII	218	Nil	Majority awaiting scrapping
BIII H₂S IIB	235	24	Most awaiting scrapping
BIII H₂S IIC	3	Nil	Awaiting scrapping
MET III	48	27	Retained for service
BV	164	Nil	Being reduced to three
BVI	361	86	Retained for service
BVI (French)	24	18	For French Air Force
MET VI	6	3	All tropicalised
AVII	62	Nil	Disposal being considered
BVII	39	2	Disposal being considered
CVIII	54	22	Eight deficient of equipment
BIX	17	Nil	All under modification

The Merlin-engined versions were all declared obsolete two months later.

57

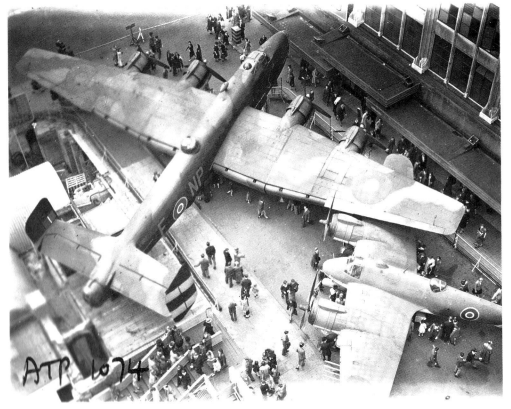

ATP 1074

Top:
With the war in Europe over, but continuing in the East, the quest was for transports. Here, in April 1945, NA195, an ex-No 10 Squadron BIII, is under conversion to a CIII.
MAP 13660D

Above:
In mid-1945 one of the prototype BVIs, LV838, was adapted as a CVI transport, but a problem was the small clearance between the ground and the freight pannier under the bomb-bay.
MAP 15151A

Left:
A Halifax near London's central shopping area: the Ministry of Aircraft Production held an exhibition of British aircraft on a bombed site off Oxford Street, to which pride of place was given to Halifax BIII LV907 *Friday the 13th. ATP 1047*

Right:
Based on the BVI, the CVIII was a purpose-built transport version of the Halifax with a lengthened faired rear fuselage.

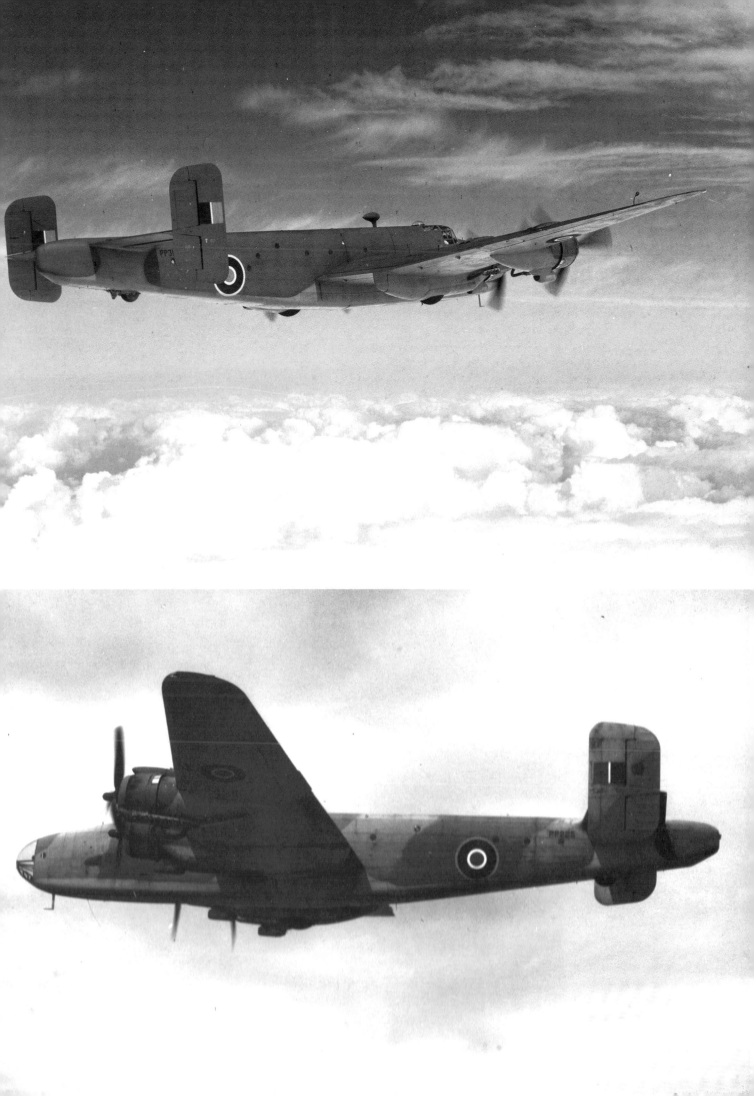

Below:
CVIIIs PP219 with pannier
attachment point under the
former bomb-bay position, and
PP332 of No 301 (Polish)
Squadron with pannier fitted.

60

Below:
A sure sign of hostilities ended, the re-introduction of aircraft serial numbers marked large under the wing as on this Halifax AVII of No 620 Squadron.

Bottom:
A marking feature of the CVIII was its light blue undersurfaces with, unlike bomber versions, roundels on this surface.

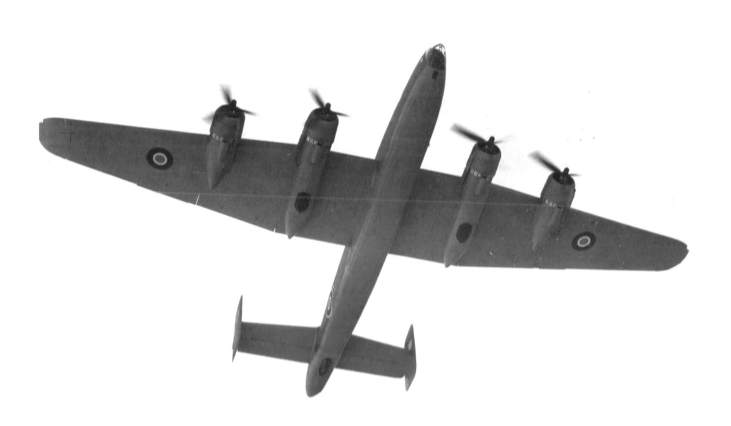

Postwar Phaseout

A postwar airborne force was initially planned with an establishment of 100 Halifaxes and 50 Stirlings, but as only 72 suitable Halifaxes were on hand the deficiency was made up with the holding of 98 Stirlings. However, with the RAF slimming rapidly, by March 1946 the establishment was changed to 25 each Halifaxes and Stirlings and by June to 35 Halifaxes only.

Transport Command was then the main Halifax user. Crews trained in No 4 (Training) Group on Halifaxes and Dakotas, types equipping No 38 Group, tasked with the development of transport support and mobility by air. Secondary tasks involved army paratroop training and advanced practice for glider pilots. The Halifaxes of No 297 Squadron in particular gave demonstrations to British and Allied army units. For general transport, No 46 Group of the command was established at 20/20 Halifax for long and medium haul.

During November 1946 an unusual mountain rescue attempt was ordered by a Halifax-Horsa combination when an American C-47 crashed on a glacier in the Swiss Alps. It was thought that the glider could bring in clothing and appliances to keep the survivors alive. The combination left Fairford for Orly to liaise with the American authorities. There, the Halifax captain flew over the glacier and judged a Horsa landing feasible, but fortunately a land party had by then reached the wreckage.

In the Levant where the United Nations had endorsed the unhappy burden of the Palestinian Mandate, Britain vainly tried to maintain the status quo between Arab and Jew. With such Jews as had survived the Holocaust in Europe clamouring for sanctuary in Palestine, which the Arabs were doing everything in their power to prevent, Britain's task was growing impossible and servicemen were being killed and maimed by terrorists. A decision in February 1946 to evacuate British women and children was achieved in two days by Halifaxes of No 113 Squadron flying 508 passengers with baggage from Aqir to Egypt. Worse was to follow with

Halifaxes wrecked as a result of Lancaster operations. As part of British measures to maintain the status quo, Lancaster GR3s engaged in sea searches to detect ships bringing in illegal Jewish immigrants and reporting their position to the Royal Navy to escort the ships away from the coast. For this reason armed Jewish terrorist organisations made determined attacks against RAF installations. On 20 February the radar of No 582 Air Ministry Experimental Station was blown up; five nights later, the RAF stations of Lydda, Petah Tiqva and Qastina were attacked simultaneously. Fortunately no RAF lives were lost, but aircraft losses included two Halifaxes destroyed and nine others written off damaged.

Later in the year when Halifaxes of No 113 Squadron took their turn at sea searches, security at their Aqir base was stepped up. In early December an attempt was made to bomb Air Headquarters (AHQ) Levant, situated opposite the Damascus Gate, Jerusalem. First a bomb was exploded at a nearby police billet, to cause a diversion, while a terrorist convoy of two taxis and a truck, all loaded with explosives, left to drive into the AHQ. However, this was thwarted by one vehicle, approaching at speed, hitting a road island and detonating its explosives, causing the other two vehicles to make off. That same month the Jewish Agency were asking the AHQ for help.

On 8 December an illegal immigrant ship, the SS *Athina*, foundered near the island of Syrina, with some 750 passengers; most reached the island in safety, but were bereft of their belongings. AHQ Levant on receiving a plea for dropping food, clothing and medical supplies, ordered three Halifaxes from No 113 Squadron to effect this which they achieved in spite of very poor weather. The Jewish Agency presented each crew with a crate of beer.

In March 1947, while Halifaxes of No 113 Squadron were joining Lancasters on sea patrols two vessels, *Abril* and *San Filipe*, were spotted at night. Alerted, the Navy boarded both ships but a third, the *Suzannah*, was not discovered until dawn, beached at Jaffa with people landing through the surf. This time it was the army that was alerted to cordon off the area. But this concluded the Halifaxes' part as the squadron was disbanded on 1 April.

In May 1948, Britain thankfully relinquished the mandate and the State of Israel was declared. Egypt, anticipating increasing conflict between Jew and Arab, built up its forces which included Halifax IXs.

Airborne Forces demonstrations had continued in the UK throughout 1947 with No 38 Group devising a standard form of support and mobility display using Horsa and Hamilcar gliders with Halifax tugs. Other types of demonstration were varied for the occasion, such as a representative paradrop from three Halifaxes in connection with the unveiling of a memorial commemorating the Bruneval raid.

That summer the British public at large saw more of the Halifax than ever before. On four occasions in July Halifaxes gave demonstrations at Blackpool, while on routine work over 6,000 parachute descents were made during the month and the Territorial troops of the 16th Airborne Division were exercised. In August the Army Cadet Force were shown Halifax-Hamilcar combinations while Exercises

Left:
After wartime service in Nos 431 and 434 (Canadian) Squadrons, this Mk III was switched in May 1945 to transport work with No 190 Squadron which that month had its Stirlings replaced by Halifaxes. *MoD H1247*

Right:
Serving with No 47 Squadron in 1946, this AIX went on to No 295 Squadron, ending its days by an undercarriage collapse whilst landing at Fairford on 3 February 1948.

'Blithe Spirit' and 'Long Drop' involved the 2nd Parachute Brigade and heavy equipment drops.

Up to the beginning of 1948, Halifax transports in Nos 47, 295 and 297 Squadrons were making training flights to the Middle East, but with the new Handley Page Hastings coming on to the scene, the Halifax went out of Command service during the year.

Following the partition of India and the emergence of Pakistan in 1947, a Pakistani purchasing commission in Britain chose the Halifax as a suitable bomber transport for which Air Tech Ltd received a conversion order. They were urgently needed for population exchanges and for supplying areas of besieged Pakistani peoples. The arrival in 1949 of six of the seven Halifaxes ordered greatly helped matters,

and they were allotted to No 12 Squadron where one was adapted to carry a spare Hercules engine. At critical times they were supplemented by three Halifax CVIIIs from Pakistan Airways. Halifaxes remained in service to 1954.

By that time the Halifax had also left RAF service. Although the wartime meteorological squadrons had been disbanded in mid-1946, the Cold War that developed in the late 1940s resulted in two squadrons, Nos 202 and 224, maintaining Halifax MET6s in service until the early 1950s. These, the last Halifaxes in service, were finally withdrawn in January 1952. Only when they had been scrapped was it realised that not one representative example of this famous aircraft type existed.

Left:
From July 1945 the Empire Air Navigation School (EANS) gave star names to its aircraft. Under the new peacetime coding system introduced in 1946, Mk VI *Sirius* ST814 depicted is 'B' of 'G-F' — the EANS code — in 'F' for Flying Training Command. *J. J. Halley*

Below:
A Halifax BVI of No 346 (French) Squadron awaits disposal postwar, still with its tactical day formating fin and rudder markings. *Ken Merrick*

Below:
Many of the former Free French BVIs went into French Air Force service where rudders were given Tricolour striping.
M. J. F. Bowyer

Bottom:
The long distance flights of the Lancaster *Aries* eclipsed the round-the-world flight of Halifax Mk III PN441, *Kerchal* of the EANS, seen here at Barrackpur, India.

Left:
Still in wartime finish, BIII
ex-NR169, once HD-T of
No 466 (RAAF) Squadron,
purchased by G. N. Wickner, is
seen en route to Australia where
it became VH-BDT.

Below:
BOAC had 18 civil CVIIIs for
service, plus one for spares of
which 12 were converted to
Halton standard as shown.
G-AHDU went later to other
airlines. *S&H J773*

Above right:
Civil Halifaxes were operated in
all five continents including a
number by European carriers.
Two were operated in Norway
by Vingtor Airways, the example
shown being ex-CVIII PP337.

Right:
Ex-LN-OAT is seen at the time it
operated on the Berlin Air Lift in
1949 as *Red Eagle* of Eagle
Aviation Ltd. *M. J. F. Bowyer*

Above:
A 2½ton Humber car being
delivered to Madrid from
Bovingdon in May 1948 by
British American Air Services.
170280 DAW

Right:
A surviving hulk at Radlett,
PN323, was used for radio
installation tests. *J. J. Halley*

Technical Treatise

In terms of cost and production manhours, the engines and their systems of a Halifax outstripped airframe manufacture. To a large extent Halifax production was dictated by engine availability. The Ministry of Aircraft Production had set great store by an early arrangement for the manufacture of Rolls-Royce Merlin engines in America to ensure a continuous supply for Halifaxes and Lancasters. When America came into the war there were initial fears that concern with Pacific fronts would affect supplies for Britain. As an insurance, Bristol Hercules production was increased. There was even a version of the Lancaster, the Mk II, built with Hercules engines and the Halifax went over completely to the Bristol engine. In spite of Bomber Command wishing to sacrifice Halifax manufacture for increased Lancaster production, the use of the Merlin in Spitfires and Mustangs being built in large quantities meant that if the Command was to reach its planned establishments for 1944, it could only be achieved by a continuing production of a Hercules-engined Halifax III.

The Bristol Hercules XVI was a 14-cylinder sleeve-valve, air-cooled, two-row radial engine of 5.75in bore and 6.5in stroke with 2,366cu in (38.7 litres) capacity. Besides its primary task of driving 3-blade Rotol constant speed, fully feathering propellers, each supplied power for the various aircraft systems as follows:

Port Outer: 1500W 24V AC Generator
Port Inner: 1500W 24V DC Generator, Pesco vacuum pump supplying instrument flying panel, Heyword compressor for pneumatic system including wheel brakes and RAE Compressor for the auto-pilot
Starboard Inner: 1500W 24V DC Generator (or alternatives with special radio installations), Pesco vacuum pump for Mk XVI bombsight, Lockheed pump for hydraulic system
Starboard Outer: 500W 24V AC Generator for radio installations

Unfortunately, the power to systems differed from the Merlin-engined versions, causing some confusion and necessitating a conversion period from Mks II to III almost as lengthy as squadrons changing to a completely new aircraft type.

Like the other four-engined bombers, the Halifax was a complex structure and it was for these aircraft that a new crew member had been introduced — the flight engineer. It was said, that if ever an aircraft needed a flight engineer that aircraft was the Halifax. He was the technical member of any crew, capable of advising, but not instructing, the pilot in the general operation of the aircraft. During flight he was expected to log data from the instruments for which Bomber Command had introduced their Form 10. On the ground, he was the liaison member between air and ground crews.

In conjunction with the pilot, the flight engineer controlled fuel distribution. The Halifax III had a 1,808gal capacity contained in six self-sealing tanks in each main plane. For each side, tank No 2 was in the leading edge of the centre-section, Nos 1, 3 and 4 between the engines and Nos 5 and 6 in the outer plane. As well as manipulating the cocks and checking readings there were the immersion pumps, normally delivering 350gal/hr, to check. As the fuel was used, an explosive air/petrol vapour could form in the emptying tanks. To prevent this the nitrogen system was brought into play, filling the empty spaces with nitrogen at low pressure, supplied from bottles held in the wing roots.

With such a fuel distribution and connecting Flexatex fuel pipes, there was the ever present threat of fire by damage from enemy action or heavy landing. Each engine had an extinguishing system of a Graviner bottle with perforated pipelines leading around cylinders and carburetters. An explosive cartridge, fired electrically, broke the seal in the bottle releasing the fire-dowsing methyl bromide driven out by the pressure of nitrogen in the bottles. Additionally, throughout the aircraft there were two large Type III and five small Type V portable hand extinguishers.

The Halifax was planned to have Messier undercarriage legs retracting backwards into the inner engine nacelles operated hydraulically, with auxiliary hand pumps, but when Rootes Securities joined the contractors producing the Merlin-engined Mk IIs in 1942, airframe production outstripped the output of Messier units, so that a Dowty system was accepted, as used in the Lancaster, which had already been tried

experimentally in Halifax L9250 in 1941. Mk II
Halifaxes so fitted with Dowty units became Mk Vs,
but were otherwise identical to the Mk IIs. Unfortunately, to facilitate production, Dowty substituted
forgings for castings which proved brittle and apt to
crack under heavy landings. As a result the Mk V was
limited to 40,000lb maximum landing weight.
Although initial deliveries from August 1942 were to
operational bomber squadrons (Nos 408 (RCAF) and
77 in that order), within two months the decision was
taken to deliver the bulk of Mk V output direct to
HCUs and use the Mk V for offsets from Bomber
Command to meet the needs of the Airborne Forces
and Coastal Command.

During 1943 with the mounting bomber offensive,
Bomber Command was compelled to put the Mk V
back into the first line, but in whatever unit, there
were a distressing number of accidents through
undercarriage collapses precipitated by any swing in
take-off or landing.

In the original Halifax specification, an 8000lb
bomb load was the maximum envisaged with 2000lb
bombs the largest to be carried. The Bomber
Command call for larger bombs meant that the
Halifax would need a larger bomb bay, a modification
difficult to effect with the needs for a ventral
armament defensive position and later H_2S housing.
The original Type A doors would not close on a
4000lb bomb and an alternative Type B door proved
unsuitable as did new Type C doors contracted out to
Evans Bellhouse and used on BIII/BVI production.
As a result the original Type A were fitted with new
hinges and side flaps as Type D doors. This allowed

Above right:
Halifax crews varied from six to
eight, although averaging seven
normally: pilot (top), flight
engineer (at rear), navigator,
wireless operator (below) and air
gunners.

Right:
Internal .303in ammunition
tracking in a Halifax fuselage.
Tail guns had a 1,700 rounds per
gun allocation, plus 4,000
rounds reserve. *IWM CH7899*

Facing page:
Twin-mounted Vickers gas-
operated guns in the beam
positions. *via Chaz Bowyer*

carriage of 4000lb on early production aircraft, but after 1942 the largest HE bomb carried operationally by Halifaxes was 2000lb.

An 8000lb bomb was fitted in the first production Halifax on tests at Boscombe Down in early 1942 and flown with partially closed bomb doors. A No 76 Squadron Halifax dropped an 8000-pounder on Essen the night of 10/11 April 1941 — the first and last time a Halifax dropped a bomb over 4000lb in weight in operations. Yet up to 1945, flight engineers were still being trained in procedures for partially closing the bomb doors on to the large block-busters to keep the Halifax force potentially capable of switching to the larger bombs. The fear at the time was that with the large amount of explosive going into the 4000lb bombs that Lancasters and Mosquitos were delivering, there would be a resultant shortage of the smaller bombs — a situation saved by Lend Lease supplies. During 1944-45 about half of all 1000lb bombs dropped by the Halifax force were of American manufacture.

Above left:
A Bristol B12 Mk I mid-upper
turret with four .303in
Brownings, fitted alternatively to
a Boulton Paul turret in a No 76
Squadron Halifax.
via Chaz Bowyer

Left:
Boulton Paul 'E' rear turret with
4 × .303in Brownings. *RP1704*

Above:
The Halifax was built in sections
which were mated together, this
being the central centre-
section. *ATP 759*

Right:
The Messier undercarriage leg
pictured here was appropriate to
all but Mk V Halifaxes. *ATP 761*

Left:
'This way in!' A test pilot points out the crew entrance hatch which opened inwards and upwards. *ATP 757*

Centre left:
The pitot head for airspeed indication, painted white, was directly below the bomb aimer's position. *ATP 145*

Bottom left:
In all plants producing Halifaxes a large percentage of the workforce was female, particularly in the spray-painting areas. *ATP 758*

Above right:
Maintenance was a job that had to be carried out in all conditions. A wintry scene at No 1663 HCU, Rufforth. *IWM CH12431*

Right:
Even in fine weather maintenance could be a hazardous job with the risk of falling 20ft on to a hard-standing surface. *Ken Merrick*

Basic Data

Wing span: 98ft 8in initially, 104ft 2in late production

Length: 69ft 9in initially, 71ft 7in from Mk II/V Srs 1A and 73ft 7in CVIII

Height (tail down, overall): 21ft 4in

Maximum loaded weight: 55,000-68,000lb according to mark and period

Speeds: Maximum varied from 250 to 305mph and economical cruising from 190 to 256mph according to mark

Range: From 920 miles with full bomb load to 2,650 miles with auxiliary tankage

Service ceiling: 18,000 to 25,000ft with maximum load according to variant

DEFENSIVE ARMAMENT

(*Note:* BP=Boulton Paul, FN=Frazer Nash, GO=gas operated)

Nose: BP 'C' Mk II turret with 2×.303in Browning machine guns in early bomber versions, replaced by gimbal-mounted .303in Vickers GO gun in the majority, but a .5in machine gun in most Coastal versions

Dorsal: BP 'C' Mk I, II or V turret with 2×.303in Brownings or BP 'A' Mk III Srs II or Mk VIII turret with 4×.303in Brownings, but no armament in this position for transports, glider tugs and many bombers where it was omitted to save weight and increase performance

Beam: Pillar-mounted .303in Vickers GO gun (one or two each side) initially on bombers and then normally only fitted when dorsal turrets were not installed. Not applicable to transports

Ventral: Nil in early versions except for first production then optional fittings of .303in or .5in machine guns in FN64 or BP 'R' Mk II turrets or single .5in Browning in Preston-Green mounting designed in service

Tail: Boulton Paul 'E' Mks I, II or III or 'D' Mk I Srs II turrets in late production was standard for all except the CVIII and certain other transport conversions

BOMB LOAD

Maximum load 7,500 to 15,000lb depending on bomb types and mark. Normally not more than two 4000lb or four 2000lb or six 1000lb bombs were carried in any one sortie, the rest being made up by smaller bombs. GR versions could take up to eight 250lb depth charges. For mining two 1500lb mines were carried per aircraft with three the maximum that could be carried. The bomb 'mix' was very varied as the actual operational dropping listing shows.

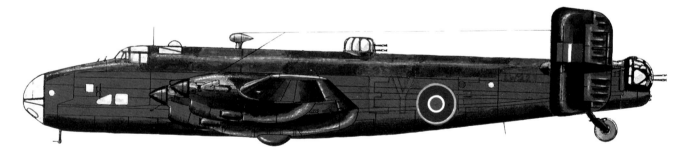

Above:
From early 1941 the non-reflecting black undersurfaces were extended to include all the aircraft except the strict plan view. This late production BII shows this variation in finish and in configuration by differing armament and the introduction of increased area rectangular fins. LW223 shown operated with No 78 Squadron from August 1943, flying a total of 144hr. *Peter G. Cooksley*

Right:
A directive was issued on 8 January 1943 that Halifax aircraft diverted for coastal work would have extra dark sea grey plan view surfaces. This was followed by instructions the following month that it was policy for coastal aircraft to have all but strict plan view surfaces in white, which was also appropriate for the aircraft of meteorological squadrons represented here by Mk V LL469 serving in No 517 Squadron *Peter G. Cooksley*

Variants

Designations					
Firm's	**Service**	**Power Units**	**Remarks giving basic progressive differences**	**Introduced**	**Declared obsolete**
HP56	Prototype	Vulture X	Twin-engined, 4-crew proposal	Project	—
HP57	1st Prototype	Merlin X	L7244 No armament	Oct 39	Aug 42
HP57	2nd Prototype	Merlin X	L7245 BP 'C' nose and BP 'E' rear turrets	Aug 40	Dec 42
HP57	BI Srs I	Merlin X	50 armed as above, plus Vickers GO beam guns	Oct 40	Jun 44
HP57	BI Srs II	Merlin X	25 stressed for up to 60,000lb loaded	Jun 41	Jun 44
HP57	BI Srs III	Merlin X, XX	As above with increased tankage from L9600	Oct 41	Jun 44
HP58	BII	Merlin XX	Cannon armed 'day bomber'	Project	—
HP59	BII Srs I	Merlin XX	Production refinements BP 'C' dorsal turret. No beam guns	Oct 41	Feb 46
HP59	BII Srs I (Spec)	Merlin XX	Faired over nose, BP 'A' Mk VIII turret optional	Dec 41	Feb 46
HP59	BII Srs IA	Merlin 22	Moulded plastic nose. Armament as I (Special)	Mar 42	Feb 46
HP59	BII Srs II	Merlin XX	BIV fitted with standard power plant for initial flights	Jun 43	Jan 46
HP59	GRII	Merlin XX, 22	BIIs for Coastal Command Srs I and Srs IA	Nov 42	Feb 46
HP59	MET II	Merlin XX, 22	BII series adapted for interim meteorological duties	Jun 42	Feb 46
HP61	BIII	Hercules XVI	Introduced radial-engined versions	Aug 43	Aug 46
HP61	AIII	Hercules XVI	BIII adapted for Airborne Forces	Oct 44	Jan 47
HP61	CIII	Hercules XVI	BIII adapted as transport	Oct 44	Jan 47
HP61	GRIII	Hercules XVI	BIII adapted for Coastal Command	Jan 44	Aug 46
HP61	METIII	Hercules XVI	BIII adapted for meteorological duties	Feb 45	Aug 46
HP60A	BIV	Merlin 61, 65	One only, HR756. Used as engine test-bed	Mar 43	Reverted
HP65	—	Hercules 38	BIV development proposed 1943	Project	—
HP63	BV	Merlin XX, 22	BII Series with Dowty undercarriage	May 43	Feb 46
HP63	GRV	Merlin XX, 22	BV Series for Coastal Command	Jan 43	Feb 46
HP63	AV	Merlin XX, 22	BV Series adapted for Airborne Forces	Feb 43	Feb 46
HP63	METV	Merlin XX, 22	BV Series adapted for meteorological work	Jul 43	Feb 46
HP61	BVI	Hercules 100	Basic BIII with increased power and tankage	Oct 44	Oct 50
HP61	CVI	Hercules 100	BVI adapted as an interim transport	Jun 45	Apr 49
HP61	GRVI	Hercules 100	BVI adapted for Coastal Command late in war	Jun 45	Mar 52
HP61	METVI	Hercules 100	BVI redesigned for meteorological duty	Sep 46	Jan 52
HP61	BVII	Hercules XVI	BVI re-engined due to short supply of Hercules 100	May 44	Feb 46
HP61	AVII	Hercules XVI	BVII without dorsal turret. Towing gear fitted	Aug 45	Feb 48
HP61	CVII	Hercules XVI	BVII adapted for transport with pannier	Jul 45	Apr 49
HP64	—	Hercules	Transport version proposed 1944	Project	—
HP70	CVIII	Hercules 100	Transport. Stripped BVI airframe. No armament	Jun 45	Jan 47
HP71	BIX	Hercules XVI	Postwar export bomber	Jan 45	Feb 46
HP71	AIX	Hercules XVI	For Airborne Forces. BP 'D' Mk II rear turret	Jan 47	Mar 51
HP71	AX	Hercules 100	Proposed improved AIX	Project	—

Note that the extended wing form and rectangular type fins introduced mid-war were irrespective of mark numbers. Also over 1,200 general modifications were carried out during and after production, some minor such as an instrument replacement, others major, such as No 1105 for internal stripping and conversion for freight, stretchers or passengers. Additionally there were command modifications by Transport and Coastal Commands postwar, concerning extra oxygen points and more modern communication equipment.

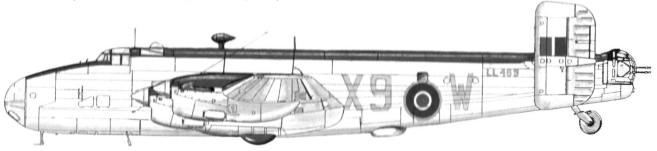

Production and Disposal 1939-52

Parent firm and main sub-contracting constructors	Quantity Ordered	Built
Handley Page Ltd, Cricklewood and Radlett	1,842	1,592
English Electric Co Ltd, Salmesbury (Preston)	2,470	2,145
Rootes Securities Ltd, Speke	1,690	1,070
Fairey Aviation, Stockport	1,030	661
London Aircraft Production Group, Leavesden	980	710
Totals:	8,012	6,178

Production by Mk numbers as built

Prototypes	2	Mk VII variants	404
BI	84	CVIII	98
Mk II variants	1,977	AIX	145
Mk III variants	2,091		
Mk V variants	904	_Total:_	6,178
Mk VI variants	473		

Serial numbers allotted to Halifaxes in production by Mk number with an indication of quantities and manufacturer

Prototypes: L7244-7245 (2 HP)

Mk I: L9485-9534, L9560-9584, L9600-9608 (84 HP)

Mk II: L9609-9624, R9363-9392, R9418-9457, R9482-9498, R9528-9540 (116 HP); V9976-9994, W1002-1021, W1035-1067, W1090-1117, W1141-1190, W1211-1253, W1270-1276 (200 EECo); W7650-7679, W7695-7720, W7745-7784, W7801-7826, W7844-7887, W7906-7939 (200 HP); BB189-223, BB236-285, BB300-344, BB357-391, BB412-446 (200 LPTB); DG219-230 (12 Rootes); DT481-526, DT539-588, DT612-649, DT665-705, DT720-752, DT767-808 (250 EECo); HR654-699, HR711-758, HR773-819, HR832-880, HR905-952, HR977-988, HX147-191, HX222-225 (299 HP); JB781-806, JB834-875, JB892-931, JB956-974, JD105-128, JD143-180, JD198-218, JD244-278, JD296-333, JD361-386, JD405-421, JD453-476 (350 EECo); JN882-926, JN941-978, JP107-137, JP159-207, JP220-259, JP275-301, JP319-338 (250 LPTB); LW223-246, LW259-301, LW313-345 (100 EECo)

Mk III: HX226-247, HX265-296, HX311-357 (101 HP); LK747-766, LK779-812, LK826-850, LK863-887 (104 Fairey); LL543-559, LL573-615 (60 Rootes); LV771-775, LV777-799, LV813-842, LV857-883, LV898-923, LV935-973, LV985-999, LW113-143, LW157-179, LW191-195 (224 HP); LW346-348, LW361-397, LW412-446, LW459-481, LW495-522, LW537-559, LW572-598, LW613-658, LW671-696, LW713-724 (260 EECo); MZ282-321, MZ334-378, MZ390-435, MZ447-495 (180 LPTB); MZ500-544, MZ556-604, MZ617-660, MZ672-717, MZ730-775, MZ787-831, MZ844-883, MZ895-939 (360 EECo); MZ945-989, NA102-150, NA162-205, NA218-263, NA275-309, NA428 & NA452 (221 Rootes); NA492-531, NA543-587, NA599-644, NA656-704 (180 Fairey); NP930-976, NP988-999, NR113-156, NR169-211, NR225-258, NR271-290 (200 EECo); PN167-207 (41 Fairey); PN365-406, PN423-60 (80 LPTB); RG345-390, RG413-446 (80 EECo)

Mk V: DG231-253, DG270-317, DG338-363, DG384-424 (138 Rootes); DJ980-999, DK114-151, DK165-207, DK223-271 (150 Fairey); EB127-160, EB178-220, EB239-258, EB274-276 (100 Rootes); LK626-667, LK680-711, LK725-246 (96 Fairey); LK890-932, LK945-976, LK988-999, LL112-153, LL167-198, LL213-258, LL270-312, LL325-267, LL380-423, LL437-469, LL481-521, LL534-542 (420 Rootes)

Mk VI: LV776, NP715, NP752-753, NP821-836, NP849-895, NP908-927, PP142-164 re-numbered TW774-796, PP165-187, PP203-216, PP225 (148 HP); RG480-513, RG527-568, RG583-625, RG639-679, RG693-736, RG749-790, RG813-853, RG867-879, ST794-818 (325 EECo)

Mk VII: LW196-210 (15 BVII HP); NA310-320, NA336-380, NA392-427, NA429-431, NA444-451, NA453-468 (119 AVII Rootes); NP681-714, NP716-723, NP736-751, NP754-781, NP793-820

(114 BVII HP); PN208, PN223-242 (21 BVII Fairey); PN243-267, PN285-327, PN343 (69 AVII Fairey); PP277, PP339-350, PP362-389 (41 AVII HP); RG447-458, RG472-479 (20 BVII EECo); RT753-757 (5 AVII HP)

Mk VIII: PP217-224, PP226-247, PP259-276, PP278-296, PP308-338 (98 CVIII HP)

Mk IX: RT758-799, RT814-856, RT868-908, RT920-938 (145 AIX HP)

Disposal of the 6,178 built

Crashed before delivery to the RAF	2
Delivered as spares or as pattern aircraft for sub-contractors	7
Missing from operational sorties at home and overseas	2,051
Written-off in the UK through crashing or damage sustained on operations	338
Destroyed by German intruder aircraft operating over the UK	16
Known to be lost by action of own forces by bombing or gunnery	10
Lost in collisions on the ground or in the air	122
Wrecked or missing on training and test flights at home and overseas	946
Lost in ground handling accidents and sabotage on the ground	29
Missing or crashed on ferry flights	24
Relegated for ground instructional use, normally after sustaining damage	109
Sold for military or civilian use (but not all registered)	179
Transferred to the French Air Force early postwar	65
Scrapped as obsolete, deteriorated beyond economical repair, etc	2,280
Total:	6,178

Bomber Command Halifax Sortie Statistics

	1941	1942	1943	1944	1945	Totals
Sorties despatched by day	55	27	—	16,288	4,918	21,288 sorties
Number of above attacking	43	4	—	14,459	4,478	18,984 sorties
Numbers lost on day raids	8	1	—	68	23	100 Halifax
Bombing sorties made by night	413	3,271	14,685	26,461	7,194	52,024 sorties
Number of abortive	33	485	1,374	2,153	507	4,552 sorties
Number lost on night raids	19	194	698	619	104	1,634 Halifax
Coastal and special duty sorties	—	292	149	3,488	2,181	6,110 sorties
Number lost on above sorties	—	1	—	33	17	51 Halifax
Number of sea mining sorties	—	157	572	2,662	325	3,716 sorties
Numbers lost sea mining	—	3	15	20	10	48 Halifax

Total number of operational sorties made by Halifaxes from the UK is 83,138. While these in the main were by Bomber Command, 1,066 were made under Coastal Command or directly under Air Ministry control

Bombs and pyrotechnics expended operationally by Halifaxes in Bomber Command

Type of bomb or pyrotechnic	No dropped	Year(s)
8000lb HC (high capacity) bomb	1	1942
4000lb HC (high capacity) bombs	467	1941-42
4000lb incendiary devices	9	1942-43
2000lb HC (high capacity) bombs	12,875	1943-45
2000lb MC (medium capacity) bombs	37	1943
2000lb AP (armour piercing) bombs	168	1941-42
1000lb GP (general purpose) bombs	28,592	1941-44
1000lb GP (general purpose) USA bombs	63	1945
1000lb MC (medium capacity) bombs	55,986	1943-45
1000lb HE (high explosive) USA bombs	19,923	1944-45
1000lb RDX (special explosive) bombs	540	1942-43
1000lb SAP (semi-armour piercing) USA bombs	50,632	1944-45
500lb GP (general purpose) bombs	198,343	1941-45
500lb MC (medium capacity) bombs	143,662	1942-45
500lb SAP (semi-armour piercing) bombs	189	1941-42
500lb SAP (semi-armour piercing) USA bombs	15,723	1944-45
500lb HE (high explosive) USA bombs	84,310	1944-45
250lb GP (general purpose) bombs	19,946	1941-45
250lb DC (depth charges)	45	1942-44
250lb TI (target indicators)	3,272	1943-45
250lb incendiary devices	524	1942-43
250lb Spot Fire devices	12	1945
50lb incendiary devices	6	1941
40lb GP (general purpose) bombs	1,065	1942-43
30lb incendiary bombs	623,527	1942-44
30lb J Type incendiaries	7,728	1944
4lb incendiaries	10,919,441	1942-45
4lb explosive incendiaries	813,715	1943-45
4lb incendiaries (in 500lb clusters)	128,048	1944
4lb No 14 incendiaries in clusters	3,765,836	1944-45
4lb No 14X explosive incendiaries	344,712	1944-45
4lb No 15 incendiaries in clusters	1,702,874	1944-45
4lb No 15X explosive incendiaries	31,758	1944-45
4lb No 17 incendiaries in clusters	332,200	1944-45

In addition 850gal of napalm were dropped during 1945

No attempt has been made to total the number of bombs as the figure including millions of 4lb bombs and a single 8000lb bomb would not be of any significance, but as a total weight, 224,207 Imp tons of bombs and pyrotechnics plus 24.5 tons of napalm were dropped on operations by Halifaxes

Below:
Of the 98 CVIII military transports built, 91 went on to the Civil Register, joining two BIIIs, 34 BVIs and 32 AIXs converted as transports. Some 25 airlines used Halifaxes or their Halton conversions and seven airlines operated them on the Berlin Air Lift in 1949. G-AHZJ depicted, formerly CVIII PP247, is shown serving with London Aero & Motor Service Ltd who had it named *Port of Marsailles*. *Peter G. Cooksley*

special occasion
Chicken

special occasion
Chicken

Entertain in style with this stunning
collection of more than 140 sophisticated
poultry, duck & game recipes

VALERIE FERGUSON

southwater

This edition is published by Southwater, an imprint of Anness Publishing Ltd, Hermes House,
88–89 Blackfriars Road, London SE1 8HA; tel. 020 7401 2077; fax 020 7633 9499

www.southwaterbooks.com; www.annesspublishing.com

If you like the images in this book and would like to investigate using them for publishing, promotions or advertising,
please visit our website www.practicalpictures.com for more information.

UK agent: The Manning Partnership Ltd; tel. 01225 478444; fax 01225 478440; sales@manning-partnership.co.uk
UK distributor: Grantham Book Services Ltd; tel. 01476 541080; fax 01476 541061; orders@gbs.tbs-ltd.co.uk
North American agent/distributor: National Book Network; tel. 301 459 3366; fax 301 429 5746; www.nbnbooks.com
Australian agent/distributor: Pan Macmillan Australia; tel. 1300 135 113; fax 1300 135 103; customer.service@macmillan.com.au
New Zealand agent/distributor: David Bateman Ltd; tel. (09) 415 7664; fax (09) 415 8892

Publisher: Joanna Lorenz
Editorial Director: Helen Sudell
Consultant Editor: Valerie Ferguson
Recipes contributed by: Catherine Atkinson, Alex Barker, Angela Boggiano, Kathy Brown, Carla Capalbo, Lesley Chamberlain, Kit Chan,
Maxine Clarke, Frances Cleary, Carole Clements, Trisha Davies, Roz Denny, Michelle Berriedale-Johnson, Patrizia Diemling,
Matthew Drennan, Sarah Edmonds, Joanna Farrow, Rafi Fernandez, Christine France, Silvana Franco, Sarah Gates, Shirley Gill,
Rosamund Grant, Carole Handslip, Rebekah Hassan, Deh-Ta Hsiung, Shehzad Husain, Christine Ingram, Judy Jackson, Soheila Kimberley,
Masaki Ko, Ruby Le Bois, Lesley Mackley, Norma MacMillan, Sue Maggs, Kathy Man, Maggie Mayhew, Norma Miller, Sallie Morris,
Elisabeth Lambert Ortiz, Maggie Pannell, Katherine Richmond, Anne Sheasby, Jenny Stacey, Liz Trigg, Hilaire Walden, Laura Washburn,
Steven Wheeler, Judy Williams, Polly Wreford, Jeni Wright and Elizabeth Wolf-Cohen
Photographs: Karl Adamson, Edward Allwright, David Armstrong, Steve Baxter, James Duncan, John Freeman, Ian Garlick,
Michelle Garrett, John Heseltine, Amanda Heywood, Ferguson Hill, Janine Hosegood, David Jordan, Don Last,
William Lingwood, Patrick McLeavey, Thomas Odulate, Juliet Piddington and Peter Reilly
Designer: Carole Perks
Editorial Reader: Richard McGinlay
Production Controller: Claire Rae

ETHICAL TRADING POLICY

Because of our ongoing ecological investment programme, you, as our customer, can have the pleasure and reassurance of knowing
that a tree is being cultivated on your behalf to naturally replace the materials used to make the book you are holding.
For further information about this scheme, go to www.annesspublishing.com/trees

Previously published as part of a larger volume, *Chicken*

NOTES

Bracketed terms are intended for American readers.
For all recipes, quantities are given in both metric and imperial measures and, where appropriate, in standard cups
and spoons. Follow one set of measures, but not a mixture, because they are not interchangeable.
Standard spoon and cup measures are level. 1 tsp = 5ml, 1 tbsp = 15ml, 1 cup = 250ml/8fl oz.
Australian standard tablespoons are 20ml. Australian readers should use 3 tsp in place of 1 tbsp for measuring small quantities.
American pints are 16fl oz/2 cups. American readers should use 20fl oz/2.5 cups in place of 1 pint when measuring liquids.
Electric oven temperatures in this book are for conventional ovens. When using a fan oven, the temperature will probably need to
be reduced by about 10–20°C/20–40°F. Since ovens vary, you should check with your manufacturer's instruction book for guidance.
Medium (US large) eggs are used unless otherwise stated.
Main front cover image shows Chicken Marengo – for recipe, see page 50.

PUBLISHER'S NOTE

Although the advice and information in this book are believed to be accurate and true at the time of going to press, neither the
authors nor the publisher can accept any legal responsibility or liability for any errors or omissions that may be made nor for any
inaccuracies nor for any harm or injury that comes about from following instructions or advice in this book.

Contents

Introduction 6

Soups & Appetizers 8

Pies, Casseroles & Baked Dishes 24

Stir-fries, Grills, Sautés & Grain Dishes 44

Chicken Roasts 62

Chicken Salads 78

Choosing a Chicken 90

Cuts of Chicken 90

Techniques 91

Index 94

Introduction

Universally popular and undoubtedly the most versatile meat in the world, chicken is the perfect choice for a family celebration, a formal dinner party, a lavish buffet, a summer barbecue or, indeed, any special occasion. It combines supremely well with a vast range of other ingredients, herbs and flavourings from rice and pasta to fruit and nuts and from soy

sauce to curry spices. It can be cooked in almost any way you can think of – roasted, baked, grilled (broiled), stir-fried, in pies, sautéed, casseroled and on the barbecue – and may be served hot or cold. You can cook a whole bird and carve it at the table or serve individual portions – from quarters to drumsticks – and it can be prepared on the bone or filleted. From soups to salads, chicken is guaranteed to delight your guests, and with this wonderful collection of recipes, it will impress them too.

Whether you are seeking inspiration for pre-dinner snacks, a tempting appetizer, a substantial main course, a summery salad or the centrepiece for a buffet, you are sure to find the ideal dish in this book. The recipes have been inspired by cuisines from around the world. Try Mexican Chicken Soup to set your guests' taste buds tingling, Persian Chicken

with Walnut Sauce for an elegant dinner party main course or French Chicken Salad for an *al fresco* lunch. A Malaysian Steamboat will certainly cause a stir and get the conversation going. The recipes range from classics, such as Coq au Vin, and traditional dishes, such as Old-fashioned Chicken Pie, to adventurous innovations, such as Chicken Salad with Lavender &

Sweet Herbs. There is something special for all occasions and every season, whatever your budget and level of skill.

This book also features a selection of sensational recipes for turkey, duck and game birds, as well as poussins. What could be more special than Roast Pheasant with Port, except, perhaps, Duck & Chestnut Casserole? Mouthwatering soups, sophisticated terrines, piquant stir-fries, delicate risottos and succulent roasts will turn a celebration into a feast.

Many of the recipes can either be cooked quickly or much of the preparation can be done in advance, allowing you to spend less time in the kitchen and more time with your guests. With fail-safe, step-by-step instructions, whatever the occasion, you can be sure that it will be as special for the cook as it is for everyone else.

SOUPS & APPETIZERS

Everybody's favourite, chicken soup – whether delicately spiced Lebanese-style or packed with fresh vegetables and pasta in the Italian manner – is not only a delicious way to start a meal, but also makes a tasty and nourishing one-pot lunch or late supper. One of the most popular dinner party appetizers must be chicken liver pâté and with this chapter you are spoilt for choice, with a mouthwatering collection of elegant, yet easy chicken and turkey pâtés, terrines and mousses, which can all be prepared well in advance. These also make wonderful dishes for the buffet table when you are entertaining on a larger scale. Chicken is the perfect choice for tempting morsels to serve with pre-dinner drinks – Chicken Cigars or Spicy Chicken Canapés, for example, are sure to impress your guests and whet their appetites. Cold appetizers are great for summer suppers and *al fresco* meals – what could be nicer than Chicken & Avocado Mayonnaise with a chilled glass of white wine served on a warm evening as the sun goes down? However, with the "fast-food" recipes in this chapter, the clever cook can, with insouciant ease, serve a succulent hot appetizer to surprise and delight the dinner guests. Richly flavoured chicken livers, attractive individual roulades or crisp-fried sticks and goujons to dip in a tasty sauce will guarantee a successful start to the evening.

Mexican Chicken Soup

For a hearty version of this simple soup, add some cooked chickpeas or rice.

Serves 6
1.5 litres/2$\frac{1}{2}$ pints/6$\frac{1}{4}$ cups
   Chicken Stock
2 cooked chicken breast fillets,
   skinned and cut into large strips
1 canned chipotle chilli or
   jalapeño chilli, drained
   and rinsed
1 avocado
salt and freshly ground
   black pepper

1 Heat the stock in a large pan and add the chicken and chilli. Simmer over a very gentle heat for 5 minutes to heat the chicken and release the flavour from the chilli.

2 Cut the avocado in half, remove the stone (pit) and peel off the skin. Slice the avocado flesh neatly.

3 Remove the chilli from the stock, using a slotted spoon, and then discard it. Taste the soup for seasoning, and add salt and pepper as necessary.

4 Pour the soup into warmed serving bowls, distributing the chicken evenly among them. Carefully add a few avocado slices to each bowl and serve immediately.

Cook's Tip
When using canned chillies, it is important to rinse them very thoroughly before adding them to the pan in order to remove the flavour of any pickling liquid.

Chicken Stellette Soup

The pasta shapes are the stars of this gently flavoured soup in two senses since despite their small size, they attract the eye and capture the interest.

Serves 4–6
900ml/1$\frac{1}{2}$ pints/3$\frac{3}{4}$ cups
   Chicken Stock
1 bay leaf
4 spring onions (scallions)
225g/8oz/3 cups button (white)
   mushrooms, sliced
115g/4oz cooked chicken
   breast portion
50g/2oz/$\frac{1}{2}$ cup stellette (tiny
   soup pasta)
150ml/$\frac{1}{4}$ pint/$\frac{2}{3}$ cup dry
   white wine
15ml/1 tbsp chopped
   fresh parsley
salt and freshly ground
   black pepper

1 Put the stock and bay leaf into a large pan and bring to the boil over a medium heat.

2 Thinly slice the spring onions and add to the pan of stock. Add the mushrooms.

3 Remove the skin from the chicken and discard. Slice the chicken thinly. Transfer to a plate and set aside.

4 Add the pasta to the pan, cover and simmer for 7–8 minutes. Just before serving, add the chicken, wine and parsley, season to taste and heat through for 2–3 minutes. Serve in warmed bowls.

Chicken Soup Lebanese-style

A substantial soup with a hint of cinnamon and cumin.

Serves 6
175g/6oz/$\frac{3}{4}$ cup chickpeas,
   soaked in water overnight
2 litres/3$\frac{1}{2}$ pints/9 cups
   Chicken Stock
90g/3$\frac{1}{2}$oz/$\frac{1}{2}$ cup long grain rice
1 onion, chopped
2 garlic cloves, crushed
30ml/2 tbsp olive oil
2.5ml/$\frac{1}{2}$ tsp ground cumin
5ml/1 tsp ground cinnamon
350g/12oz/2$\frac{1}{2}$ cups cooked
   chicken, diced
salt and freshly ground
   black pepper

1 Simmer the drained chickpeas in the stock for about 1 hour until tender, but not mushy. Add the rice and cook for 15 minutes until the rice is just tender.

2 Meanwhile, gently fry the onion and garlic in the oil for 10 minutes until soft but not browned. Stir in the spices and cook gently for 5 minutes more.

3 Add the onion mixture and the cooked chicken to the soup at the end of its cooking time, and simmer long enough to heat the chicken thoroughly. Season to taste and serve.

Chicken Soup with Vermicelli

This traditional Moroccan soup is injected with an extra burst of flavour in the form of lemon, parsley, coriander and saffron just before serving.

Serves 4–6

30ml/2 tbsp sunflower oil
15g/½oz/1 tbsp butter
1 onion, chopped
2 chicken legs or breast portions, halved or quartered
seasoned flour, for dusting
2 carrots, cut into 4cm/
    1½in pieces
1 parsnip, cut into 4cm/
    1½in pieces

1.5 litres/2½ pints/6¼ cups
    Chicken Stock
1 cinnamon stick
good pinch of paprika
pinch of saffron
2 egg yolks
juice of ½ lemon
30ml/2 tbsp chopped
    fresh coriander (cilantro)
30ml/2 tbsp chopped
    fresh parsley
150g/5oz vermicelli
salt and freshly ground
    black pepper
Moroccan bread, to serve

1 Heat the oil and butter in a pan or flameproof casserole and fry the onion for 3–4 minutes until softened. Dust the chicken pieces in seasoned flour, add to the pan or casserole and fry gently until evenly browned.

2 Transfer the chicken to a plate and add the carrots and parsnip to the pan. Cook over a gentle heat for 3–4 minutes, stirring frequently, then return the chicken to the pan. Add the chicken stock, cinnamon stick and paprika, and season to taste with salt and pepper.

3 Bring the soup to the boil, cover and simmer for 1 hour or until the vegetables are very tender.

4 While the soup is cooking, blend the saffron in 30ml/2 tbsp boiling water. Beat the egg yolks with the lemon juice in a separate bowl and add the chopped coriander and parsley. When the saffron water has cooled, stir into the egg and lemon mixture until thoroughly blended.

5 When the vegetables are tender, transfer the chicken to a plate. Spoon away any excess fat from the soup, then increase the heat a little and stir in the vermicelli. Cook for 5–6 minutes until the noodles are tender.

6 Meanwhile, remove the skin from the chicken and, if you like, bone and chop the meat into bitesize pieces. If you prefer, simply skin the chicken and leave the pieces whole.

7 When the vermicelli is cooked, reduce the heat and stir in the chicken pieces and the egg, lemon and saffron mixture. Cook over a very low heat for 1–2 minutes, stirring constantly. Adjust the seasoning and serve with Moroccan bread.

Rich Minestrone

A special minestrone made with chicken. Served with crusty Italian bread, it makes a hearty meal.

Serves 4–6

15ml/1 tbsp olive oil
2 chicken thighs
3 lean bacon rashers (strips), rinded and chopped
1 onion, finely chopped
a few fresh basil leaves, shredded
a few fresh rosemary leaves, finely chopped
15ml/1 tbsp chopped fresh flat leaf parsley
2 potatoes, cut into 1cm/
    ½in cubes

1 large carrot, cut into 1cm/
    ½in cubes
2 small courgettes (zucchini), cut into 1cm/½in cubes
1–2 celery sticks, cut into 1cm/
    ½in cubes
1 litre/1¾ pints/4 cups
    Chicken Stock
200g/7oz/1¾ cups frozen peas
115g/4oz/1 cup stellette or other tiny soup pasta
salt and freshly ground
    black pepper
coarsely shaved Parmesan cheese, and fresh basil leaves,
    to garnish

1 Heat the oil in a large pan and fry the chicken for about 5 minutes on each side. Remove and set aside. Lower the heat, add the bacon, onion, shredded basil, rosemary and parsley to the pan and stir well. Cook gently, stirring constantly, for about 5 minutes. Add all the vegetables except the frozen peas and cook for 5–7 minutes more, stirring frequently.

2 Return the chicken thighs to the pan, add the stock and bring to the boil. Cover and cook over a low heat for 35–40 minutes, stirring the soup occasionally.

3 Remove the chicken thighs using a slotted spoon. Stir the peas and pasta into the soup, and bring back to the boil. Simmer, stirring frequently, for 7–8 minutes until the pasta is *al dente*, or according to the instructions on the packet.

4 Meanwhile, skin the chicken and cut the meat into 1cm/ ½in pieces. Return it to the soup and heat through. Adjust the seasoning and serve, sprinkled with Parmesan and basil leaves.

Chicken Soup with Lockshen

To achieve the best results with this traditional Jewish dish, follow two rules: make it the day before and try to find a boiling fowl, which has much more flavour than a roasting bird.

Serves 6–8
3kg/6½lb boiling chicken, including the giblets, but not the liver

1 litre/1¾ pints/4 cups cold water
2 onions, halved
2 carrots
5 celery sticks
handful of fine vermicelli (lockshen), about 115g/4oz
salt and freshly ground black pepper
fresh bread, to serve (optional)

1 Put the chicken into a very large pan, together with the giblets. Add the water and bring to the boil over a high heat. Skim off the white froth that comes to the top and then add the halved onions, the carrots and celery. Season to taste with ground black pepper only.

2 Bring the liquid to the boil again, then turn the heat to low, cover and simmer for at least 2 hours. Keep an eye on the water level and add a little more as needed so that the chicken is always covered.

3 When the chicken is tender, remove from the pan and take the meat off the bones, reserving it for another use. Put the bones back in the soup and continue cooking for a further 1 hour. There should be at least 1 litre/1¾ pints/4 cups of soup.

4 Strain the soup into a large bowl and chill overnight. When it is quite cold, it may form a jelly and a pale layer of fat will have settled on the top. Remove the fat with a spoon and discard.

5 Bring the soup to the boil again, season to taste and add the vermicelli. Boil for about 8 minutes and serve in warmed large bowls, with fresh bread, if using.

Chicken Soup with Matzo Kleis Balls

Another classic Jewish recipe, in which herbed dumplings are cooked in delicious home-made soup.

Serves 4
2 matzot (sheets of unleavened bread)
30ml/2 tbsp oil
1 onion, chopped

handful of fresh parsley
2 eggs
pinch of ground ginger
15–30ml/1–2 tbsp medium ground matzo meal
1 litre/1¾ pints/4 cups Chicken Soup
salt and freshly ground black pepper

1 Soak the matzot in cold water for about 5 minutes, and then drain and squeeze them dry.

2 Heat the oil in a frying pan and fry the onion until golden. Chop the parsley, reserving a few sprigs for the garnish. Whisk the eggs slightly.

3 Mix together the soaked matzot, fried onion, parsley and eggs. Season with salt, pepper and ginger, and add about 15ml/1 tbsp matzo meal. Chill for at least 1 hour.

4 Bring the soup to the boil in a large pan. Roll the dumpling mixture into small balls, drop them into the fast-boiling soup and cook for about 20 minutes. Serve the soup in warmed bowls, garnished with the reserved parsley.

> **Cook's Tip**
> You can make the dumplings well in advance, but they should be kept chilled. They also freeze well, so it is a good idea to make a double quantity, and cook half and freeze half. To use frozen dumplings, leave them to thaw for about 1 hour before cooking in the soup.

Turkey & Lentil Soup

A fairly substantial soup, ideal for a cold day and a great way of using up leftover cooked turkey, or other poultry, at the end of the festive season.

Serves 4

25g/1oz/2 tbsp butter
 or margarine
1 large carrot, chopped
1 onion, chopped
1 leek, white part only, chopped
1 celery stick, chopped
115g/4oz/1½ cups
 mushrooms, chopped
45ml/3 tbsp dry white wine
1 litre/1¾ pints/4 cups
 Chicken Stock
10ml/2 tsp dried thyme
1 bay leaf
115g/4oz/½ cup brown or
 green lentils
225g/8oz cooked turkey, diced
salt and freshly ground
 black pepper

1 Melt the butter or margarine in a large pan. Add the carrot, onion, leek, celery and mushrooms. Cook over a low heat for 3–5 minutes until the vegetables are softened.

2 Stir in the wine and chicken stock. Bring to the boil and skim off any foam that rises to the surface. Add the thyme and bay leaf. Reduce the heat, cover and simmer for 30 minutes.

3 Add the lentils and continue cooking, covered, for 30–40 minutes more until they are just tender. Stir the soup from time to time.

4 Stir in the diced turkey and season to taste with salt and pepper. Cook until the turkey is just heated through. Ladle the soup into warmed bowls and serve hot.

> **Cook's Tip**
> *Lentils are one of the few pulses that do not need to be soaked before cooking. Puy lentils have the best flavour and retain their shape well.*

Asian Duck Consommé

Though a little time-consuming to make, this wonderful soup, light and rich at the same time, is well worth the effort.

Serves 4

1 duck carcass (raw or cooked),
 plus 2 legs or any giblets,
 trimmed of as much fat
 as possible
1 large onion, unpeeled, with root
 end trimmed
2 carrots, cut into 5cm/2in pieces
1 parsnip, cut into 5cm/2in pieces
1 leek, cut into 5cm/2in pieces
2–4 garlic cloves, crushed
2.5cm/1in piece fresh root ginger,
 peeled and sliced
15ml/1 tbsp black peppercorns
4–6 fresh thyme sprigs
1 small bunch fresh coriander
 (cilantro) (6–8 sprigs), leaves
 and stems separated

For the garnish

1 small carrot
1 small leek, halved lengthways
4–6 shiitake mushrooms,
 thinly sliced
soy sauce
2 spring onions (scallions),
 thinly sliced
shredded Chinese leaves
 (Chinese cabbage)
freshly ground black pepper

1 Put the duck carcass, the legs or giblets, the vegetables, spices, thyme and coriander stems in a large pan, cover with cold water and bring to the boil over a medium-high heat, skimming any foam that rises to the surface.

2 Reduce the heat and simmer for 1½–2 hours, then strain through a sieve lined with muslin (cheesecloth) into a bowl.

3 Leave the stock to cool, then chill for several hours or overnight. Skim off any congealed fat and blot the surface with kitchen paper to remove any traces of fat.

4 To make the garnish, cut the carrot and leek into julienne strips. Place in a large pan with the mushrooms. Pour over the stock, add a few dashes of soy sauce and some pepper. Bring to the boil, skimming off any foam. Stir in the spring onions and Chinese leaves. Ladle into warmed bowls, sprinkle with coriander leaves and serve.

Chicken Liver Pâté

This is a really quick pâté to make, yet it has a delicious, rich flavour. It is sealed with clarified butter, which helps maintain its freshness.

Serves 6
50g/2oz butter
1 onion, finely chopped
350g/12oz chicken
   livers, trimmed
60ml/4 tbsp medium sherry
25g/1oz full-fat soft
   (farmers) cheese
15–30ml/1–2 tbsp lemon juice
2 hard-boiled (hard-cooked) eggs,
   shelled and chopped
50–75g/2–3oz/4–6 tbsp
   Clarified Butter
salt and freshly ground
   black pepper
bay leaves, to garnish
toast or savoury biscuits
   (crackers), to serve

1 Melt the butter in a frying pan. Add the onion and livers, and cook until the onion is soft and the livers are lightly browned and no longer pink in the centre.

2 Add the sherry and boil until reduced by half. Cool slightly.

3 Turn the mixture into a food processor or blender and add the soft cheese and 15ml/1 tbsp lemon juice. Process until thoroughly blended and smooth.

4 Add the hard-boiled eggs and blend briefly. Season with salt and pepper. Taste and add more lemon juice if liked.

5 Pack the liver pâté into a mould or into individual ramekins. Smooth the surface.

6 Spoon a layer of clarified butter over the surface of the pâté. Chill until firm and garnish with bay leaves. Serve at room temperature, with hot toast or savoury biscuits.

Clarified Butter

This is a refined butter from which the milk solids have been removed.

Makes about 175g/6oz
225g/8oz butter

1 Put the butter in a heavy pan over a low heat. Melt gently. Skim off the froth from the surface. You will then see a clear yellow layer on top of a milky layer: carefully pour the clear fat into a bowl or jug (pitcher), leaving the milky residue in the pan.

2 Discard the milky residue, or add it to soups.

3 The clarified butter may be stored in the refrigerator for several weeks and for longer in the freezer. Defrost to room temperature.

Chicken Liver Pâté with Marsala

A more sophisticated version of chicken liver pâté which contains Marsala, a soft and pungent fortified wine from Sicily, and a generous quantity of garlic.

Serves 4–6
225g/8oz/1 cup butter, softened
350g/12oz chicken
   livers, trimmed
2 garlic cloves, crushed
15ml/1 tbsp Marsala
5ml/1 tsp chopped fresh sage
salt and freshly ground
   black pepper
8 sage leaves, to garnish
Melba toast, to serve

1 Melt 25g/1oz/2 tbsp of the butter in a frying pan, add the chicken livers and garlic, and fry over a medium heat for about 5 minutes or until the livers are lightly browned, but still pink in the middle.

2 Transfer the livers to a blender or food processor, using a slotted spoon, and add the Marsala and chopped sage.

3 Melt 150g/5oz/10 tbsp of the remaining butter in the frying pan, stirring to loosen any sediment, then pour into the blender or processor and process until smooth. Season well.

4 Spoon the pâté into individual pots and smooth the surface. Melt the rest of the butter in a separate pan and pour over the pâtés. Garnish with sage leaves and chill until set. Serve with triangles of Melba toast.

Cook's Tip
Sage has a special affinity with liver. However, it is very powerfully flavoured and should be used sparingly.

Chicken & Pistachio Pâté

This version of a classic of French charcuterie can be made using a whole boned bird or chicken pieces.

Serves 10–12
900g/2lb boneless chicken meat
1 chicken skinless breast fillet, about 175g/6oz
25g/1oz/ ¹/₂ cup fresh white breadcrumbs
120ml/4fl oz/¹/₂ cup whipping cream
1 egg white
4 spring onions (scallions), finely chopped
1 garlic clove, finely chopped
75g/3oz/¹/₂ cup cooked ham, cut into 1cm/¹/₂in cubes
50g/2oz/¹/₂ cup shelled pistachio nuts
45ml/3 tbsp chopped fresh tarragon
pinch of grated nutmeg
3.5ml/³/₄ tsp salt
7.5ml/1¹/₂ tsp freshly ground black pepper
oil, for greasing
green salad, to serve

1 Trim the chicken meat and cut into 5cm/2in cubes. Put in a food processor and pulse to chop the meat to a smooth purée, in two or three batches. Alternatively, pass the meat through the medium or fine blade of a mincer (grinder).

2 Preheat the oven to 180°C/350°F/Gas 4. Cut the chicken breast fillet into 1cm/ ¹/₂in cubes.

3 In a large bowl, soak the breadcrumbs in the whipping cream. Add the puréed chicken, egg white, spring onions, garlic, ham, pistachios, tarragon, nutmeg, salt and pepper. Using a wooden spoon or your fingers, stir the mixture until very well combined.

4 Lay out a piece of foil about 45cm/18in long on a work surface and lightly brush oil on a 30cm/12in square in the centre. Spoon the chicken mixture on to the foil to form a log shape about 30cm/12in long and about 9cm/3¹/₂in thick. Bring together the long sides of the foil and fold over securely. Twist the ends and tie with string.

5 Transfer to a baking tray and bake for 1¹/₂ hours. Leave to cool, then chill overnight. Serve sliced with green salad.

Chicken Liver Mousse

This mousse makes an elegant yet easy first course. The onion marmalade makes a delicious accompaniment, along with a salad of bitter leaves.

Serves 6–8
175g/6oz/³/₄ cup butter, diced
1 small onion, finely chopped
1 garlic clove, finely chopped
450g/1lb chicken livers, trimmed
2.5ml/¹/₂ tsp dried thyme
30–45ml/2–3 tbsp brandy
salt and freshly ground black pepper

For the onion marmalade
25g/1oz/2 tbsp butter
450g/1lb red onions, thinly sliced
1 garlic clove, finely chopped
2.5ml/ ¹/₂ tsp dried thyme
30–45ml/2–3 tbsp raspberry or red wine vinegar
15–30ml/1–2 tbsp clear honey
40g/1¹/₂oz/¹/₄ cup sultanas (golden raisins)

1 In a heavy frying pan, melt 25g/1oz/2 tbsp of the butter over a medium heat. Add the onion and cook for 5–7 minutes until soft and golden, then add the chopped garlic and cook for 1 minute more.

2 Increase the heat to medium-high and add the chicken livers, thyme, salt and pepper. Cook for 3–5 minutes until the livers are coloured, stirring frequently; the livers should remain pink inside. Add the brandy and cook for a further minute.

3 Using a slotted spoon, transfer the livers to a food processor fitted with the metal blade. Pour in the cooking juices and process for 1 minute or until smooth, scraping down the sides once. With the machine running, add the remaining butter, a few pieces at a time, until it is incorporated. Press the mousse mixture through a fine sieve with a wooden spoon or rubber spatula. Scrape the underside of the sieve.

4 Line a 475ml/16fl oz/2 cup loaf tin (pan) with clear film (plastic wrap), smoothing out as many wrinkles as possible. Pour the mixture into the tin. Cool, then cover and chill until firm.

5 To make the onion marmalade, heat the butter in a heavy frying pan over a medium-low heat, add the onions, and cook for 20 minutes until softened and just coloured, stirring frequently. Stir in the garlic, thyme, vinegar, honey and sultanas and cook, covered, for 10–15 minutes until the onions are completely soft and jam-like, stirring occasionally. Spoon into a bowl and cool to room temperature.

6 To serve, dip the loaf tin into hot water for 5 seconds, wipe dry and invert on to a board. Lift off the tin, peel off the clear film and smooth the surface with a knife. Serve sliced with a little of the onion marmalade.

Cook's Tip
The mousse will keep for 3–4 days. If made ahead, cover and chill until ready to use. The onion marmalade can be made up to 2 days ahead and gently reheated over a low heat or in the microwave until just warm.

Chicken & Mushroom Terrine

Ideal as an appetizer or light lunch, this delicious dish proves that low-fat cooking need not sacrifice flavour.

Serves 4
2 shallots, chopped
175g/6oz/generous 2 cups
    mushrooms, chopped
45ml/3 tbsp Chicken Stock
2 skinless chicken breast
    fillets, chopped
1 egg white
30ml/2 tbsp wholemeal (whole-
    wheat) breadcrumbs
30ml/2 tbsp chopped
    fresh parsley
30ml/2 tbsp chopped fresh sage
oil, for greasing
salt and freshly ground
    black pepper
fresh sage sprigs, to garnish
tomatoes, to serve

1 Preheat the oven to 180°C/350°F/Gas 4. Place the shallots, mushrooms and stock in a pan and cook over a low heat, stirring occasionally, until the vegetables have softened and the mixture is dry.

2 Transfer to a food processor and add the chicken, egg white, breadcrumbs and seasoning, and chop coarsely. Add the chopped herbs and process briefly.

3 Spoon into a greased 900ml/1½ pint/3¾ cup ovenproof terrine dish and smooth the surface. Cover with foil and bake for 35–40 minutes until the juices are no longer pink.

4 Remove from the oven and place a weight on top. Leave to cool, then chill. Serve sliced, garnished with sage and accompanied by tomatoes.

Potted Chicken

A simple-to-make appetizer using cooked chicken, this looks good served in attractive individual pots.

Serves 4–6
350g/12oz skinless boneless
    cooked chicken
115g/4oz/½ cup Clarified Butter
25ml/1½ tbsp dry sherry
ground cinnamon
ground mace
salt and freshly ground
    black pepper

1 Put the cooked chicken through the fine blade of a mincer (grinder) or chop finely in a food processor.
2 Heat the butter and blend half with the chicken. Add the sherry with cinnamon, mace, salt and pepper to taste.
3 Pack into individual containers and seal the tops with the remaining butter.

Chicken, Bacon & Walnut Terrine

A luxurious dish, richly textured and lightly spiced, this would make a perfect appetizer for a special occasion dinner or buffet.

Serves 8–10
2 chicken breast fillets
1 large garlic clove, crushed
½ slice bread
1 egg
350g/12oz bacon chops (the
    fattier the better), minced
    (ground) or finely chopped
225g/8oz chicken livers, trimmed
    and finely chopped
25g/1oz/¼ cup chopped
    walnuts, toasted
30ml/2 tbsp sweet sherry
    or Madeira
2.5ml/½ tsp ground allspice
2.5ml/½ tsp cayenne pepper
pinch each grated nutmeg and
    ground cloves
8 rashers (strips) streaky (fatty)
    bacon, rinded and stretched
oil, for greasing
salt and freshly ground
    black pepper
chicory (Belgian endive) leaves,
    chives and chopped walnuts,
    to garnish

1 Cut the chicken into thin strips and season lightly. Mash the garlic, bread and egg together. Work in the chopped bacon (using your hands is really the best way) and then the finely chopped livers. Stir in the chopped walnuts, sherry or Madeira, spices and seasoning to taste.

2 Preheat the oven to 200°C/400°F/Gas 6. Line a 675g/1½lb loaf tin (pan) with the bacon rashers and pack in half the meat mixture. Lay the chicken strips on the top and spread the rest of the mixture over. Cover the loaf tin with lightly greased foil, seal well and press down firmly.

3 Place the terrine in a roasting pan half full of hot water and bake for 1–1½ hours or until firm to the touch. Remove from the oven, place a weight on top and leave to cool, draining off any excess fat or liquid while the terrine is still warm. Chill.

4 To serve, turn out the terrine and cut into thick slices. Garnish with a few chicory leaves and chives, and a scattering of chopped walnuts.

Chicken & Pork Terrine

A delicate-flavoured, smooth pâté with a contrasting strip of coarser-textured meat in the centre.

Serves 6–8
225g/8oz rindless streaky
  (fatty) bacon
375g/13oz skinless chicken
  breast fillet
15ml/1 tbsp lemon juice
225g/8oz lean minced
  (ground) pork
½ small onion, finely chopped
2 eggs, beaten
30ml/2 tbsp chopped
  fresh parsley
5ml/1 tsp salt
5ml/1 tsp green
  peppercorns, crushed
oil, for greasing
green salad, radishes and lemon
  wedges, to serve

1 Preheat the oven to 160°C/325°F/Gas 3. Put the bacon on a board and stretch it using the back of a heavy knife so that it can be arranged in overlapping slices over the base and sides of a 900g/2lb loaf tin (pan).

2 Cut 115g/4oz of the chicken into strips about 10cm/4in long. Sprinkle with lemon juice. Put the rest of the chicken in a food processor or blender with the minced pork and the onion. Process until fairly smooth.

3 Add the eggs, parsley, salt and peppercorns to the meat mixture and process again briefly. Spoon half the mixture into the loaf tin and then level the surface.

4 Arrange the chicken strips on top, then spoon in the remaining meat mixture and smooth the top. Give the tin a couple of sharp taps to knock out any pockets of air.

5 Cover with a piece of oiled foil and put in a roasting pan. Pour in enough hot water to come halfway up the sides of the loaf tin. Bake for about 45–50 minutes, until firm.

6 Allow the terrine to cool in the tin before turning out and chilling. Serve sliced, with a green salad, radishes and wedges of lemon to squeeze over.

Turkey, Juniper & Green Peppercorn Terrine

This is an ideal dish for entertaining as it can be made several days in advance and looks beautiful.

Serves 10–12
225g/8oz chicken livers, trimmed
450g/1lb minced (ground) turkey
450g/1lb minced (ground) pork
225g/8oz cubetti pancetta
50g/2oz/½ cup shelled pistachio
  nuts, roughly chopped
5ml/1 tsp salt
2.5ml/½ tsp ground mace
2 garlic cloves, crushed
5ml/1 tsp green peppercorns in
  brine, drained
5ml/1 tsp juniper berries
120ml/4fl oz/½ cup dry
  white wine
30ml/2 tbsp gin
finely grated rind of 1 orange
8 large vacuum-packed vine
  leaves in brine
oil, for greasing
pickle or chutney, to serve

1 Chop the chicken livers finely. Put them in a bowl and add the turkey, pork, pancetta, pistachio nuts, salt, mace and garlic. Mix well. Lightly crush the peppercorns and juniper berries, and add them to the mixture. Stir in the wine, gin and orange rind. Cover and chill overnight.

2 Preheat the oven to 160°C/325°F/Gas 3. Rinse the vine leaves under cold running water. Drain them thoroughly. Lightly oil a 1.2 litre/2 pint/5 cup ovenproof terrine dish or loaf tin (pan). Line the terrine or tin with the leaves, letting the ends hang over the sides. Pack the meat mixture into the terrine or tin and fold the leaves over to enclose. Brush lightly with oil.

3 Cover the terrine. Place it in a roasting pan and pour in boiling water to come halfway up the sides of the terrine. Bake for 1¾ hours, checking the level of the water occasionally.

4 Leave the terrine to cool, then pour off the surface juices. Cover with clear film (plastic wrap), then foil, and place a weight on top. Chill overnight.

5 Serve in slices, at room temperature, with pickle or chutney.

Spicy Chicken Canapés

These little cocktail sandwiches have a spicy filling, finished with different flavours of toppings.

Makes 18
75g/3oz/generous ½ cup finely chopped cooked chicken

2 spring onions (scallions), finely chopped
30ml/2 tbsp chopped red (bell) pepper
90ml/6 tbsp Curry Mayonnaise
6 slices white bread
15ml/1 tbsp paprika
15ml/1 tbsp chopped fresh parsley
30ml/2 tbsp chopped salted peanuts

1 Mix the chicken with the chopped spring onions and red pepper and half the curry mayonnaise.

2 Spread the mixture over three of the bread slices and sandwich with the remaining bread. Spread the remaining curry mayonnaise over the top and cut into 4cm/1½in circles using a plain cutter. Dip into paprika, chopped parsley or chopped nuts and arrange on a serving platter.

Curry Mayonnaise

**Makes about 300ml/
½ pint/1¼ cups**
2 egg yolks
5ml/1 tsp French mustard
15–20ml/3–4 tbsp curry paste
150ml/5fl oz/⅔ cup extra virgin olive oil
150ml/5fl oz/⅔ cup groundnut (peanut) oil
10ml/2 tsp white wine vinegar
salt and freshly ground black pepper

1 Place the egg yolks, mustard and curry paste in a food processor and blend smoothly.
2 Add the olive oil a little at a time while the processor is running. When the mixture is thick, add the remainder of the oil in a slow, steady stream. Add the vinegar and season to taste with salt and pepper.

Chicken & Avocado Mayonnaise

You will need quite firm 'scoops' or forks to eat this appetizer, so don't be tempted to pass it around as finger food.

Serves 4
30ml/2 tbsp mayonnaise
15ml/1 tbsp fromage frais or cream cheese
2 garlic cloves, crushed
115g/4oz/scant 1 cup chopped cooked chicken
1 large ripe but firm avocado
30ml/2 tbsp lemon juice
salt and freshly ground black pepper
nacho chips or tortilla chips, to serve

1 Mix together the mayonnaise, fromage frais or cream cheese, garlic and seasoning to taste in a small bowl. Stir in the chopped chicken.

2 Peel, stone (pit) and chop the avocado and immediately toss in the lemon juice, then stir gently into the chicken mixture. Taste and adjust the seasoning as necessary. Chill until required.

3 Serve in small dishes, with nacho or tortilla chips as scoops.

Cook's Tip
This mixture also makes a great, chunky filling for sandwiches, baps or pitta bread. Alternatively, serve it as a main-course salad, heaped on to a base of mixed salad leaves.

Chicken Livers in Sherry

This dish, which could hardly be quicker to prepare, makes an excellent simple appetizer. Serve with crusty bread.

Serves 4
225g/8oz chicken livers
1 small onion
2 small garlic cloves
15ml/1 tbsp olive oil
5ml/1 tsp fresh thyme leaves
30ml/2 tbsp sweet sherry
30ml/2 tbsp sour or
  double (heavy) cream
salt and freshly ground
  black pepper
fresh thyme sprigs, to garnish

1 Trim any green spots and sinews from the chicken livers. Finely chop the onion and garlic.

2 Heat the oil in a frying pan and fry the onion, garlic, chicken livers and thyme leaves for 3 minutes or until the livers are coloured on the outside but still slightly pink in the middle.

3 Stir in the sherry and cook gently for 1 minute. Add the sour or double cream and cook over a low heat for a further 1–2 minutes.

4 Stir in salt and pepper to taste, and serve immediately, garnished with thyme sprigs.

Fresh Tomato Sauce

Adding a little tomato purée gives extra strength of flavour to this sauce.

Makes 300ml/½ pint/
1¼ cups

1 onion, finely chopped
1 garlic clove, crushed
15ml/1 tbsp olive oil
450g/1lb tomatoes, peeled
  and chopped
10ml/2 tsp tomato
  purée (paste)
5ml/1 tsp granulated
  sugar (optional)
salt and freshly ground
  black pepper

1 Cook the chopped onion and crushed garlic in the olive oil for about 5 minutes until softened but not browned.

2 Add the tomatoes, tomato purée, sugar (if using imported, out of season tomatoes) and seasoning to taste.
3 Cover and simmer for 15–20 minutes, stirring occasionally. If the sauce seems a little thin, remove the lid and simmer for a few more minutes to reduce slightly.

Polenta with Chicken Livers

The richness of the livers is perfectly balanced here by the mild-flavoured polenta and fresh tomato sauce.

Serves 4
750ml/1¼ pints/3 cups Chicken
  Stock or water
130g/4½oz/generous
  1 cup polenta
about 50g/2oz/4 tbsp butter
30ml/2 tbsp olive oil
450g/1lb chicken livers, trimmed
  and cut in half
1–2 garlic cloves, finely chopped
60ml/4 tbsp chopped fresh
  parsley, preferably flat leaf
5ml/1 tsp chopped fresh oregano
  or 2.5ml/½ tsp dried oregano
squeeze of lemon juice
salt and freshly ground
  black pepper
350ml/12fl oz/1½ cups Fresh
  Tomato Sauce, heated

1 Bring the stock or water to the boil in a large pan. If using water, add a little salt. Gradually stir in the polenta and cook over a low heat until very thick, stirring constantly. Pour the polenta into a buttered 20cm/8in round tin (pan). Set aside for at least 30 minutes to firm up.

2 Invert the block of polenta on to a board. Cut it into four wedges. Fry in 40g/1½oz of the butter until golden brown on both sides, turning once.

3 Heat the remaining butter and the oil in a frying pan over moderately high heat. Add the livers and fry for 2–3 minutes or until they are starting to brown, turning once. Add the garlic, herbs, lemon juice and seasoning. Continue cooking for a further 1–2 minutes or until the livers are lightly browned on the outside but still pink in the centre.

4 Place a wedge of polenta on each warmed plate. Spoon the tomato sauce over and put the chicken livers on top.

Variation
Use 450g/1lb/6½ cups sliced mushrooms sautéed in 40g/1½oz butter in place of the chicken livers.

Chicken Roulades

These attractive chicken rolls, stuffed with a nutty spinach filling, make an impressive hot first course for a dinner party.

Makes 4
4 skinless boneless chicken thighs
115g/4oz chopped
　frozen spinach
15g/½oz/1 tbsp butter
25g/1oz/2 tbsp pine nuts
pinch of grated nutmeg
25g/1oz/½ cup fresh
　white breadcrumbs
4 rashers (strips) rindless streaky
　(fatty) bacon
30ml/2 tbsp olive oil
150ml/¼ pint/⅔ cup white wine
　or Chicken Stock
10ml/2 tsp cornflour (cornstarch)
30ml/2 tbsp single (light) cream
15ml/1 tbsp chopped fresh chives
salt and freshly ground
　black pepper
salad leaves, to garnish

1 Preheat the oven to 180°C/350°F/Gas 4. Place the chicken between clear film (plastic wrap) and flatten with a rolling pin.

2 Put the spinach and butter into a pan, heat gently until the spinach has thawed, then increase the heat and cook rapidly, stirring occasionally, until all the moisture has been driven off. Add the pine nuts, seasoning, nutmeg and breadcrumbs.

3 Divide the spinach mixture between the chicken pieces and roll up neatly. Wrap a rasher of bacon around each piece and secure with string.

4 Heat the oil in a large frying pan and brown the roulades all over. Drain through a slotted spoon and place in a shallow, ovenproof dish.

5 Pour over the wine or stock, cover and bake for about 15–20 minutes or until tender. Transfer the chicken to a serving plate and remove the string. Strain the cooking liquid into a pan. Mix the cornflour to a thin, smooth paste with a little cold water and add to the juices in the pan, with the cream. Bring to the boil to thicken, stirring constantly. Adjust the seasoning, if necessary, and add the chives. Pour the sauce around the chicken and serve with a garnish of salad leaves.

Mini Spring Rolls

Eat these light, crispy parcels with your fingers. If you like slightly spicier food, sprinkle them with cayenne pepper.

Makes 20
1 fresh green chilli
120ml/4fl oz/½ cup vegetable oil
1 small onion, finely chopped
1 garlic clove, crushed
75g/3oz cooked chicken
　breast portion
1 small carrot, cut into
　fine batons
1 spring onion (scallion),
　thinly sliced
1 small red (bell) pepper, seeded
　and cut into fine batons
25g/1oz beansprouts
5ml/1 tsp sesame oil
4 large sheets filo pastry
1 small egg white, lightly beaten
fresh chives, to garnish (optional)
light soy sauce, to serve

1 Carefully remove the seeds from the chilli and chop finely, wearing rubber gloves to protect your hands, if necessary.

2 Heat a wok or heavy frying pan, then add 30ml/2 tbsp of the vegetable oil. When hot, add the onion, garlic and chilli. Stir-fry for 1 minute.

3 Slice the chicken thinly, then add to the wok and fry over a high heat, stirring constantly until browned.

4 Add the carrot, spring onion and red pepper, and stir-fry for 2 minutes. Add the beansprouts, stir in the sesame oil, then remove from the heat and leave to cool.

5 Cut each sheet of filo pastry into five short strips. Place a small amount of filling at one end of each strip, then fold in the long sides and roll up the pastry to make a neat parcel. Seal and glaze the parcels with the egg white, then chill, uncovered, for 15 minutes before frying.

6 Wipe out the wok with kitchen paper, heat it again and add the remaining vegetable oil. When the oil is hot, fry the rolls, in batches, until crisp and golden brown. Drain on kitchen paper and keep warm. Serve garnished with chives, if you like, accompanied by light soy sauce for dipping.

Chicken Cigars

These small, crispy rolls can be served warm as canapés with a drink before a meal, or as a first course with a crisp, colourful salad.

Serves 4
275g/10oz filo pastry
45ml/3 tbsp olive oil
fresh flat leaf parsley, to garnish

For the filling
350g/12oz minced
  (ground) chicken
1 egg, beaten
2.5ml/½ tsp ground cinnamon
2.5ml/½ tsp ground ginger
30ml/2 tbsp raisins
15ml/1 tbsp olive oil
1 small onion, finely chopped
salt and freshly ground
  black pepper

1 To make the filling, combine all the ingredients, except the oil and onion, in a bowl. Heat the oil in a frying pan and cook the onion until tender. Cool, then stir into the chicken mixture.

2 Preheat the oven to 180°C/350°F/Gas 4. Once the filo pastry packet has been opened, keep the pastry covered at all times with a damp dishtowel. Work fast, as the pastry dries out very quickly when exposed to the air. Unravel the pastry and cut into 10 × 25cm/4 × 10in strips.

3 Take one strip (cover the remainder), brush with a little oil and place a small spoonful of the filling about 1cm/½in from the end.

4 To encase the filling, fold the sides inwards to a width of 5cm/2in and roll into a cigar shape. Place on a greased baking sheet and brush with oil. Bake for about 20–25 minutes until golden brown and crisp. Garnish with parsley and serve.

Aubergine with Sesame Chicken

Sweet, delicate-tasting, small aubergines are stuffed with seasoned chicken and deep fried in a crispy sesame seed coating.

Serves 4
175g/6oz skinless chicken breast
  portion or thigh
1 spring onion (scallion), green
  part only, finely chopped
15ml/1 tbsp dark soy sauce
15ml/1 tbsp mirin or sweet sherry

2.5ml/½ tsp sesame oil
1.5ml/¼ tsp salt
4 small aubergines (eggplants),
  about 10cm/4in long
15ml/1 tbsp sesame seeds
flour, for dusting
vegetable oil, for deep-frying

For the dipping sauce
60ml/4 tbsp dark soy sauce
60ml/4 tbsp dashi or
  vegetable stock
45ml/3 tbsp mirin or sweet sherry

1 Remove the chicken meat from the bone and mince (grind) it finely in a food processor. Add the spring onion, soy sauce, mirin or sherry, sesame oil and salt.

2 Make four slits in each aubergine, leaving them joined at the stem. Spoon the minced chicken mixture into the aubergines, opening them slightly to accommodate the mixture. Dip the fat end of each stuffed aubergine in the sesame seeds, then dust in flour. Set aside.

3 To make the dipping sauce, combine the soy sauce, dashi or stock and mirin or sherry. Pour into a shallow serving bowl and set aside.

4 Heat the vegetable oil in a deep-fat fryer to 196°C/385°F or until a cube of day-old bread browns in 45 seconds. Fry the aubergines, two at a time, for 3–4 minutes. Lift out using a slotted spoon on to kitchen paper to drain. Serve hot, accompanied by the dipping sauce.

Chicken Croquettes

These tasty bites are a great way to "stretch" a small quantity of chicken to make an appetizer for four people.

Serves 4
25g/1oz/2 tbsp butter
25g/1oz/¼ cup plain (all-purpose) flour
150ml/¼ pint/⅔ cup milk
15ml/1 tbsp olive oil

1 chicken breast fillet with skin, about 75g/3oz, diced
1 garlic clove, finely chopped
1 small egg, beaten
50g/2oz/1 cup fresh white breadcrumbs
vegetable oil, for deep-frying
salt and freshly ground black pepper
flat leaf parsley, to garnish
lemon wedges, to serve

1 Melt the butter in a small pan. Add the flour and cook over a low heat, stirring constantly, for 1 minute. Gradually beat in the milk to make a smooth, very thick sauce. Cover with a lid and remove from the heat.

2 Heat the olive oil in a frying pan and cook the chicken with the garlic for 5 minutes until the chicken is lightly browned and cooked through.

3 Tip the contents of the frying pan into a food processor and process until finely chopped, stopping the motor once to push the contents down with a spatula. Stir into the sauce. Add plenty of salt and freshly ground black pepper to taste, then leave to cool completely.

4 Shape the chicken mixture into eight small sausages using moistened hands. Dip each one in beaten egg and then in breadcrumbs.

5 Heat the oil in a heavy pan or deep-fat fryer. It is ready when a cube of bread tossed into the oil sizzles on the surface. Deep fry the croquettes in the oil for 4 minutes or until crisp and golden. Drain on kitchen paper.

6 Pile the croquettes on to a serving plate, garnish with flat leaf parsley and serve with lemon wedges.

Chicken Goujons

Serve as a first course for eight people or as a filling main course for four.

Serves 4–8
4 skinless chicken breast fillets
175g/6oz/3 cups fresh breadcrumbs
5ml/1 tsp ground coriander
10ml/2 tsp ground paprika
2.5ml/½ tsp ground cumin
45ml/3 tbsp plain (all-purpose) flour
2 eggs, beaten

oil, for deep-frying
salt and freshly ground black pepper
lemon wedges and fresh coriander (cilantro) sprigs, to garnish

For the dip
300ml/½ pint/1¼ cups Greek (US strained plain) yogurt
30ml/2 tbsp lemon juice
60ml/4 tbsp chopped fresh coriander (cilantro)
60ml/4 tbsp chopped fresh parsley

1 Divide the chicken breast portions into two natural fillets. Place them between two sheets of clear film (plastic wrap) and, using a rolling pin, flatten each one to a thickness of 5mm/¼in. Cut on the diagonal into 2.5cm/1in strips.

2 Mix the breadcrumbs with the spices and seasoning in a bowl. Place the flour and beaten eggs in separate bowls.

3 Toss the chicken fillet pieces (goujons) in the flour, keeping them separate. Dip the goujons into the beaten egg and finally coat in the breadcrumb mixture.

4 To make the dip, thoroughly mix all the ingredients together and season to taste. Pour into a serving bowl and chill.

5 Heat the oil in a heavy pan or deep-fat fryer. It is ready when a cube of bread tossed into the oil sizzles on the surface. Fry the goujons, in batches, until golden and crisp. Drain on kitchen paper and keep warm in the oven.

6 Arrange the goujons on a warmed serving plate and garnish with lemon wedges and sprigs of fresh coriander. Serve at once with the dip.

Turkey Sticks with Sour Cream Dip

Pasta Bonbons

Crisp morsels of turkey
with a quick-to-prepare dip.

I small egg, lightly beaten
salt and freshly ground
  black pepper

Serves 4
350g/12oz skinless turkey
  breast fillets
50g/2oz/1 cup fine
  fresh breadcrumbs
1.5ml/¼ tsp paprika

For the sour cream dip
45ml/3 tbsp sour cream
15ml/1 tbsp ready-made
  Fresh Tomato Sauce
15ml/1 tbsp mayonnaise

1 Preheat the oven to 190°C/375°F/Gas 5. Cut the turkey into strips. In a bowl, mix the breadcrumbs and paprika, and season with salt and pepper. Put the beaten egg into another bowl.

2 Dip the turkey strips into the egg, then into the breadcrumbs, turning until evenly coated. Place on a greased baking sheet.

3 Cook the turkey at the top of the oven for 20 minutes until crisp and golden. Turn once during the cooking time.

4 To make the dip, mix all the ingredients together and season to taste. Serve the turkey sticks accompanied by the dip.

These little pasta parcels are
filled with a turkey stuffing.

Serves 4–6
I quantity of Basic Pasta Dough
flour, for dusting
I egg white, beaten
salt and freshly ground
  black pepper

For the filling
I small onion, finely chopped
I garlic clove, crushed
150ml/¼ pint/ ⅔ cup
  Chicken Stock

225g/8oz minced (ground) turkey
2–3 fresh sage leaves, chopped
2 canned anchovy fillets, drained

For the sauce
150ml/¼ pint/⅔ cup
  Chicken Stock
200g/7oz/scant 1 cup
  cream cheese
15ml/1 tbsp lemon juice
5ml/1 tsp caster (superfine) sugar
2 tomatoes, peeled, seeded and
  finely diced
½ red onion, finely chopped
6 small pickled gherkins, sliced

1 To make the filling, put the onion, garlic and stock into a pan. Cover and simmer for 5 minutes. Uncover and boil for 5 minutes, or until the stock has reduced to 30ml/2 tbsp.

2 Add the turkey and stir until it is no longer pink. Add the sage and anchovies and season. Cook, uncovered, for 5 minutes until all the liquid has been absorbed. Leave to cool.

3 Divide the pasta dough in half. Roll into thin sheets and cut into 9 × 6cm/3½ × 2½in rectangles. Lay on a lightly floured dishtowel. Repeat with the remaining dough. Place a teaspoon of the filling on the centre of each rectangle, brush around the meat with egg white and roll up the pasta, pinching in the ends. Transfer to a floured dishtowel and rest for 1 hour.

4 To make the sauce, put the stock, cream cheese, lemon juice and sugar into a pan. Heat gently and whisk until smooth. Add the tomatoes, onion and gherkins. Keep warm.

5 Cook the pasta bonbons in a large pan of boiling, salted water for 5 minutes. Remove with a slotted spoon, drain well and serve immediately with the sauce poured over.

Basic Pasta Dough

200g/7oz/1¾ cups plain
  (all-purpose) flour
pinch of salt
2 eggs
10ml/2 tsp cold water

1 Sift the flour and salt on to a work surface. Make a well in the centre. Break the eggs and add the water to the well.

2 Using a fork, beat the eggs gently together, then draw in the flour to make a thick paste.
3 Use your hands to mix to a firm dough.
4 Knead for 5 minutes, until smooth. Wrap the pasta in clear film (plastic wrap) and leave to rest for 20–30 minutes.

PIES, CASSEROLES & BAKED DISHES

One of the easiest and most enjoyable ways to entertain and to ensure that you spend plenty of time with your guests is to choose a main course dish that can be wholly or partly prepared in advance. This chapter offers a dazzling array of pies, succulent casseroles and fabulous baked dishes, which can be left to cook to perfection while you join the party. The recipes have been inspired by cuisines from all over the world – Greece, Hungary, Morocco, the Middle East, Italy, China and Iran – and range from the traditional to the innovative. What could make your guests feel more welcome on a cold winter's night than a richly flavoured, hearty casserole or a steaming dish of chicken-filled baked pasta served piping hot straight from the oven? Equally delicious on a warm summer evening would be a cold chicken pie topped with crisp, golden pastry. For more lavish occasions, there are some superb buffet dishes from a light-as-air bouchée to an elegant Chinese combination of chicken and ham that looks almost too pretty to eat. Whatever the occasion, this chapter has just the right special dish.

Traditional Chicken Pie

Chicken, vegetables and herbs in a creamy white sauce with a top crust of rich pastry: a perennial family favourite.

Serves 6
50g/2oz/4 tbsp butter
  or margarine
1 medium onion, chopped
3 carrots, cut into 1cm/½in dice
1 parsnip, cut into 1cm/½in dice
45ml/3 tbsp plain (all-
  purpose) flour
350ml/12fl oz/1½ cups
  Chicken Stock
90ml/6 tbsp medium sherry
90ml/6 tbsp dry white wine
175ml/6fl oz/¾ cup
  whipping cream

115g/4oz/1 cup frozen
  peas, thawed
350g/12oz cooked chicken meat,
  in chunks
5ml/1 tsp dried thyme
15ml/1 tbsp finely chopped
  fresh parsley
salt and freshly ground
  black pepper

For the pastry
165g/5½oz/1⅓ cups plain flour,
  plus extra for dusting
2.5ml/½ tsp salt
115g/4oz/½ cup lard (shortening)
  or vegetable fat
30–45ml/2–3 tbsp iced water
1 egg
30ml/2 tbsp milk

1 To make the pastry, sift the flour and salt into a mixing bowl. Using a pastry blender, cut in the fat until the mixture resembles coarse breadcrumbs. Sprinkle in the water, 15ml/1 tbsp at a time, tossing lightly with a fork until the dough forms a ball. Dust with flour, wrap and chill until required.

2 Preheat the oven to 200°C/400°F/Gas 6. Heat half of the butter or margarine in a pan. Add the onion, carrots and parsnip, and cook for about 10 minutes until softened. Remove the vegetables from the pan using a slotted spoon.

3 Melt the remaining butter or margarine in the pan. Add the flour and cook for 5 minutes, stirring constantly. Stir in the stock, sherry and wine. Bring the sauce to the boil and continue boiling for 1 minute, stirring constantly.

4 Add the cream, peas, chicken, thyme and parsley to the sauce. Season to taste with salt and pepper. Simmer for 1 minute, stirring. Transfer to a 2 litre/3½ pint/8¾ cup ovenproof dish. Dampen the rim of the dish.

5 On a lightly floured surface, roll out the pastry to 1cm/½in thickness. Lay the pastry over the dish and trim off the excess. Using a fork, press the pastry to the rim to seal.

6 Lightly whisk the egg with the milk. Brush the pastry all over with the egg glaze. Cut decorative shapes from the pastry trimmings and arrange on top of the pie. Brush again with the egg glaze. Make one or two holes in the crust so that steam can escape during baking.

7 Bake the pie for about 35 minutes until the pastry is golden brown. Serve hot.

Old-fashioned Chicken Pie

The chicken can be roasted and the sauce prepared a day in advance.

Serves 4
1.75kg/4lb chicken
1 onion, quartered
1 fresh tarragon or
  rosemary sprig
25g/1oz/2 tbsp butter
115g/4oz/1½ cups button
  (white) mushrooms

30ml/2 tbsp plain (all-
  purpose) flour
300ml/½ pint/1¼ cups
  Chicken Stock
115g/4oz/¾ cup cooked
  ham, diced
30ml/2 tbsp chopped
  fresh parsley
450g/1lb ready-made puff or
  flaky pastry
1 egg, beaten
salt and freshly ground
  black pepper

1 Preheat the oven to 200°C/400°F/Gas 6. Put the chicken into a casserole with the onion and herbs. Add 300ml/½ pint/1¼ cups water and season. Cover with a lid and cook in the oven for about 1¼ hours or until tender.

2 Remove the chicken from the casserole and strain the cooking liquid into a measuring jug (cup). Leave to cool and remove any fat. Make up to 300ml/½ pint/1¼ cups with water.

3 Remove the bones and skin from the chicken and dice the meat. Melt the butter in a pan and cook the mushrooms for 2–3 minutes. Sprinkle in the flour and blend in the stock. Bring to the boil, season and add the ham, chicken and parsley. Turn into a pie dish and cool before covering with pastry.

4 Roll out the pastry to 5cm/2in larger than the pie dish. Cut a narrow strip, dampen with a little water and stick to the rim. Brush with egg. Lay the pastry over the pie and press firmly on to the rim. Trim away the excess and knock up the sides. Crimp the edge and cut a hole in the centre to allow steam to escape. Decorate with pastry leaves cut from the trimmings.

5 Brush the top of the pie with beaten egg and bake in the oven for about 35 minutes or until the pastry is golden brown.

Chicken en Croûte

Chicken breasts layered with herbs and orange-flavoured stuffing and wrapped in a light puff pastry make an impressive dinner-party dish.

Serves 8
450g/1lb ready-made puff pastry
4 large skinless chicken
   breast fillets
1 egg, beaten
lightly cooked vegetables,
   to serve

For the stuffing
115g/4oz leeks, thinly sliced
50g/2oz/ ⅓ cup streaky (fatty)
   bacon, chopped
25g/1oz/2 tbsp butter
115g/4oz/2 cups fresh
   white breadcrumbs
30ml/2 tbsp chopped fresh herbs,
   e.g. parsley, thyme, marjoram
   and chives
grated rind of 1 large orange
1 egg, beaten
salt and freshly ground
   black pepper

1 To make the stuffing, cook the leeks and bacon in the butter until soft. Put the breadcrumbs, herbs and seasoning in a bowl. Add the leeks and butter with the orange rind and bind with beaten egg. If the mixture is too dry, add a little orange juice.

2 Preheat the oven to 200°C/400°F/Gas 6. Roll out the pastry to a large rectangle 30 × 40cm/12 × 16in. Trim the edges and reserve the trimmings for the decoration.

3 Place the chicken between two pieces of clear film (plastic wrap) and flatten to a thickness of 5mm/¼in with a rolling pin or meat mallet. Spread one-third of the stuffing over the centre of the pastry. Lay two chicken fillets, side by side, over the stuffing. Cover with another third of the stuffing, then repeat with two more chicken fillets and the rest of the stuffing.

4 Cut diagonally from each corner of the pastry to the chicken. Brush with beaten egg. Bring up the sides and overlap them slightly. Trim away any excess and fold the ends over like a parcel. Turn over on to a greased baking sheet. Using a sharp knife, lightly criss-cross the pastry into a diamond pattern. Brush with beaten egg and cut leaves from the trimmings to decorate the top. Bake for 50–60 minutes. Serve hot with vegetables.

Chicken & Apricot Filo Pie

The filling for this pie has a Middle Eastern flavour – chicken combined with apricots, bulgur wheat, nuts and spices.

Serves 6
75g/3oz/ ½ cup bulgur wheat
75g/3oz/6 tbsp butter
1 onion, chopped
450g/1lb minced (ground) chicken
50g/2oz/¼ cup ready-to-eat dried
   apricots, finely chopped
25g/1oz/ ¼ cup blanched
   almonds, chopped
5ml/1 tsp ground cinnamon
2.5ml/ ½ tsp ground allspice
50ml/2fl oz/ ¼ cup Greek
   (US strained plain) yogurt
15ml/1 tbsp chopped fresh chives
30ml/2 tbsp chopped
   fresh parsley
6 large sheets filo pastry, thawed
   if frozen
salt and freshly ground
   black pepper
fresh whole chives, to garnish

1 Preheat the oven to 200°C/400°F/Gas 6. Put the bulgur wheat in a bowl with 120ml/4fl oz/½ cup boiling water. Soak for 5–10 minutes until the water is absorbed.

2 Heat 25g/1oz/2 tbsp of the butter in a pan and gently fry the onion and chicken until pale golden, stirring frequently. Add the apricots, almonds and bulgur wheat, and cook for a further 2 minutes. Remove from the heat and stir in the cinnamon, allspice, yogurt, chives and parsley. Season to taste.

3 Melt the remaining butter. Unroll the filo pastry and cut into 25cm/10in rounds. Keep the pastry rounds covered with a clean, damp dishtowel to prevent them from drying out.

4 Line a 23cm/9in loose-based flan tin (tart pan) with three of the pastry rounds, brushing each with melted butter as you layer them. Spoon in the chicken mixture and cover with three more pastry rounds, brushed with melted butter as before.

5 Crumple the remaining pastry rounds and place them on top of the pie, then brush over any remaining melted butter. Bake for about 30 minutes until the pastry is golden brown and crisp. Serve hot or cold, garnished with whole chives.

Chicken Bouchée

A spectacular centrepiece, this light pastry case contains a delicious chicken and mushroom filling.

Serves 4

450g/1lb ready-made puff pastry
1 egg, beaten

For the filling

15ml/1 tbsp oil
450g/1lb minced (ground) chicken
25g/1oz/¼ cup plain
   (all-purpose) flour
150ml/¼ pint/⅔ cup milk
150ml/¼ pint/⅔ cup
   Chicken Stock
4 spring onions
   (scallions), chopped
25g/1oz/¼ cup redcurrants
75g/3oz/generous 1 cup button
   (white) mushrooms, sliced
15ml/1 tbsp chopped
   fresh tarragon
salt and freshly ground
   black pepper

1 Preheat the oven to 200°C/400°F/Gas 6. Roll out half the pastry on a lightly floured surface to a 25cm/10in oval. Roll out the remainder to an oval of the same size and draw a smaller 20cm/8in oval in the centre.

2 Brush the edge of the first pastry shape with the beaten egg and place the smaller oval on top. Place on a dampened baking sheet and cook for 30 minutes in the oven.

3 To make the filling, heat the oil in a large pan. Fry the chicken for 5 minutes, stirring frequently. Add the flour and cook for a further 1 minute. Stir in the milk and stock, and bring to the boil. Add the spring onions, redcurrants and mushrooms. Cook for 20 minutes. Stir in the tarragon and season to taste.

4 Place the pastry bouchée on a serving plate, remove the oval centre and spoon in the filling. Replace the "lid" and serve.

Variation
You can also use shortcrust (unsweetened) pastry for this dish and cook as a traditional chicken pie.

Kotopitta

This is based on a Greek chicken pie. Serve hot or cold with a Greek salad of tomatoes, cucumber and cubes of feta cheese.

Serves 4

275g/10oz filo pastry, thawed
   if frozen
30ml/2 tbsp olive oil
75g/3oz/¾ cup chopped
   toasted almonds
30ml/2 tbsp milk
Greek salad, to serve

For the filling

15ml/1 tbsp olive oil
1 medium onion, finely chopped
1 garlic clove, crushed
450g/1lb boneless cooked chicken
50g/2oz feta cheese, crumbled
2 eggs, beaten
15ml/1 tbsp chopped fresh parsley
15ml/1 tbsp chopped
   fresh coriander (cilantro)
15ml/1 tbsp chopped fresh mint
salt and freshly ground
   black pepper

1 To make the filling, heat the oil in a large frying pan and cook the onion gently until soft. Add the garlic and cook for a further 2 minutes. Transfer to a bowl.

2 Remove the skin from the chicken and mince (grind) or chop the meat finely. Add to the onion with the rest of the filling ingredients. Mix together thoroughly and season to taste with salt and pepper.

3 Preheat the oven to 190°C/375°F/Gas 5. Have a damp dishtowel ready to keep the filo pastry covered. Unravel the pastry and cut the whole batch into a 30cm/12in square. Taking half the sheets (cover the remainder), brush one sheet with a little olive oil, lay it on a well-greased 1.5 litre/2½ pint/6¼ cup ovenproof dish and sprinkle with a few chopped, toasted almonds. Repeat with the other uncovered sheets of filo, overlapping them alternately into the dish. Spoon in the filling and cover the pie in the same way with the rest of the pastry.

4 Fold in the overlapping edges and mark a diamond pattern on the surface of the pie with a sharp knife. Brush with milk and sprinkle on any remaining almonds. Bake for 20–30 minutes or until golden brown on top. Serve with Greek salad.

Bisteeya

This intriguing dish is a simplified version of a Moroccan speciality.

Serves 4
30ml/2 tbsp sunflower oil, plus
   extra for brushing
25g/1oz/2 tbsp butter
3 chicken quarters,
   preferably breast portions
1½ Spanish onions, grated or
   very finely chopped
good pinch of ground ginger
good pinch of saffron powder
10ml/2 tsp ground cinnamon, plus
   extra for dusting
40g/1½ oz/4 tbsp
   flaked almonds
1 large bunch fresh coriander
   (cilantro), finely chopped
1 large bunch fresh parsley,
   finely chopped
3 eggs, beaten
about 175g/6oz filo pastry
5–10ml/1–2 tsp icing
   (confectioners') sugar
   (optional), plus extra for dusting
salt and freshly ground
   black pepper

1 Heat the oil and butter in a large, flameproof casserole or pan and brown the chicken pieces for about 4 minutes. Add the onions, ginger, saffron, 2.5ml/ ¼ tsp of the cinnamon and enough water (about 300ml/ ½ pint/1¼ cups) so that the chicken braises, rather than boils. Season well.

2 Bring to the boil, then cover and simmer very gently for 45–55 minutes or until the chicken is tender. Meanwhile, dry-fry the almonds until golden and set aside.

3 Transfer the chicken to a plate and leave to cool. When it is cool enough to handle, remove the skin and bones and cut the flesh into pieces.

4 Stir the coriander and parsley into the pan, and simmer the sauce until well reduced and thick. Add the beaten eggs and cook over a very gentle heat until they are lightly scrambled.

5 Preheat the oven to 180°C/350°F/Gas 4. Oil a shallow, round ovenproof dish, about 25cm/10in in diameter. Place one or two sheets of filo pastry in a single layer over the base of the dish (it will depend on the size of your filo pastry), so that it is completely covered and the edges of the pastry sheets hang over the sides. Brush lightly with oil and make two more layers of filo, brushing with oil between the layers. Place the chicken on the pastry and then spoon the egg mixture on top.

6 Place a single layer of filo pastry on top of the filling (you may need to use more than one sheet of filo pastry) and scatter with the almonds. Sprinkle with the remaining cinnamon and the icing sugar, if using.

7 Fold the edges of the filo over the almonds and then make four further layers of filo (using one or two sheets per layer, depending on size), brushing each layer with a little oil. Tuck the filo edges under the pie (as if you were making a bed) and brush the top layer with oil.

8 Bake in the oven for 40–45 minutes until golden. Dust the top with icing sugar and use the extra cinnamon to make criss-cross or diagonal lines. Serve immediately.

Chicken in Badacsonyi Wine

A Hungarian recipe, originally made with a Balatan wine called *Badacsonyi Këkryalii* ("Blue Handled"), which has a full body and distinctive bouquet.

Serves 4
50g/2oz/4 tbsp butter
4 spring onions
   (scallions), chopped
115g/4oz rindless smoked
   bacon, diced
2 bay leaves
1 fresh tarragon sprig
1.5kg/3½ lb corn-fed chicken
60ml/4 tbsp sweet sherry
   or mead
115g/4oz/1½ cups button
   (white) mushrooms, sliced
300ml/ ½ pint/1¼ cups
   Badacsonyi or dry white wine
salt
fresh tarragon and bay leaves,
   to garnish
steamed rice, to serve

1 Heat the butter in a large, heavy pan or flameproof casserole and sweat the spring onions for 1–1½ minutes. Add the bacon, bay leaves and tarragon, stripping the leaves from the stem. Cook for a further 1 minute.

2 Add the whole chicken to the pan and pour in the sherry or mead. Cook, covered, over a very low heat for 15 minutes.

3 Sprinkle the mushrooms into the pan and pour in the wine. Cook, covered, for 1 hour. Remove the lid, baste the chicken with the wine mixture and cook, uncovered, for a further 30 minutes, until almost all the liquid has evaporated.

4 Skim the fat from the cooking liquid remaining in the pan. Taste and adjust the seasoning as necessary. Transfer the chicken, vegetables and bacon to a serving dish. Garnish with tarragon and bay leaves, and serve with rice.

Cook's Tip
Traditionally, this recipe also used a sweet drink with a honeyed caramel flavour called marc. If you can obtain this, use it instead of the sweet sherry or mead.

Curried Apricot & Chicken Casserole

A mild curried and fruity chicken dish served with almond rice, this makes a good winter meal.

Serves 4
15ml/1 tbsp oil
8 large skinless boneless chicken thighs
1 medium onion, finely chopped
5ml/1 tsp medium curry powder
30ml/2 tbsp plain (all-purpose) flour

450ml/ ¾ pint/scant 2 cups Chicken Stock
juice of 1 large orange
8 dried apricots, halved
15ml/1 tbsp sultanas (golden raisins)
salt and freshly ground black pepper

For the almond rice
225g/8oz/1 cup cooked rice
15g/½oz/1 tbsp butter
50g/2oz/ ½ cup toasted almonds

1 Preheat the oven to 190°C/375°F/Gas 5. Heat the oil in a large frying pan. Cut the chicken into cubes and brown quickly all over in the oil.

2 Add the onion and cook gently until soft and lightly browned.

3 Transfer to a large, flameproof casserole, sprinkle in the curry powder and cook again for a few minutes. Add the flour, and blend in the stock and orange juice. Bring to the boil and season with salt and pepper.

4 Add the apricots and sultanas, cover and cook in the oven for 1 hour or until tender. Adjust the seasoning to taste.

5 To make the almond rice, reheat the precooked rice with the butter and season to taste. Stir in the toasted almonds. Serve with the chicken.

> **Variation**
> *This recipe would also work well with diced turkey breast or other boneless turkey meat.*

Spiced Chicken & Apricot Pie

This pie is unusually sweet-sour and very moreish. Use boneless turkey instead of chicken if you wish, or even some leftovers from a roast turkey – the dark, moist leg meat is best.

Serves 6
30ml/2 tbsp sunflower oil
1 large onion, chopped
450g/1lb boneless chicken, roughly chopped
15ml/1 tbsp curry paste or powder

30ml/2 tbsp apricot or peach chutney
115g/4oz/ ½ cup ready-to-eat dried apricots, halved
115g/4oz cooked carrots, sliced
5ml/1 tsp dried mixed herbs
60ml/4 tbsp crème fraîche
350g/12oz ready-made shortcrust (unsweetened) pastry
a little egg or milk, to glaze
salt and freshly ground black pepper
cooked vegetables, to serve

1 Heat the oil in a large, heavy frying pan and fry the onion and chicken until just colouring. Add the curry paste or powder and fry, stirring constantly, for 2 minutes more.

2 Add the chutney, apricots, carrots, herbs and crème fraîche to the pan, and season to taste with salt and pepper. Mix well, then transfer to a deep 900ml–1.2 litre/1½–2 pint/3¾–5 cup pie dish.

3 Preheat the oven to 190°C/375°F/Gas 5. Roll out the pastry to 2.5cm/1in wider than the pie dish. Cut a strip of pastry from the edge. Dampen the rim of the dish, press on the strip, then brush this strip with water and place the sheet of pastry on top. Press to seal and trim to fit.

4 Use the pastry trimmings to decorate the top of the pie if you wish. Brush all over with beaten egg or milk, to glaze, and bake in the oven for 40 minutes until crisp and golden. Serve hot with vegetables.

Chicken Fricassée Forestier

The term fricassée is used to describe a light stew, usually of chicken that is first sautéed in butter. The accompanying sauce can vary, but here wild mushrooms and bacon provide a rich flavour.

Serves 4

3 chicken breast portions, sliced
50g/2oz/4 tbsp unsalted (sweet) butter
15ml/1 tbsp vegetable oil
115g/4oz rindless streaky (fatty) bacon, cut into pieces
75ml/5 tbsp dry sherry or white wine
1 medium onion, chopped
350g/12oz/4½ cups assorted wild mushrooms, such as chanterelles, ceps, horn of plenty, chicken of the woods and closed field (portabello) mushrooms, trimmed and sliced
40g/1½oz/3 tbsp plain (all-purpose) flour
550ml/18fl oz/2½ cups Chicken Stock
10ml/2 tsp lemon juice
60ml/4 tbsp chopped fresh parsley
salt and freshly ground black pepper
boiled rice, carrots and baby corn, to serve

1 Season the chicken with pepper. Heat half of the butter with the oil in a large, heavy frying pan or flameproof casserole, and brown the chicken and bacon pieces. Transfer to a shallow dish and pour off any excess fat.

2 Return the pan to the heat and brown the sediment. Pour in the sherry or wine and stir to deglaze the pan. Pour the sherry or wine liquid over the chicken and wipe the pan clean.

3 Fry the onion in the remaining butter until golden brown. Add the mushrooms and cook, stirring frequently, for 6–8 minutes until their juices begin to run. Stir in the flour, then remove from the heat. Gradually add the chicken stock and stir well until the flour is completely absorbed.

4 Add the reserved chicken and bacon with the sherry or wine juices, return to the heat and stir to thicken. Simmer for about 10–15 minutes and then add the lemon juice, parsley and seasoning. Serve with boiled rice, carrots and baby corn.

Coq au Vin

This classic French dish was originally made with an old rooster, marinated then slowly braised until tender.

Serves 4

1.5–1.75kg/3½–4lb chicken, cut into portions
25ml/1½ tbsp olive oil
225g/8oz baby onions
15g/½oz/1 tbsp butter
225g/8oz/3 cups mushrooms, quartered if large
30ml/2 tbsp plain (all-purpose) flour
750ml/1¼ pints/3 cups dry red wine
250ml/8fl oz/1 cup Chicken Stock, or more to cover
bouquet garni
salt and freshly ground black pepper

1 Pat the chicken pieces dry and season with salt and pepper. Place in a large, heavy frying pan, skin side down, and cook over a medium-high heat for 10–12 minutes or until golden brown. Transfer to a plate.

2 Meanwhile, heat the oil in a large, flameproof casserole over a medium-low heat, add the onions and cook, covered, until evenly browned, stirring frequently.

3 Wipe the frying pan clean and melt the butter in it over a medium heat. Add the mushrooms and sauté, stirring, until golden brown.

4 Sprinkle the onions in the casserole with flour and cook for 2 minutes, stirring frequently, then add the wine and boil for 1 minute, stirring. Add the chicken, mushrooms, stock and bouquet garni. Bring to the boil, reduce the heat to very low and simmer, covered, for 45–50 minutes until the chicken is tender and the juices run clear when the thickest part of the meat is pierced with a skewer or knife.

5 Transfer the chicken pieces and vegetables to a plate. Strain the cooking liquid, skim off the fat and return the liquid to the pan. Boil to reduce by one-third, then return the chicken and vegetables to the casserole and simmer for 3–4 minutes to heat through. Serve immediately.

Chicken with Shallots

Shallots are cooked whole in this casserole, which makes the most of their superb, mild onion flavour.

Serves 4
1.3kg/3lb chicken or
   4 chicken portions
seasoned flour, for coating
30ml/2 tbsp sunflower oil
25g/1oz/2 tbsp butter
115g/4oz/⅔ cup unsmoked
   streaky (fatty) bacon, rinded
   and chopped

2 garlic cloves
450ml/ ¾ pint/scant 2 cups
   red wine
1 bay leaf
2 fresh thyme sprigs
250g/9oz shallots
115g/4oz/1½ cups button (white)
   mushrooms, halved if large
10ml/2 tsp plain (all-
   purpose) flour
salt and freshly ground
   black pepper

1 Preheat the oven to 180°C/350°F/Gas 4. If using a whole chicken, cut into four or eight pieces. Place the seasoned flour in a plastic bag, add the chicken pieces and shake to coat.

2 Heat half the oil and half the butter in a flameproof casserole and fry the bacon and garlic for 3–4 minutes. Add the chicken and fry until lightly browned. Add the wine, bay leaf and thyme, and bring to the boil. Cover and cook in the oven for 1 hour.

3 Boil the shallots in salted water for 10 minutes. Heat the remaining oil in a small frying pan and fry the shallots for 3–4 minutes until beginning to brown. Add the mushrooms and fry for a further 2–3 minutes.

4 Stir the shallots and mushrooms into the chicken casserole, and cook for a further 8–10 minutes. Using a fork, blend the flour with the remaining butter to make a thick paste.

5 Transfer the chicken, shallots and mushrooms to a serving dish and keep warm. Bring the liquid to the boil, then add small pieces of the flour paste, stirring vigorously after each addition. When the sauce is thick, either pour it over the chicken pieces or return the chicken to the casserole, and serve.

Old-fashioned Chicken Fricassée

A fricassée is a classic dish in which poultry is first seared in fat, then braised with liquid until cooked. This recipe is finished with a little cream, but you can leave it out if you wish.

Serves 4–6
1.2–1.3kg/2½–3lb chicken, cut
   into portions
50g/2oz/4 tbsp butter
30ml/2 tbsp vegetable oil
25g/1oz/ ¼ cup plain (all-
   purpose) flour
250ml/8fl oz/1 cup dry
   white wine

750ml/1¼ pints/3 cups
   Chicken Stock
bouquet garni
1.5ml/ ¼ tsp white pepper
225g/8oz/3 cups button (white)
   mushrooms, trimmed
5ml/1 tsp lemon juice
16–24 small white onions, peeled
120ml/4fl oz/ ½ cup water
5ml/1 tsp sugar
90ml/6 tbsp whipping cream
salt
30ml/2 tbsp chopped fresh
   parsley, to garnish

1 Wash the chicken pieces, then pat dry with kitchen paper. Melt half the butter with the oil in a large, heavy flameproof casserole over a medium heat. Add half the chicken pieces and cook for 10 minutes, turning occasionally, or until just golden. Transfer to a plate, then cook the remaining pieces.

2 Return the seared chicken pieces to the casserole. Sprinkle with the flour, turning the pieces to coat. Cook over a low heat for about 4 minutes, turning occasionally.

3 Pour in the wine, bring to the boil and add the stock. Push the chicken pieces aside and scrape the base of the casserole, stirring until well blended.

4 Bring the liquid to the boil, add the bouquet garni and season with a pinch of salt and the white pepper. Cover and simmer over a medium heat for 25–30 minutes until the chicken is tender and the juices run clear when the thickest part of the thigh is pierced with a knife or skewer.

5 Meanwhile, in a frying pan, heat the remaining butter over a medium-high heat. Add the mushrooms and lemon juice, and cook for 3–4 minutes until the mushrooms are golden, stirring.

6 Add the onions, water and sugar to the pan, swirling to dissolve the sugar. Simmer for about 10 minutes, until just tender. Tip the onions and any juices into a bowl with the mushrooms and set aside.

7 When the chicken is cooked, transfer the pieces to a deep serving dish and cover with foil to keep warm. Discard the bouquet garni. Add any cooking juices from the vegetables to the casserole. Bring to the boil and cook, stirring frequently, until the sauce is reduced by half.

8 Whisk the cream into the sauce and cook for 2 minutes. Add the mushrooms and onions, and cook for a further 2 minutes. Adjust the seasoning, then pour the sauce over the chicken, sprinkle with parsley and serve.

Chicken Casserole with Spiced Figs

A Spanish recipe which, rather unusually, combines chicken with succulent figs.

Serves 4

150g/5oz/ ⅔ cup granulated sugar
120ml/4fl oz/ ½ cup white
   wine vinegar
1 lemon slice
1 cinnamon stick
450g/1lb fresh figs
120ml/4fl oz/ ½ cup medium
   sweet white wine
pared rind of ½ lemon
1.5kg/3½lb chicken, cut into
   8 portions
50g/2oz lardons, or thick streaky
   (fatty) bacon cut into strips
15ml/1 tbsp olive oil
50ml/2fl oz/ ¼ cup Chicken Stock
salt and freshly ground
   black pepper

1 Put the sugar, vinegar, lemon slice and cinnamon stick in a pan with 120ml/4fl oz/ ½ cup water. Bring to the boil, then simmer for 5 minutes. Add the figs, cover and simmer for 10 minutes. Remove from the heat, cover and leave to stand for 3 hours.

2 Preheat the oven to 180°C/350°F/Gas 4. Drain the figs and place in a bowl. Add the wine and lemon rind. Season the chicken with salt and pepper.

3 In a large frying pan, cook the lardons or streaky bacon strips until the fat melts and they turn golden. Transfer to a shallow, ovenproof dish, leaving any fat in the pan. Add the oil to the pan and brown the chicken pieces all over.

4 Drain the figs, adding the wine to the chicken in the frying pan. Boil until the sauce has reduced and is syrupy. Transfer the contents of the frying pan to the ovenproof dish and cook in the oven, uncovered, for about 20 minutes.

5 Add the figs and chicken stock, cover and return to the oven for a further 10 minutes. Taste and adjust the seasoning as necessary. Serve hot.

Chicken with Chianti

Together the robust, full-flavoured Italian red wine and red pesto give this sauce a rich colour and almost spicy flavour, while the grapes add a delicious touch of sweetness.

Serves 4

45ml/3 tbsp olive oil
4 skinless part-boned chicken
   breast portions
1 medium red onion
30ml/2 tbsp red pesto
300ml/ ½ pint/1¼ cups Chianti
300ml/ ½ pint/1¼ cups water
115g/4oz red grapes, halved
   lengthways and seeded
   if necessary
salt and freshly ground
   black pepper
fresh parsley leaves, to garnish
rocket (arugula) salad, to serve

1 Heat 30ml/2 tbsp of the oil in a large frying pan, add the chicken breast portions and sauté over a medium heat for about 5 minutes until they have changed colour on all sides. Remove using a slotted spoon and drain on kitchen paper.

2 Cut the onion in half, through the root. Trim off the root, then slice the onion halves lengthways to create thin wedges.

3 Heat the remaining oil in the pan, add the onion wedges and red pesto, and cook gently, stirring constantly, for about 3 minutes until the onion is softened, but not browned.

4 Add the Chianti and water to the pan and bring to the boil, stirring constantly. Return the chicken to the pan and season with salt and pepper to taste.

5 Reduce the heat, then cover the pan and simmer gently for about 20 minutes or until the chicken is tender and cooked through, stirring occasionally.

6 Add the grapes to the pan and cook over a low to medium heat until heated through. Taste the sauce and adjust the seasoning as necessary. Serve the chicken hot, garnished with parsley and accompanied by the rocket salad.

Chicken Kdra with Chickpeas & Almonds

A kdra is a type of Moroccan tagine. The almonds in this recipe are precooked until soft, adding an interesting texture and flavour to the chicken.

Serves 4
75g/3oz/¾ cup blanched almonds
75g/3oz/scant ½ cup chickpeas, soaked in water overnight
4 skinless part-boned chicken breast portions
50g/2oz/4 tbsp butter
2.5ml/ ½ tsp saffron
2 Spanish onions, thinly sliced
900ml/1½ pints/3¾ cups Chicken Stock
1 small cinnamon stick
60ml/4 tbsp chopped fresh flat leaf parsley, plus extra to garnish
lemon juice, to taste
salt and freshly ground black pepper

1 Place the almonds in a pan of water and simmer for 1½–2 hours until fairly soft. Drain and set aside.

2 Cook the chickpeas for 1–1½ hours until soft. Drain, then place in a bowl of cold water and rub with your fingers to remove the skins. Discard the skins and drain.

3 Place the chicken portions in a flameproof casserole together with the butter, half of the saffron, salt and plenty of black pepper. Heat gently, stirring, until the butter has melted.

4 Add the onions and stock, bring to the boil and then add the chickpeas and cinnamon stick. Cover and cook very gently for 45–60 minutes until the chicken is completely tender.

5 Transfer the chicken to a serving plate and keep warm. Bring the sauce to the boil and simmer until well reduced, stirring frequently. Remove and discard the cinnamon stick. Add the cooked almonds, the parsley and remaining saffron to the sauce, and cook for a further 2–3 minutes. Sharpen the sauce with a little lemon juice, then pour over the chicken and serve, garnished with extra parsley.

Chicken with Preserved Lemon & Olives

This is one of the most famous Moroccan dishes. You must use preserved lemon, as fresh lemon simply doesn't have the mellow flavour required.

Serves 4
30ml/2 tbsp olive oil
1 Spanish onion, chopped
3 garlic cloves
1cm/ ½in piece fresh root ginger, grated, or 2.5ml/ ½ tsp ground ginger
2.5–5ml/ ½–1 tsp ground cinnamon
pinch of saffron
4 chicken quarters, preferably breast portions, halved if liked
750ml/1¼ pints/3 cups Chicken Stock
30ml/2 tbsp chopped fresh coriander (cilantro)
30ml/2 tbsp chopped fresh parsley
1 preserved lemon
115g/4oz/ ⅔ cup Moroccan tan olives
salt and freshly ground black pepper
lemon wedges and fresh coriander (cilantro) sprigs, to garnish

1 Heat the oil in a large, flameproof casserole and fry the onion for 6–8 minutes over a moderate heat until lightly golden, stirring occasionally.

2 Crush the garlic and blend with the ginger, cinnamon, saffron and seasoning. Stir into the pan and fry for 1 minute. Add the chicken pieces and fry over a moderate heat for 2–3 minutes until lightly browned. Add the stock, coriander and parsley, bring to the boil, then cover and simmer very gently for 45 minutes.

3 Rinse the preserved lemon under cold water, discard the flesh and cut the peel into small pieces. Stir into the pan with the olives and simmer for a further 15 minutes until the chicken is very tender.

4 Transfer the chicken to a plate and keep warm. Bring the sauce to the boil and cook for 3–4 minutes until reduced and fairly thick. Pour over the chicken and serve, garnished with lemon wedges and coriander sprigs.

Stuffed Chicken Breast Fillets with Cream Sauce

The chicken meat encloses a delicately flavoured leek filling with a hint of lime.

Serves 4
4 large skinless chicken breast
   fillets or chicken suprêmes
50g/2oz/4 tbsp butter
3 large leeks, white and pale
   green parts only, thinly sliced
5ml/1 tsp grated lime rind
250ml/8fl oz/1 cup Chicken
   Stock or half stock and half dry
   white wine
120ml/4fl oz/¹⁄₂ cup double
   (heavy) cream
15ml/1 tbsp lime juice
salt and freshly ground
   black pepper
lime twists and fresh parsley
   sprigs, to garnish

1 Cut horizontally into the thickest part of each chicken fillet or suprême to make a deep, wide pocket. Take care not to cut all the way through. Set the chicken aside.

2 Melt half the butter in a large, heavy frying pan over a low heat. Cook the leeks and lime rind, stirring occasionally, for 15–20 minutes or until the leeks are soft but not coloured. Turn them into a bowl, season and leave to cool.

3 Divide the leeks among the chicken pockets, packing them full. Secure the openings with wooden cocktail sticks (toothpicks).

4 Melt the remaining butter in a clean frying pan over a moderate heat. Add the chicken pockets and brown lightly on both sides. Pour in the stock, and wine if using, and bring to the boil. Cover and simmer for about 10 minutes or until the chicken is cooked through.

5 Using a slotted spoon, remove the chicken from the pan and keep warm. Boil the cooking liquid until it is reduced by half. Stir the cream into the cooking liquid and boil until reduced by about half again. Stir in the lime juice and season to taste. Remove the cocktail sticks. Cut each pocket into 1cm/½in slices. Pour the sauce over and garnish with lime and parsley.

Lavender Chicken

Here, lavender flowers are used to perfume and flavour chicken cooked with red wine, oranges and thyme. The heady aroma of this dish will be a talking point among your guests.

Serves 4
15ml/1 tbsp butter
15ml/1 tbsp olive oil
8 chicken portions
8 shallots
30ml/2 tbsp plain (all-
   purpose) flour
250ml/8fl oz/1 cup red wine
250ml/8fl oz/1 cup Chicken Stock
4 fresh thyme sprigs
10ml/2 tsp fresh thyme flowers,
   removed from stalk
10ml/2 tsp lavender flowers
grated rind and juice of 1 orange
salt and freshly ground
   black pepper

To garnish
1 orange, divided into segments
12 fresh lavender sprigs
20ml/4 tsp fresh lavender flowers

1 Heat the butter and oil in a heavy pan and add the chicken portions. Fry until brown all over, then transfer to a large casserole. Add the shallots to the frying pan and cook for 2 minutes. Transfer to the casserole.

2 Add the flour to the frying pan and cook, stirring constantly, for 2 minutes. Pour in enough wine and stock to make a thin sauce, bring to the boil, stirring constantly, and season to taste. Stir in the thyme sprigs, thyme and lavender flowers, orange rind and juice. Pour the sauce over the chicken. Cover and simmer for 30–40 minutes until the chicken is tender.

3 Remove the thyme sprigs. Serve, garnished with orange segments and lavender sprigs and flowers.

> **Cook's Tip**
> *Do not use lavender flowers that may have been sprayed with a toxic substance, or that grow near a busy road and so may have been polluted by traffic fumes.*

Chicken with Sloe Gin & Juniper

Juniper is used in the manufacture of gin, and the reinforcement of the flavour by using both sloe gin and juniper berries is delicious. Sloe gin is easy to make, but can also be bought.

Serves 8
25g/1oz/2 tbsp butter
30ml/2 tbsp sunflower oil
8 chicken breast fillets

350g/12oz carrots, cooked
1 garlic clove, crushed
15ml/1 tbsp finely chopped
    fresh parsley
50ml/2fl oz/ ¼ cup
    Chicken Stock
50ml/2fl oz/ ¼ cup red wine
50ml/2fl oz/ ¼ cup sloe gin
5ml/1 tsp crushed juniper berries
salt and freshly ground
    black pepper
chopped fresh basil, to garnish

1 Heat the butter with the oil in a pan and sauté the chicken until browned on all sides.

2 In a food processor, combine all the remaining ingredients, except the basil, and process to a smooth purée. If the mixture seems too thick, add a little more red wine or water until a thinner consistency is reached.

3 Put the chicken fillets in a heavy pan, pour the sauce over the top of them and cook for about 15 minutes until the chicken is cooked through.

4 Adjust the seasoning to taste and serve, garnished with chopped fresh basil.

> **Variation**
> *Instead of sloe gin, you could make this dish with a herb-flavoured liqueur, such as Benedictine or Galliano, a plum brandy, such as slivovitz or kirsch, or a herb- or plum-flavoured vodka, but still using the juniper berries.*

Herbed Chicken with Apricot & Pecan Potato Baskets

The potato baskets make a pretty addition to the chicken and could easily have different fillings when you need a change.

Serves 8
8 skinless chicken breast fillets
30ml/2 tbsp butter
6 mushrooms, chopped
15ml/1 tbsp chopped pecan nuts
115g/4oz/ ⅓ cup chopped
    cooked ham
50g/2oz/1 cup wholemeal (whole-
    wheat) breadcrumbs
15ml/1 tbsp chopped fresh
    parsley, plus a few whole leaves
    to garnish
salt and freshly ground
    black pepper

For the sauce
10ml/2 tsp cornflour (cornstarch)
120ml/4fl oz/ ½ cup white wine
50g/2oz/4 tbsp butter
50g/2oz apricot chutney

For the potato baskets
4 large baking potatoes
175g/6oz pork sausage (bulk
    sausage) meat
225g/8oz can apricots in natural
    juice, drained and quartered
1.5ml/ ¼ tsp ground cinnamon
2.5ml/ ½ tsp grated orange rind
30ml/2 tbsp maple syrup
25g/1oz/2 tbsp butter
25g/1oz/ ¼ cup chopped pecan
    nuts, plus some pecan halves
    to garnish

1 Preheat the oven to 160°C/325°F/Gas 3. Place the potatoes in the oven to bake. Place the chicken breast fillets between two sheets of clear film (plastic wrap) and beat lightly with a rolling pin or meat mallet to flatten.

2 Melt the butter in a pan and sauté the mushrooms, pecans and ham. Stir in the breadcrumbs and parsley, and season.

3 Divide the mushroom mixture among the chicken fillets. Roll up and secure each one with a wooden cocktail stick (toothpick). Chill while making the sauce.

4 To make the sauce, mix the cornflour with a little of the wine to make a smooth paste. Put the remaining wine in a pan and add the paste. Simmer until smooth, then add the butter and chutney, and cook for about 5 minutes, stirring constantly.

5 Place the chicken breasts in a shallow, ovenproof dish and pour over the sauce. Bake in the oven (do not adjust the temperature) for 20 minutes, basting several times.

6 To make the potato baskets, cut the baked potatoes in half and scoop out the inside, leaving a reasonable layer within the shell. Mash the potato and place in a mixing bowl.

7 Fry the sausagemeat, discarding some of the fat that comes off. Add the remaining ingredients and cook for 1 minute. Add the mixture to the mashed potato, blend and use to fill the potato shells. Sprinkle the pecan halves over the top, place in the oven with the chicken and bake for another 30 minutes.

8 Remove the chicken from the oven and drain the sauce into a jug (pitcher). Slice the chicken, arrange on plates and pour the sauce over. Garnish and serve with the potato baskets.

Steamboat

This Malaysian dish is named after the utensil in which it is cooked – a type of fondue with a funnel and a moat. The moat is filled with stock, which traditionally is kept hot with charcoal. An electric steamboat or any traditional fondue pot can be used instead.

Serves 8

8 Chinese dried mushrooms, soaked for 30 minutes in warm water to cover
1.5 litres/2½ pints/6¼ cups Chicken Stock
10ml/2 tsp rice wine or medium-dry sherry
10ml/2 tsp sesame oil
225g/8oz lean pork, thinly sliced
225g/8oz rump (round) steak, thinly sliced
1 skinless chicken breast fillet, thickly sliced

2 chicken livers, trimmed and sliced
225g/8oz raw prawns (shrimp), peeled
450g/1lb white fish fillets, skinned and cubed
200g/7oz fish balls
115g/4oz fried beancurd (tofu), each piece halved
leafy green vegetables, such as lettuce, Chinese leaves (Chinese cabbage), spinach leaves and watercress, cut into 15cm/ 6in lengths
225g/8oz Chinese rice vermicelli
8 eggs
selection of sauces, including soy with sesame seeds; soy with crushed ginger; chilli; plum and hot mustard
½ bunch spring onions (scallions), chopped
salt and freshly ground white pepper

1 Drain the mushrooms, reserving the soaking liquid. Cut off and discard the stems; slice the caps thinly.

2 Pour the stock into a large pan and add the rice wine or sherry, sesame oil and reserved mushroom liquid. Bring the mixture to the boil, then season with salt and pepper. Reduce the heat and simmer gently.

3 Put the meat, fish, beancurd, vegetables and mushrooms in bowls. Soak the vermicelli in hot water for about 5 minutes, drain and place in eight soup bowls. Crack an egg in a small bowl for each diner and set aside. Put the sauces in bowls.

4 Add the spring onions to the pan of stock, bring it to a full boil and fuel the steamboat. Pour the stock into the moat and seat your guests. Each guest lowers a few chosen morsels into the boiling stock, using chopsticks or fondue forks, leaves them for 1–2 minutes, then removes them with a small wire mesh ladle, a fondue fork or pair of chopsticks.

5 When all the meat, fish, beancurd and vegetables have been cooked, the stock will be concentrated. Add a little boiling water if necessary. Bring the soup bowls containing the soaked noodles to the table, pour in the hot soup and slide a whole egg into each, stirring until it cooks and forms threads.

> **Cook's Tip**
> Fresh or frozen fish balls are available from Asian foodstores and Chinese supermarkets.

Drunken Chicken

In China, "drunken" foods are usually served cold as part of an appetizer to a Chinese meal or as canapés.

Serves 4–6

1 chicken, about 1.3kg/3lb
1cm/½in piece fresh root ginger, thinly sliced
2 spring onions (scallions)
1.75 litres/3 pints/7½ cups water or to cover
15ml/1 tbsp salt
300ml/½ pint/1¼ cups dry sherry
15–30ml/1–2 tbsp brandy
shredded spring onions (scallions) and fresh herbs, to garnish

1 Rinse and dry the chicken inside and out. Place the ginger and spring onions in the body cavity. Put the chicken in a large pan or flameproof casserole and just cover with water. Bring to the boil, skim and cook for 15 minutes.

2 Turn off the heat, cover the pan or casserole tightly and leave the chicken in the cooking liquid for 3–4 hours, by which time it will be cooked. Drain well. Pour 300ml/½ pint/1¼ cups of the stock into a jug (pitcher). Freeze the remainder if you like.

3 Leaving the skin on the chicken, joint it neatly. Divide each leg into a drumstick and thigh. Make two more portions from the wings and some from the breast. Finally cut away the remainder of the breast pieces (still on the bone) and divide each breast into two even-size portions.

4 Arrange the chicken portions in a shallow dish. Rub salt into the skin and cover with clear film (plastic wrap). Leave in a cool place for several hours or overnight in the refrigerator.

5 Next day, lift off and discard any fat from the stock. Mix the sherry and brandy in a jug, add the stock and pour over the chicken. Cover again and leave in the refrigerator to marinate for 2–3 days, turning occasionally.

6 When ready to serve remove the chicken skin. Cut the chicken through the bone into chunky pieces and arrange on a serving platter, garnished with spring onion shreds and herbs.

Chicken, Leek & Bacon Casserole

A moist whole chicken, braised on a bed of leeks and bacon, and topped with a creamy tarragon sauce.

Serves 4–6
15ml/1 tbsp vegetable oil
25g/1oz/2 tbsp butter
1.5kg/3½lb chicken

225g/8oz streaky (fatty) bacon
450g/1lb leeks
250ml/8fl oz/1 cup Chicken Stock
250ml/8fl oz/1 cup double
  (heavy) cream
15ml/1 tbsp chopped
  fresh tarragon
salt and freshly ground
  black pepper

1 Preheat the oven to 180°C/350°F/Gas 4. Heat the oil and melt the butter in a large, flameproof casserole. Add the chicken and cook it, breast side down, for 5 minutes until golden. Remove from the casserole and set aside.

2 Dice the streaky bacon and add to the casserole. Cook for 4–5 minutes until golden brown. Trim the leeks, cut them into 2.5cm/1in pieces and add to the bacon. Cook for another 5 minutes until the leeks begin to brown.

3 Return the chicken to the casserole, placing it on top of the bacon and leeks. Cover and put into the oven. Cook for 1½ hours or until the juices run clear when the thickest part of the thigh is pierced with a skewer or knife.

4 Remove the chicken, bacon and leeks from the casserole and keep warm. Skim the fat from the juices. Pour in the stock and cream and bring to the boil. Cook for 4–5 minutes until slightly reduced and thickened.

5 Stir in the tarragon and seasoning to taste. Carve the chicken and serve with the bacon, leeks and a little sauce.

Stuffed Chicken Rolls

These are simple to make, but sophisticated enough to serve at a dinner party.

Serves 4
25g/1oz/2 tbsp butter
1 garlic clove, chopped
150g/5oz/1¼ cups cooked white
  long grain rice
45ml/3 tbsp ricotta cheese
10ml/2 tsp chopped fresh flat
  leaf parsley

5ml/1 tsp chopped fresh tarragon
4 skinless chicken breast fillets
3–4 slices prosciutto
15ml/1 tbsp olive oil
120ml/4fl oz/ ½ cup white wine
salt and freshly ground
  black pepper
fresh flat leaf parsley sprigs,
  to garnish
cooked tagliatelle and sautéed
  blewit mushrooms,
  to serve (optional)

1 Preheat the oven to 180°C/350°F/Gas 4. Melt about 10g/ ¼oz/1 ½ tsp of the butter in a small pan and fry the garlic for a few seconds without browning. Spoon into a bowl. Add the rice, ricotta, parsley and tarragon to the garlic and season with salt and pepper. Stir to mix.

2 Place each chicken breast fillet in turn between two sheets of clear film (plastic wrap) and flatten by beating lightly, but firmly, with a rolling pin or meat mallet.

3 Lay a slice of prosciutto over each chicken fillet, trimming it to fit if necessary. Place a spoonful of the rice stuffing at the wider end of each fillet. Roll up carefully and tie in place with cooking string or secure with a wooden cocktail stick (toothpick).

4 Heat the oil and the remaining butter in a frying pan and lightly fry the chicken rolls until browned on all sides. Place side by side in a shallow, ovenproof dish and pour over the wine.

5 Cover the dish with greaseproof (waxed) paper and cook in the oven for 30–35 minutes until the chicken is tender.

6 Cut the rolls into slices and serve on a bed of tagliatelle with sautéed blewit mushrooms, if you like. Garnish with fresh, flat leaf parsley.

Soy-braised Chicken

This chicken is cooked whole and divided after cooking. It can be served hot or cold as part of a buffet-style meal.

Serves 6–8
1.3–1.5kg/3–3½lb chicken
15ml/1 tbsp ground
  Sichuan peppercorns
30ml/2 tbsp grated fresh
  root ginger

45ml/3 tbsp light soy sauce
30ml/2 tbsp dark soy sauce
45ml/3 tbsp Chinese rice wine or
  dry sherry
15ml/1 tbsp light brown sugar
vegetable oil, for deep-frying
about 600ml/1 pint/
  2½ cups water
10ml/2 tsp salt
25g/1oz rock sugar
lettuce leaves, to serve

1 Rub the chicken both inside and out with the ground pepper and fresh ginger. In a bowl, mix together the soy sauces, wine or sherry and sugar. Place the chicken in a bowl, pour over the soy mixture and leave to marinate for at least 3 hours, turning several times.

2 Heat the oil in a pan or preheated wok. Remove the chicken from the marinade and deep-fry for 5–6 minutes or until brown all over. Remove and drain.

3 Pour off the excess oil from the pan or wok. Add the marinade with the water, salt and rock sugar, and bring to the boil. Return the chicken to the wok and braise in the sauce for 35–40 minutes, covered, turning once or twice.

4 Remove the chicken from the pan or wok and let it cool a little before cutting it into approximately 30 bitesize pieces. Arrange the pieces on a bed of lettuce leaves, then pour some of the sauce over the chicken and serve. Any leftover sauce can be stored in the refrigerator for use in another dish.

Cook's Tip
Rock sugar is also known as crystal sugar.

Chicken & Ham with Green Vegetables

This dish originates from China, where its name means "Golden Flower and Jade Tree Chicken". It makes a marvellous buffet-style dish for all occasions.

Serves 6–8
1–1.3kg/2¼–3lb chicken
2 spring onions (scallions)
2–3 pieces fresh root ginger
15ml/1 tbsp salt
225g/8oz honey-roast ham
275g/10oz broccoli
45ml/3 tbsp vegetable oil
5ml/1 tsp light brown sugar
10ml/2 tsp cornflour (cornstarch)

1 Place the chicken in a large pan and add sufficient cold water to cover. Add the spring onions, ginger and about 10ml/2 tsp of the salt. Bring to the boil, then cover with a tight-fitting lid, reduce the heat and simmer for 10–15 minutes. Remove from the heat and set aside to let the chicken cook itself in the hot water for at least 4–5 hours – you must not lift the lid as this will let out the residual heat.

2 Remove the chicken from the pan, reserving the liquid, and carefully cut the meat off the bones, keeping the skin on. Slice both the chicken and ham into pieces, each about 5 × 4cm/ 2 × 3in, and arrange the meats in alternating layers on a large serving plate.

3 Cut the broccoli into small florets. Heat the oil in a wok and stir-fry the broccoli with the remaining salt and the sugar for about 2–3 minutes. Arrange the broccoli between the rows of chicken and ham, and around the edge of the plate, making a border around the meat.

4 Heat a small amount of the reserved chicken stock and thicken with the cornflour. Stir until smooth, then pour it evenly all over the chicken and ham so that it forms a thin coat of transparent jelly resembling "jade". Allow to cool before serving.

Duck & Chestnut Casserole

Serve this casserole with a mixture of mashed potatoes and celeriac, to soak up the rich duck juices.

Serves 4–6
2kg/4½lb duck
45ml/3 tbsp olive oil
175g/6oz small onions
50g/2oz/1 cup field (portabello) mushrooms, sliced
50g/2oz/1 cup shiitake mushrooms, sliced
300ml/½ pint/1¼ cups red wine
300ml/½ pint/1¼ cups beef stock
225g/8oz canned, peeled, unsweetened chestnuts, drained
salt and freshly ground black pepper
mashed potatoes and celeriac, to serve
fresh parsley, to garnish

1 Joint the duck into eight pieces. Heat the oil in a large frying pan and brown the duck pieces. Remove from the frying pan using a slotted spoon and set aside.

2 Add the onions to the pan and cook for about 10 minutes until well browned.

3 Add the field and shiitake mushrooms and cook for a few minutes more. Deglaze the pan with the red wine and boil to reduce the volume by half. Meanwhile, preheat the oven to 180°C/350°F/Gas 4.

4 Pour the contents of the frying pan into a casserole and stir in the stock. Add the browned duck and the chestnuts, season well and cook in the oven for 1½ hours until the duck is tender. Serve immediately with mashed potatoes and celeriac, garnished with parsley.

Cook's Tip
Unlike some poultry, duck freezes well because its high fat content ensures that it retains its flavour and moisture when it is thawed. However, the flesh can easily be damaged, so check the packaging carefully before buying. Fresh duck is also available all year round.

Duck Stew with Olives

In this provençal recipe, the sweetness of the onions counterbalances the saltiness of the olives.

Serves 6–8
2 × 1.3kg/3lb ducks, quartered, or 8 duck leg quarters
225g/8oz small onions
30ml/2 tbsp plain (all-purpose) flour
350ml/12fl oz/1½ cups dry red wine
475ml/16fl oz/2 cups duck or Chicken Stock
bouquet garni
115g/4oz/1 cup pitted green or black olives, or a combination
salt, if needed, and freshly ground black pepper

1 Put the duck pieces, skin side down, in a large frying pan over a medium heat and cook for 10–12 minutes until well browned, turning to colour evenly and cooking in batches if necessary. Pour off the fat from the pan.

2 Heat 15ml/1 tbsp of the duck fat in a large, flameproof casserole. Add the onions and cook, covered, over a medium-low heat until evenly browned, stirring frequently. Sprinkle with the flour and continue cooking, uncovered, for 2 minutes, stirring frequently.

3 Stir in the wine and bring to the boil, then add the duck pieces, stock and bouquet garni. Bring back to the boil, then reduce the heat to very low and simmer, covered, for about 40 minutes, stirring occasionally.

4 Rinse the olives in several changes of cold water. If they are very salty, put them into a pan, cover with water and bring to the boil, then drain and rinse. Add the olives to the casserole and cook for a further 20 minutes until the duck is very tender.

5 Transfer the duck pieces, onions and olives to a plate. Strain the cooking liquid, skim off the fat and return the liquid to the pan. Boil to reduce by about one-third, then adjust the seasoning and return the duck and vegetables to the casserole. Simmer gently to heat through before serving.

Persian Chicken with Walnut Sauce

This distinctive dish is traditionally served on festive occasions in Iran.

Serves 4
30ml/2 tbsp oil
4 chicken portions (leg or breast)
1 large onion, grated
250ml/8fl oz/1 cup water
115g/4oz/1 cup finely
    chopped walnuts
75ml/4 tbsp pomegranate
    purée (paste)
15ml/1 tbsp tomato
    purée (paste)
30ml/2 tbsp lemon juice
15ml/1 tbsp sugar
3–4 saffron threads dissolved in
    15ml/1 tbsp boiling water
salt and freshly ground
    black pepper
rice and salad leaves, to serve

1 Heat 15ml/1 tbsp of the oil in a large pan or flameproof casserole and sauté the chicken portions until golden brown. Add half of the grated onion and fry until slightly softened.

2 Add the water and seasoning, and bring to the boil. Cover the pan, reduce the heat and simmer for 15 minutes.

3 Heat the remaining oil in a small pan or frying pan and fry the rest of the onion for 2–3 minutes until soft. Add the walnuts and fry for a further 2–3 minutes over a low heat, stirring frequently and taking care that the walnuts do not burn.

4 Stir in the pomegranate and tomato purées, lemon juice, sugar and the dissolved saffron. Season to taste and then simmer over a low heat for 5 minutes.

5 Pour the walnut sauce over the chicken, ensuring that it is well covered. Cover and simmer for 30–35 minutes until the meat is cooked and the oil of the walnuts has risen to the top. Serve at once with rice and salad leaves.

> **Cook's Tip**
> *Pomegranate purée is available from Middle Eastern delicatessens and specialist foodstores.*

Chicken with Prosciutto & Cheese

An Italian way of making a special meal of chicken, using Fontina cheese and cured ham.

Serves 4
2 thin slices prosciutto
2 thin slices Fontina cheese
4 skinless part-boned chicken
    breast portions
4 fresh basil sprigs
30ml/2 tbsp olive oil
15g/½oz/1 tbsp butter
120ml/4fl oz/ ½ cup dry
    white wine
salt and freshly ground
    black pepper
tender young salad leaves,
    to serve

1 Preheat the oven to 200°C/400°F/Gas 6. Lightly oil an ovenproof dish. Cut the ham and cheese slices in half crossways.

2 Open out the slit in the centre of each chicken portion. Fill each cavity with half a ham slice and a fresh basil sprig.

3 Heat the oil and butter in a wide, heavy frying pan until foaming. Cook the chicken portions over a medium heat for 1–2 minutes on each side until they change colour.

4 Transfer the chicken to the ovenproof dish. Add the wine to the pan juices, stir until sizzling, then pour over the chicken and season to taste.

5 Top each chicken breast portion with a slice of Fontina. Bake for 20 minutes or until the chicken is tender. Serve hot, with tender young salad leaves.

> **Cook's Tip**
> *There is nothing quite like the buttery texture and nutty flavour of Fontina cheese, and it also has superb melting qualities, but you could use a Swiss or French mountain cheese, such as Gruyère or Emmenthal. Ask for the cheese to be sliced thinly on the machine slicer, as you will find it difficult to slice it sufficiently thinly yourself.*

Rolled Stuffed Cannelloni

These cannelloni are made by rolling cooked lasagne sheets around the herbed chicken filling.

Serves 4
12 sheets lasagne
30ml/2 tbsp grated
  Parmesan cheese
fresh basil leaves, to garnish

For the filling
2–3 garlic cloves, crushed
1 small onion, finely chopped
150ml/ ¼ pint/ ⅔ cup
  white wine
450g/1lb minced (ground) chicken

15ml/1 tbsp dried basil
15ml/1 tbsp dried thyme
40g/1½ oz/ ¾ cup fresh
  white breadcrumbs
salt and freshly ground
  black pepper

For the sauce
25g/1oz/2 tbsp low-fat margarine
25g/1oz/ ¼ cup plain (all-
  purpose) flour
300ml/ ½ pint/1¼ cups
  skimmed milk
4 sun-dried tomatoes, chopped
15ml/1 tbsp chopped mixed fresh
  herbs (basil, parsley, marjoram)

1 To make the filling, put the garlic, onion and half the wine into a pan. Cover and cook for 5 minutes. Add the chicken and break up with a spoon. Cook until all the liquid has evaporated and the chicken begins to brown, stirring constantly. Add the remaining wine, seasoning and herbs. Cover and simmer for 20 minutes. Remove from the heat and stir in the breadcrumbs.

2 Cook the lasagne sheets in a large pan of boiling salted water according to the packet instructions until *al dente*. Drain and rinse in cold water. Pat dry on a clean dishtowel.

3 Spread out the lasagne. Spoon the chicken mixture along one short edge and roll up into a tube. Cut the tubes in half.

4 Preheat the oven to 200°C/400°F/Gas 6. To make the sauce, put the margarine, flour and milk into a pan, heat and whisk until thickened. Add the tomatoes and herbs. Season to taste. Spoon a layer of sauce into an ovenproof dish and place a layer of cannelloni on top. Repeat, then sprinkle with Parmesan. Bake for 10–15 minutes. Garnish and serve.

Lasagne

You can still enjoy classic pasta dishes even if you are reducing the fat content of your diet, as this version of lasagne, made with chicken or turkey, shows.

Serves 6–8
1 large onion, chopped
2 garlic cloves, crushed
500g/1¼ lb minced (ground)
  chicken or turkey
450g/1lb passata (bottled
  strained tomatoes)
5ml/1 tsp dried mixed herbs
225g/8oz frozen leaf
  spinach, thawed

200g/7oz lasagne verdi
200g/7oz/scant 1 cup low-fat
  cottage cheese
salt and freshly ground
  black pepper
mixed salad, to serve

For the sauce
25g/1oz/2 tbsp low-fat margarine
25g/1oz/ ¼ cup plain (all-
  purpose) flour
300ml/ ½ pint/1¼ cups
  skimmed milk
1.5ml/ ¼ tsp grated nutmeg
25g/1oz/ ⅓ cup grated
  Parmesan cheese

1 Put the onion, garlic and minced chicken or turkey into a non-stick pan. Brown quickly for 5 minutes, stirring with a wooden spoon to break up any lumps.

2 Add the passata, herbs and seasoning. Bring to the boil, cover and simmer for 30 minutes.

3 To make the sauce, put all the ingredients, except the grated Parmesan cheese, into a pan. Heat gently to thicken, whisking constantly until bubbling and smooth. Season to taste, add the cheese to the sauce and stir.

4 Preheat the oven to 190°C/375°F/Gas 5. Lay the spinach leaves out on kitchen paper and pat dry.

5 Layer the chicken or turkey mixture, dried lasagne, cottage cheese and spinach in a 2 litre/3½ pint/9 cup ovenproof dish, starting and ending with a layer of chicken or turkey. Spoon the sauce over the top to cover and bake for 45–50 minutes or until bubbling. Serve with a mixed salad.

Baked Poussins

The important factor in this recipe is a good, long marinating time before cooking, which allows the spicy yogurt mixture to penetrate and the flavours to permeate the birds.

Serves 4
475ml/16fl oz/2 cups natural (plain) yogurt
60ml/4 tbsp olive oil
1 large onion, grated
2 garlic cloves, crushed
2.5ml/½ tsp paprika
2–3 saffron threads, soaked in 15ml/1 tbsp boiling water
juice of 1 lemon
4 poussins, halved
oil, for greasing
salt and freshly ground black pepper
lettuce leaves, to serve

1 In a bowl, blend together the yogurt, olive oil, grated onion, crushed garlic, paprika, saffron threads with their soaking water and lemon juice, and season to taste with salt and freshly ground black pepper.

2 Place the poussin halves in a shallow dish and pour over the yogurt mixture, ensuring that they are well coated, spreading with the back of a spoon or your fingers. Cover and leave to marinate overnight in a cool place or for at least 4 hours in the refrigerator.

3 Preheat the oven to 180°C/350°F/Gas 4. Arrange the poussins in a greased ovenproof dish and bake for about 30–45 minutes, basting frequently until cooked. Serve with a lettuce salad.

> **Cook's Tip**
> *The poussins can also be barbecued (grilled), which makes them, if anything, even more delicious.*

Parmesan Chicken Bake

The tomato sauce may be made the day before and left to cool. Serve with crusty bread and salad.

Serves 4
4 skinless chicken breast fillets
60ml/4 tbsp plain (all-purpose) flour
45ml/3 tbsp olive oil
salt and freshly ground black pepper

For the tomato sauce
15ml/1 tbsp olive oil
1 onion, finely chopped
1 celery stick, finely chopped
1 red (bell) pepper, seeded and diced

1 garlic clove, crushed
400g/14oz can chopped tomatoes, with their juice
150ml/¼ pint/⅔ cup Chicken Stock
15ml/1 tbsp tomato purée (paste)
10ml/2 tsp caster (superfine) sugar
15ml/1 tbsp chopped fresh basil
15ml/1 tbsp chopped fresh parsley

To assemble
225g/8oz mozzarella cheese, sliced
60ml/4 tbsp grated Parmesan cheese
30ml/2 tbsp fresh breadcrumbs

1 To make the tomato sauce, heat the oil in a frying pan. Gently cook the onion, celery, pepper and garlic until tender. Add the tomatoes with their juice, the stock, tomato purée, sugar and herbs. Season and bring to the boil. Simmer for 30 minutes.

2 Divide each chicken fillet into two natural pieces, place between sheets of clear film (plastic wrap) and flatten to a thickness of 5mm/¼in with a rolling pin or meat mallet. Season the flour. Toss the chicken portions in the flour to coat.

3 Preheat the oven to 180°C/350°F/Gas 4. Heat the oil in a large frying pan and cook the chicken quickly in batches for 3–4 minutes until coloured.

4 To assemble, layer the chicken pieces in an ovenproof dish with the cheeses and thick tomato sauce, finishing with a layer of cheese and breadcrumbs on top. Bake, uncovered, for 20–30 minutes or until golden brown. Serve immediately.

STIR-FRIES, GRILLS, SAUTÉS & GRAIN DISHES

Dishes that are cooked quickly and served immediately are perfect for family occasions and informal entertaining. If you wash and chop the vegetables and get the other preparation done in advance, it can be fun – and subtly impressive – to chat to your guests over a glass of wine in the kitchen while you casually pull together a colourful stir-fry or gently mix a creamy risotto. If you prefer to cook without an audience, the speedy recipes in this chapter will ensure that you are missing for the shortest possible time between courses. Perhaps the best of both worlds is a barbecue, when everyone wants to help, but any hard work has been completed in the kitchen beforehand. Chicken is the perfect choice for these summer parties and is perennially popular, so success is virtually guaranteed. Apart from the recipes specifically designed for cooking on a barbecue, many of the other recipes in this chapter can easily be adapted for cooking over charcoal. Indoors or outdoors, you are sure to find something special.

Minty Yogurt Chicken

Marinating skinned chicken in yogurt infused with fresh mint and lime or lemon juice is an excellent way to give it flavour with the minimum of fat.

Serves 4

8 skinless chicken thighs
15ml/1 tbsp clear honey
30ml/2 tbsp lime or lemon juice
30ml/2 tbsp natural (plain) yogurt
60ml/4 tbsp chopped fresh mint
salt and freshly ground
   black pepper
boiled new potatoes and tomato
   salad, to serve

1 Slash the flesh of the chicken thighs at intervals with a sharp knife. Place in a bowl.

2 In another small bowl, mix the honey, lime or lemon juice, yogurt, seasoning and half the mint.

3 Spoon the yogurt mixture over the chicken and leave to marinate for 30 minutes. Preheat the grill (broiler) and line a grill pan with foil.

4 Cook the chicken under a moderately hot grill until thoroughly cooked and golden brown, turning occasionally during cooking.

5 Sprinkle the chicken with the remaining mint and serve immediately with new potatoes and tomato salad.

Cook's Tip
There are several different types of yogurt. Ordinary plain yogurt is made by adding a culture to full-fat (whole) milk. Its fat content varies, but can be as high as 7.5 per cent. Low-fat yogurt is made from concentrated skimmed milk and has a fat content of 0.5–2 per cent. Very low-fat yogurt, made from skimmed milk, contains less than 0.5 per cent fat.

Lemon Chicken with Guacamole Sauce

Guacamole, which is very easy to prepare and looks stunning on the plate, is a great partner for chicken.

salt and freshly ground
   black pepper
chopped fresh coriander (cilantro)
   and frisée lettuce, to garnish

Serves 4

juice of 2 lemons
45ml/3 tbsp olive oil
2 garlic cloves, finely chopped
4 chicken breast portions, about
   200g/7oz each
2 tomatoes, cored and cut in half

For the guacamole sauce

1 ripe avocado
60ml/4 tbsp sour cream
45ml/3 tbsp fresh lemon juice
2.5ml/ ½ tsp salt
about 50ml/2fl oz/ ¼ cup water

1 Combine the lemon juice, oil, garlic, 2.5ml/ ½ tsp salt and a little pepper in a bowl. Arrange the chicken portions, in a single layer, in a shallow non-metallic dish. Pour over the lemon mixture and turn to coat evenly. Cover and leave to marinate for at least 1 hour at room temperature or chill overnight.

2 To make the sauce, halve the avocado, remove the stone (pit) and scrape the flesh into a food processor. Add the sour cream, lemon juice and salt, and process until smooth. Add the water and process to blend. If necessary, add a little more water to thin the sauce. Transfer to a bowl and set aside.

3 Preheat the grill (broiler) and heat a ridged frying pan. Remove the chicken from the marinade and pat dry. When the frying pan is hot, add the chicken portions and cook for about 10 minutes, turning frequently, until they are cooked through.

4 Meanwhile, arrange the tomato halves, cut sides up, on a baking sheet and season lightly. Grill (broil) for about 5 minutes until hot and bubbling.

5 To serve, place a chicken portion, tomato half and a spoon of sauce on each plate. Garnish with coriander and lettuce.

Poussins with Citrus Glaze

This recipe is suitable for many kinds of small birds, including snipe and partridges, provided they are young and tender.

Serves 4
2 poussins, about 675g/
  1½lb each
50g/2oz/4 tbsp butter, softened
30ml/2 tbsp olive oil
2 garlic cloves, crushed
2.5ml/½ tsp dried thyme
1.5ml/¼ tsp cayenne pepper
grated rind and juice of 1 lemon
grated rind and juice of 1 lime
30ml/2 tbsp clear honey
salt and freshly ground
  black pepper
fresh dill, to garnish
tomato salad, to serve

1 Using kitchen scissors or poultry shears, cut along both sides of the backbone of each bird; remove and discard. Cut the birds in half along the breastbone, then use a rolling pin to flatten them.

2 Beat the butter in a small bowl, then beat in 15ml/1 tbsp of the olive oil, the garlic, thyme, cayenne, salt and pepper, half the lemon and lime rind and 15ml/1 tbsp each of the lemon and lime juice.

3 Using your fingertips, carefully loosen the skin of each poussin breast. Using a round-bladed knife, spread the butter mixture evenly between the skin and breast meat.

4 Preheat the grill (broiler) and line a grill pan with foil. In a small bowl, mix together the remaining olive oil, lemon and lime juices, and rind and the honey. Place the bird halves, skin side up, in the grill pan and brush with the juice mixture.

5 Grill (broil) for 10–12 minutes, basting once or twice with the juices. Turn over and grill for 7–10 minutes, basting once, or until the juices run clear when the thigh is pierced with a knife. Serve with tomato salad, garnished with dill.

Spatchcocked Poussins

These little, herb-marinated chickens can be cooked conventionally, but taste best if they are cooked over charcoal.

Serves 4
2 large or 4 small poussins
fresh herbs, to garnish
mixed salad leaves, to serve

For the marinade
150ml/¼ pint/⅔ cup olive oil
1 onion, grated
1 garlic clove, crushed
15ml/1 tbsp chopped fresh mint
15ml/1 tbsp chopped fresh flat
  leaf parsley
15ml/1 tbsp chopped
  fresh coriander (cilantro)
5–10ml/1–2 tsp ground cumin
5ml/1 tsp paprika
pinch of cayenne pepper

1 Tuck the wings of each poussin under the body and remove the wishbone. Turn the birds over and cut along each side of the backbone using kitchen scissors or poultry shears, then remove and discard.

2 Push down on each bird to break the breastbone. Keeping the bird flat, push a skewer through the wings and breast. Push another skewer through the thighs.

3 To make the marinade, blend together all the ingredients in a bowl. Spread the marinade over both sides of the poussins. Place in a large, shallow dish, cover with clear film (plastic wrap) and marinate for at least 4 hours or overnight.

4 Prepare a barbecue or preheat the grill (broiler). Barbecue the poussins for about 25–35 minutes, turning and brushing with the marinade occasionally. If grilling (broiling), cook under a medium grill about 7.5cm/3in from the heat for 25–35 minutes, turning and basting occasionally.

5 When the birds are cooked, cut them in half. Garnish with herbs and serve immediately with salad leaves.

Baby Chickens with Lime & Chilli

Kept succulent with a sun-dried tomato-flavoured butter, these poussins make a splendid barbecue meal for friends, though they also cook well conventionally.

Serves 4
4 poussins, about 450g/1lb each
45ml/3 tbsp butter

30ml/2 tbsp sun-dried
  tomato purée (paste)
finely grated rind of 1 lime
10ml/2 tsp chilli sauce
juice of ½ lime
fresh flat leaf parsley sprigs,
  to garnish
lime wedges, to serve

1 Prepare the barbecue or preheat the grill (broiler). Spatchcock the poussins and turn the flattened birds breast side up. Lift the breast skin carefully and gently ease your fingertips underneath, to loosen it from the flesh.

2 In a bowl, mix together the butter, tomato purée, lime rind and chilli sauce. Spread about three-quarters of the mixture under the skin of each poussin, smoothing it evenly.

3 To hold the poussins flat during cooking, thread two skewers through each bird, crossing at the centre. Each skewer should pass through a wing and then out through a drumstick.

4 Combine the remaining butter mixture with the lime juice and brush it over the skin of the poussins. Cook on a medium-hot barbecue or under the grill, turning occasionally, for 25–30 minutes or until the juices run clear when the thickest part of the thigh is pierced with a skewer or knife. Garnish with flat leaf parsley and serve with lime wedges.

Cook's Tip
If you wish to serve half a poussin per portion, you may find it easier simply to cut the birds in half lengthways. Use poultry shears or a large, sharp knife to cut through the breastbone and backbone.

Duck with Chestnut Sauce

This autumnal dish makes use of delicious sweet chestnuts that can be gathered in the woods.

Serves 4–5
1 fresh rosemary sprig, plus extra
  to garnish
1 garlic clove, thinly sliced
30ml/2 tbsp olive oil
4 duck breast fillets, skin and
  fat removed

For the sauce
450g/1lb chestnuts
5ml/1 tsp oil
350ml/12fl oz/1½ cups milk
1 small onion, finely chopped
1 carrot, finely chopped
1 small bay leaf
salt and freshly ground
  black pepper
30ml/2 tbsp double (heavy)
  cream, warmed

1 Pull the leaves from the sprig of rosemary. Combine them with the garlic and oil in a shallow bowl. Pat the duck fillets dry with kitchen paper and lay them in a shallow dish. Brush with the flavoured oil and leave to marinate for at least 2 hours.

2 Preheat the oven to 180°C/350°F/Gas 4. To make the sauce, cut a cross in the flat side of each chestnut with a sharp knife. Place the chestnuts in a roasting pan with the oil and shake the pan until the nuts are well coated. Bake in the oven for about 20 minutes, then peel.

3 Place the chestnuts in a heavy pan with the milk, onion, carrot and bay leaf. Cook for about 10–15 minutes until the chestnuts are very tender. Season with salt and pepper. Discard the bay leaf. Press the mixture through a sieve.

4 Return the chestnut sauce to the pan and heat gently. Preheat the grill (broiler) or prepare a barbecue.

5 Cook the duck for about 6–8 minutes until medium rare. The meat should be pink when sliced. Slice into rounds and arrange on warmed plates.

6 Stir the cream into the sauce just before serving. Garnish the sliced duck with rosemary and serve with the sauce.

Turkey with Sage, Prunes & Brandy

This stir-fry has a very rich sauce based on a good-quality brandy – use the best you can afford.

Serves 4
115g/4oz/½ cup prunes
675g/1½ lb turkey breast fillet
300ml/½ pint/1¼ cups brandy
15ml/1 tbsp chopped fresh sage
150g/5oz smoked bacon, in one piece
50g/2oz/4 tbsp butter
24 baby (pearl) onions, peeled and quartered
salt and freshly ground black pepper
fresh sage sprigs, to garnish

1 Stone (pit) the prunes and cut them into slivers. Remove the skin from the turkey and cut the breast into thin pieces.

2 Mix together the prunes, turkey, brandy and chopped sage in a non-metallic dish. Cover and set aside to marinate overnight in the refrigerator.

3 Next day, strain the turkey and prunes, reserving the marinade, and pat dry with kitchen paper. Dice the bacon.

4 Heat a wok or heavy frying pan and add half the butter. When the butter is hot, add the onions and stir-fry for 4 minutes until crisp and golden. Set aside.

5 Add the bacon to the wok and stir-fry for 1 minute until it begins to release some fat. Add the remaining butter, and stir-fry the turkey and prunes for 3–4 minutes until the turkey and bacon are crisp and golden.

6 Push the turkey mixture to the side of the wok, add the reserved marinade and simmer until thickened. Stir the turkey into the sauce, season well with salt and pepper and serve, garnished with sage.

> **Cook's Tip**
> "VSOP" on the label is a guarantee of the quality of the brandy.

Stir-fried Duck with Blueberries

Serve this conveniently quick dinner-party dish with sprigs of fresh mint, which will give a wonderful fresh aroma as you bring the meal to the table.

Serves 4
2 duck breast fillets, about 175g/6oz each
30ml/2 tbsp sunflower oil
15ml/1 tbsp red wine vinegar
5ml/1 tsp sugar
5ml/1 tsp red wine
5ml/1 tsp crème de cassis
115g/4oz/1 cup fresh blueberries
15ml/1 tbsp chopped fresh mint
salt and freshly ground black pepper
fresh mint sprigs, to garnish

1 Cut the duck breast fillets into neat slices. Season well with salt and pepper.

2 Heat a wok, then add the oil. When the oil is hot, add the duck and stir-fry for 3 minutes.

3 Add the red wine vinegar, sugar, red wine and crème de cassis. Bubble for 3 minutes to reduce to a thick syrup.

4 Stir in the blueberries, sprinkle over the chopped mint and serve, garnished with sprigs of mint.

> **Variations**
> *You could substitute blackcurrants, redcurrants or cranberries for the blueberries. If using cranberries – and if you can obtain a bottle – substitute Karpi, a Finnish liqueur made from cranberries, for the crème de cassis. Otherwise, use crème de cassis, which is a classic French liqueur made from blackcurrants.*

Chicken Kiev

This popular recipe is a modern Russian invention. Prepare these chicken breast portions filled with garlic butter in advance to allow time for chilling.

Serves 4

115g/4oz/ ½ cup butter, softened
2 garlic cloves, crushed
finely grated rind of 1 lemon
30ml/2 tbsp chopped
   fresh tarragon
pinch of grated nutmeg
4 skinless chicken breast fillets
   with wing bones attached
1 egg, lightly beaten
115g/4oz/2 cups
   fresh breadcrumbs
oil, for deep-frying
salt and freshly ground
   black pepper
lemon wedges, to garnish
potato wedges, to serve

1 Mix the butter in a bowl with the garlic, lemon rind, tarragon and nutmeg. Season to taste with salt and pepper. Shape the butter into a rectangular block about 5cm/2in long, wrap in foil and chill for 1 hour.

2 Place the chicken on a piece of oiled clear film (plastic wrap). Cover with a second piece of clear film and gently beat the chicken pieces with a meat mallet or rolling pin until fairly thin.

3 Cut the butter lengthways into four pieces and put one in the centre of each chicken fillet. Fold the edges over the butter and secure with wooden cocktail sticks.

4 Put the beaten egg and the breadcrumbs into separate dishes. Dip the chicken pieces first in the beaten egg and then in the breadcrumbs to coat evenly. Dip them a second time in egg and crumbs, then put them on a plate and chill for at least 1 hour.

5 Heat the oil in a large pan or deep-fat fryer to 180°C/350°F. Deep-fry the chicken for 6–8 minutes or until the chicken is cooked and the coating golden brown and crisp. Drain on kitchen paper and remove the cocktail sticks. Garnish with wedges of lemon and serve with potato wedges.

Chicken Marengo

This dish was created especially for Napoleon after the battle of Marengo.

Serves 4

120ml/4fl oz/ ½ cup olive oil
8 skinless chicken thighs on
   the bone
1 onion, finely chopped
1 celery stick, finely chopped
1 garlic clove, crushed
350g/12oz ripe Italian plum
   tomatoes, peeled and
   coarsely chopped
250ml/8fl oz/1 cup dry
   white wine
2.5ml/ ½ tsp finely chopped
   fresh rosemary
15g/½oz/1 tbsp butter
8 small triangles thinly sliced
   white bread, without crusts
175g/6oz large raw
   prawns (shrimp), peeled
salt and freshly ground
   black pepper
finely chopped flat leaf parsley,
   to garnish

1 Heat 30ml/2 tbsp of the oil in a frying pan and sauté the chicken over a medium heat for 5 minutes until it has changed colour on all sides. Transfer to a flameproof casserole.

2 Add the onion and celery to the pan and cook gently, stirring frequently, for 3 minutes until softened. Add the garlic, tomatoes, wine, rosemary and seasoning. Bring to the boil, stirring.

3 Pour the tomato sauce over the chicken. Cover and cook gently for 40 minutes or until the chicken juices run clear when the thickest part is pierced with a knife or skewer.

4 About 10 minutes before serving, heat the remaining oil and the butter in the frying pan. Add the triangles of bread and fry until crisp and golden on each side. Drain on kitchen paper.

5 Add the prawns to the casserole and heat until they are cooked. Taste the sauce and adjust the seasoning as necessary.

6 Dip one of the tips of each fried bread triangle into the chopped parsley. Serve the chicken dish hot, garnished with the bread triangles.

Chicken with Morels

Morels are among the tastiest dried mushrooms and, although they are expensive, a small quantity goes a long way and is certainly worth investing in for this wonderful dinner party dish.

Serves 4

40g/1½ oz dried
   morel mushrooms
250ml/8fl oz/1 cup Chicken Stock
50g/2oz/4 tbsp butter
5 or 6 shallots, thinly sliced
115g/4oz/1½ cups button
   (white) mushrooms, thinly sliced
1.5ml/¼ tsp dried thyme
30–45ml/2–3 tbsp brandy
175ml/6fl oz/¾ cup double
   (heavy) or whipping cream
4 skinless chicken breast fillets,
   about 200g/7oz each
15ml/1 tbsp vegetable oil
175ml/6fl oz/¾ cup Champagne
   or dry sparkling wine
salt and freshly ground
   black pepper

1 Put the morels in a sieve and rinse well under cold running water, shaking to remove as much grit as possible. Put them in a pan with the stock and bring to the boil over a medium heat. Remove the pan from the heat and set aside for 1 hour.

2 Remove the morels from the cooking liquid. Strain the liquid through a very fine sieve lined with muslin (cheesecloth) and set aside. Reserve a few whole morels and slice the rest.

3 Melt half the butter in a frying pan over a medium heat. Add the shallots and cook for 2 minutes until softened, then add the morels and button mushrooms and cook, stirring frequently, for 2–3 minutes.

4 Season and add the thyme, brandy and 100ml/3½fl oz/⅓ cup of the cream. Reduce the heat and simmer gently for 10–12 minutes until any liquid has evaporated, stirring occasionally. Remove the mixture from the pan and set aside.

5 Pull off the small fillet (the finger-shaped piece on the underside) from each chicken breast fillet and reserve for another use. Make a pocket in each chicken portion by cutting a slit along the thicker edge, but do not to cut right through.

6 Using a small spoon, fill each pocket with a quarter of the mushroom mixture, then, if necessary, close with a wooden cocktail stick (toothpick).

7 Melt the remaining butter with the oil in a heavy frying pan over a medium-high heat and cook the chicken breast portions on one side for 6–8 minutes until golden. Transfer to a plate. Add the Champagne or sparkling wine to the pan and boil to reduce by half. Add the reserved strained morel cooking liquid and boil to reduce by half again.

8 Add the remaining cream and cook over a medium heat for 2–3 minutes until the sauce thickens slightly and coats the back of a spoon. Adjust the seasoning. Return the chicken to the pan with any accumulated juices and the reserved whole morels, and simmer for 3–5 minutes over a medium-low heat until the chicken is hot and the juices run clear when the thickest part is pierced with a knife or skewer. Serve immediately.

Pan-fried Marinated Poussin

These small birds are full of flavour when marinated for several hours before they are cooked.

Serves 3–4

2 poussins, about 450g/1lb each
5–6 fresh mint leaves, torn
   into pieces
1 leek, sliced into thin rings
1 garlic clove, finely chopped
60ml/4 tbsp olive oil
30ml/2 tbsp lemon juice
50ml/2fl oz/¼ cup dry
   white wine
salt and freshly ground
   black pepper
fresh mint leaves, to garnish

1 Cut the poussins in half down the backbone, dividing the breast. Flatten the four halves with a meat mallet. Place them in a bowl with the mint, leek and garlic. Season with pepper, and sprinkle with oil and half the lemon juice. Cover and leave to stand in a cool place for 6 hours.

2 Heat a large, heavy frying pan. Place the poussins and their marinade in the pan, cover and cook over a moderate heat for about 45 minutes, turning them occasionally. Season with salt to taste during the cooking. Transfer the poussins to a warmed serving platter.

3 Tilt the pan and spoon off any fat on the surface of the liquid. Pour in the white wine and the remaining lemon juice and cook until the sauce reduces by about half.

4 Strain the white wine sauce, pressing the vegetables with a ladle or wooden spoon to extract all the juices. Place the poussins on individual plates and spoon over the sauce. Garnish with mint and serve.

Cook's Tip

While bottled lemon juice is very convenient, it does not have the same flavour as freshly squeezed juice. Let citrus fruits come to room temperature before squeezing for the maximum quantity of juice.

Chicken with Asparagus

Canned asparagus may be used, but will not require any cooking – simply add at the very end to warm through.

Serves 4

4 large skinless chicken
   breast fillets
15ml/1 tbsp ground coriander
30ml/2 tbsp olive oil

20 slender asparagus spears, cut
   into 7.5–10cm/3–4in lengths
300ml/ ½ pint/1¼ cups
   Chicken Stock
15ml/1 tbsp cornflour
   (cornstarch)
15ml/1 tbsp lemon juice
salt and freshly ground
   black pepper
15ml/1 tbsp chopped fresh
   parsley, to garnish

1 Divide each chicken breast fillet into two natural pieces. Place each between two sheets of clear film (plastic wrap) and flatten to a thickness of 5mm/¼in with a rolling pin. Cut into 2.5cm/1in strips diagonally across the fillets. Sprinkle over the ground coriander and toss to coat each piece.

2 Heat the oil in a large frying pan and fry the chicken very quickly, in small batches, for 3–4 minutes until lightly coloured. Season each batch with a little salt and pepper. Remove from the pan and keep warm while frying the rest of the chicken.

3 Add the asparagus and chicken stock to the pan, and bring to the boil. Cook for a further 4–5 minutes or until the asparagus is tender.

4 Mix the cornflour to a thin paste with a little cold water and stir into the sauce to thicken. Return the chicken to the pan together with the lemon juice. Reheat and then serve immediately, garnished with the chopped parsley.

> **Cook's Tip**
> *You can use green or white asparagus for this dish, but whichever you choose, the buds should be plump and the stems evenly coloured.*

Chicken with White Wine, Olives & Garlic

The chicken portions are browned without fat before being simmered in a rich white wine sauce.

Serves 4

1.5kg/3½lb chicken, cut into
   serving portions
15ml/1 tbsp olive oil
1 onion, sliced

3–5 garlic cloves, to taste, crushed
5ml/1 tsp dried thyme
475ml/16fl oz/2 cups dry
   white wine
16–18 green olives, pitted
1 bay leaf
15ml/1 tbsp lemon juice
15–30ml/1–2 tbsp butter
salt and freshly ground
   black pepper

1 Heat a deep, heavy, non-stick frying pan, add the chicken portions, skin side down, and cook over a medium heat for about 10 minutes until browned. Turn the chicken portions and cook for a further 5–8 minutes to brown the other side. (Work in batches if necessary.) Transfer the chicken to a large plate and set aside.

2 Heat the olive oil in the same pan. Add the sliced onion and a pinch of salt, and cook for 5 minutes, stirring occasionally until just soft. Add the crushed garlic and dried thyme and cook for 1 minute.

3 Add the wine and stir, scraping up any sediment that clings to the bottom of the pan. Bring to the boil and boil for 1 minute. Stir in the green olives.

4 Return the partially cooked chicken to the pan. Add the bay leaf and season lightly with freshly ground pepper. Lower the heat, cover the pan and simmer for 20–30 minutes until the chicken is cooked through.

5 Transfer the chicken portions to a warmed platter. Stir the lemon juice into the sauce. Whisk in the butter, a little at a time, to thicken the sauce slightly. Spoon the sauce over the chicken and serve immediately.

Chicken with Red Wine Vinegar

This is an easy version of the modern classic invented by a French master chef.

Serves 4
4 skinless chicken breast fillets, about 200g/7oz each
50g/2oz/4 tbsp unsalted (sweet) butter
8–12 shallots, halved

60ml/4 tbsp red wine vinegar
2 garlic cloves, finely chopped
60ml/4 tbsp dry white wine
120ml/4fl oz/ ½ cup Chicken Stock
15ml/1 tbsp chopped fresh parsley
freshly ground black pepper
green salad, to serve

1 Cut each chicken breast in half crossways to make eight pieces. Melt half the butter in a large, heavy frying pan over a medium heat. Add the chicken and cook for 3–5 minutes until golden brown, turning once, then season with pepper.

2 Add the shallot halves to the pan, cover and cook over a low heat for 5–7 minutes, shaking the pan and stirring occasionally.

3 Transfer the chicken pieces to a plate. Add the red wine vinegar to the pan and cook, stirring frequently, for about 1 minute until the liquid is almost evaporated. Add the garlic, wine and stock, and stir to blend. Return the chicken to the pan with any juices. Cover and simmer for 2–3 minutes until the chicken is tender.

4 Transfer the chicken and shallots to a serving dish and keep warm. Increase the heat and boil the cooking liquid until it has reduced by half. Remove the pan from the heat. Gradually add the remaining butter, whisking until the sauce is slightly thickened and glossy. Stir in the parsley, and pour the sauce over the chicken pieces and shallots. Serve with a green salad.

Variation
You could use different flavoured vinegars. Try tarragon vinegar and substitute fresh tarragon for the parsley.

Chicken Cordon Bleu

Perennially popular, this dish consists of breast portions of chicken stuffed with smoked ham and Gruyère cheese, then coated in egg and breadcrumbs, and fried.

Serves 4
4 skinless chicken breast fillets, about 130g/3½ oz each
4 very thin slices smoked ham, halved and rind removed

about 90g/3½ oz Gruyère cheese, thinly sliced
plain (all-purpose) flour, for coating
2 eggs, beaten
75g/3oz/generous 1 cup natural-coloured dried breadcrumbs
5ml/1 tsp dried thyme
40g/1½ oz/3 tbsp butter
30ml/2 tbsp olive oil
salt and freshly ground black pepper
mixed leaf salad, to serve

1 Slit the chicken breast fillets about three-quarters of the way through, then open them up and lay them flat. Place a slice of ham on each cut side of the chicken, trimming to fit if necessary. Top with the Gruyère slices, making sure that they are well within the ham slices. Fold over the chicken and reshape, pressing well to seal and ensuring that no cheese is visible.

2 Put the flour into a shallow bowl. Pour the beaten eggs into another bowl, and mix the breadcrumbs with the thyme and seasoning in a third bowl. Toss each stuffed fillet in the flour, then coat in egg and breadcrumbs, shaking off any excess. Lay the crumbed fillets flat on a plate, cover and chill for 1 hour.

3 To cook, heat the butter and oil in a frying pan. Slide in the coated fillets, two at a time. Fry over a medium-low heat for about 5 minutes on each side, turning carefully with a fish slice (spatula). Drain on kitchen paper and keep hot while you cook the remaining fillets. Serve with a side salad.

Variation
Instead of Gruyère, try one of the herb-flavoured hard cheeses, such as double Gloucester with chives.

Chicken with Grapes

Reducing the sauce is important for really concentrating the flavour, so take the time to do this fully before adding the cream.

Serves 4
4 chicken breast fillets, about 200g/7oz each, well trimmed
25g/1oz/2 tbsp butter
1 large or 2 small shallots, chopped
120ml/4fl oz/ ½ cup dry white wine
250ml/8fl oz/1 cup Chicken Stock
120ml/4fl oz/ ½ cup whipping cream
150g/5oz seedless green grapes
salt and freshly ground black pepper
fresh parsley sprigs, to garnish

1 Season the chicken breast fillets. Melt half the butter in a frying pan over a medium-high heat and cook the chicken for 4–5 minutes on each side until golden.

2 Transfer the chicken to a plate and cover to keep warm. Add the remaining butter to the pan and sauté the shallots until just softened, stirring frequently.

3 Add the wine, bring to the boil and boil to reduce by half, then add the stock and continue boiling to reduce by half again.

4 Add the cream to the sauce, bring back to the boil and pour in any juices from the chicken. Add the grapes and cook gently for 5 minutes. Slice the chicken and serve with the sauce, garnished with parsley.

Variation

This recipe also works well with poussins. Cook 4 poussins and the shallots as in steps 1 and 2 in a flameproof casserole. After adding the wine and stock in step 3, return the poussins to the casserole and simmer for 20–25 minutes. Transfer to a serving platter and finish the sauce as above.

Tarragon Chicken

The original version of this dish, created in France, uses a whole chicken, but boneless breast portions are quick to cook and elegant. The combination of dried and fresh tarragon makes a wonderfully aromatic sauce.

Serves 4
4 skinless chicken breast fillets, about 150–175g/ 5–6oz each
120ml/4fl oz/ ½ cup dry white wine
about 300ml/ ½ pint/1¼ cups Chicken Stock
15ml/1 tbsp dried tarragon
1 garlic clove, finely chopped
175ml/6fl oz/ ¾ cup whipping cream
15ml/1 tbsp chopped fresh tarragon
salt and freshly ground black pepper
fresh tarragon sprigs, to garnish

1 Season the chicken breast fillets lightly with salt and pepper, and put them in a pan just large enough to hold them in a single layer. Pour over the wine and stock, adding more stock to cover, if necessary, then add the dried tarragon and garlic.

2 Bring the stock just to a simmer over a medium heat and cook gently for 8–10 minutes until the chicken juices run clear when the thickest part is pierced with a knife or skewer.

3 Using a slotted spoon, transfer the chicken to a plate and cover to keep warm. Strain the cooking liquid into a small pan, skim off any fat and boil to reduce by two-thirds.

4 Add the cream and boil to reduce by half. Stir in the fresh tarragon and adjust the seasoning to taste. Slice the chicken, spoon over a little sauce, garnish with fresh tarragon sprigs and serve immediately.

Cook's Tip

Tarragon is traditionally paired with chicken, but you could, of course, use chopped fresh basil or parsley instead. Do not use dried versions of these two herbs.

Chicken with Wild Mushrooms & Vermouth

Tender chicken slices are folded into a rich sour-cream sauce, spiked with dry white vermouth.

Serves 4
30ml/2 tbsp oil
1 leek, finely chopped
4 skinless chicken breast
  fillets, sliced
225g/8oz/3 cups wild
  mushrooms, sliced if large
15ml/1 tbsp brandy
pinch of grated nutmeg
1.5ml/¼ tsp chopped fresh thyme
150ml/¼ pint/⅔ cup dry
  white vermouth
150ml/¼ pint/⅔ cup
  Chicken Stock
6 green olives, pitted
  and quartered
150ml/¼ pint/⅔ cup
  sour cream
salt and freshly ground
  black pepper
fresh thyme sprigs and croûtons,
  to garnish

1 Heat the oil and fry the leek until softened but not browned. Add the chicken slices and mushrooms. Fry, stirring occasionally, until just beginning to brown.

2 Pour over the brandy and ignite. When the flames have died down, stir in the nutmeg, chopped thyme, vermouth and stock, with salt and pepper to taste.

3 Bring to the boil, lower the heat and simmer for 5 minutes. Stir in the olives and most of the sour cream. Reheat gently, but do not let the mixture boil.

4 Garnish with the remaining sour cream, the thyme sprigs and croûtons. Serve immediately.

> **Cook's Tip**
> Chinese dried mushrooms work well in this dish. Soak them for 1 hour in cold water before use.

Duck with Peppercorns

Thick, meaty duck breast, like steak, should be served medium-rare. Green peppercorns make a zingy sauce, but choose pink peppercorns if you prefer a milder flavour.

Serves 2
5ml/1 tsp vegetable oil
2 duck breast fillets, about
  225g/8oz each, skinned
60ml/4 tbsp duck or
  Chicken Stock
90ml/6 tbsp whipping cream
5ml/1 tsp Dijon mustard
15ml/1 tbsp green or pink
  peppercorns in vinegar, drained
salt
fresh parsley, to garnish

1 Heat the oil in a heavy frying pan. Add the duck breast fillets and cook over a medium-high heat for about 3 minutes on each side.

2 Transfer the duck to a plate and cover to keep warm. Pour off any fat from the pan and stir in the stock, cream, mustard and peppercorns. Boil for 2–3 minutes until the sauce thickens slightly, then season with salt.

3 Pour any accumulated juices from the duck into the sauce, then slice the fillets diagonally.

4 Arrange the sliced duck on two warmed individual serving plates, pour over a little of the sauce, garnish with parsley and serve immediately.

> **Cook's Tip**
> Green peppercorns are the unripe berries of the same plant from which both black and white peppercorns come, Piper nigrum, although they have a milder flavour. They have a special affinity with poultry, especially duck. Pink peppercorns, however, are not really peppercorns at all, but the processed berries of a South American plant that is related to poison ivy.

Turkey with Fig, Orange & Mint Marmalade

This unusual fruity sauce gives a tremendous lift to the rather bland flavour of turkey breast fillets.

Serves 4

450g/1lb dried figs
1/2 bottle sweet, fruity white wine
15ml/1 tbsp butter

4 turkey breast fillets, about
    175–225g/6–8oz each
30ml/2 tbsp dark
    orange marmalade
10 fresh mint leaves, finely
    chopped, plus extra to garnish
juice of 1/2 lemon
salt and freshly ground
    black pepper

1 Place the dried figs in a pan with the white wine and bring to the boil, then simmer very gently for about 1 hour. Leave the figs to cool in the cooking liquid and chill overnight.

2 Melt the butter in a frying pan and fry the turkey fillets, turning them once, until they are cooked through. Transfer to a warmed serving dish and keep warm.

3 Drain any fat from the pan and pour in the cooking liquid from the figs. Bring to the boil and reduce until about 150ml/ 1/4 pint/ 2/3 cup remains.

4 Add the marmalade, chopped mint and lemon juice, and simmer for a few minutes. Season to taste with salt and pepper. Add the figs and heat through.

5 When the sauce is thick and shiny, pour it over the meat and serve, garnished with plenty of mint leaves.

Cook's Tip
Some of the more unusual varieties of mint would be ideal for this dish. Try apple or pineapple, for example. A variety with variegated leaves would make an attractive garnish.

Turkey with Marsala Cream Sauce

Marsala makes a very rich and tasty sauce. The addition of lemon juice gives it a sharp edge, which helps to balance the richness.

Serves 6

6 turkey breast steaks
45ml/3 tbsp plain (all-
    purpose) flour
30ml/2 tbsp olive oil

25g/1oz/2 tbsp butter
175ml/6fl oz/ 3/4 cup dry Marsala
60ml/4 tbsp lemon juice
175ml/6fl oz/ 3/4 cup
    double (heavy) cream
salt and freshly ground
    black pepper
lemon wedges and chopped fresh
    parsley, to garnish
steamed mangetouts (snow peas)
    and green beans, to serve

1 Put each turkey steak between two sheets of clear film (plastic wrap) and pound with a meat mallet or rolling pin to flatten and stretch. Cut each steak in half or into quarters.

2 Spread out the flour in a shallow dish and season well. Dip the turkey steaks in the flour, turning them to coat thoroughly.

3 Heat the oil and butter in a wide pan or frying pan. Add as many pieces of turkey as the pan will hold in a single layer and sauté over a medium heat for 3 minutes on each side until coloured on the outside and cooked. Transfer to a warmed serving dish and keep hot. Repeat with the remaining turkey.

4 Lower the heat. Mix the Marsala and lemon juice in a jug (pitcher), add to the pan and raise the heat. Bring to the boil, stirring in the sediment, then add the cream. Simmer, stirring constantly, until the sauce is reduced and glossy. Taste and adjust the seasoning. Spoon over the turkey, garnish with lemon and parsley, and serve with mangetouts and green beans.

Variations
Chicken breast fillets can be used instead of the turkey, and 50g/2oz/1/4 cup mascarpone cheese can be substituted for the double (heavy) cream.

Turkey Escalopes with Capers

These thin slices of turkey, coated in breadcrumbs, cook very quickly. Here they are enhanced with the fresh, sharp flavours of lemon, capers and sage.

Serves 2
4 thin turkey breast escalopes (scallops), about 75g/3oz each
1 large unwaxed lemon
2.5ml/ ½ tsp chopped fresh sage
60–75ml/4–5 tbsp extra virgin olive oil
50g/2oz/ ¾ cup fine dry breadcrumbs
15ml/1 tbsp capers, rinsed and drained
salt and freshly ground black pepper
fresh sage leaves and lemon wedges, to garnish

1 Place the turkey escalopes between two sheets of clear film (plastic wrap) and pound with the flat side of a meat mallet or rolling pin to flatten to a thickness of about 5mm/ ¼in.

2 With a vegetable peeler, remove four thin pieces of rind from the lemon. Cut them into fine julienne strips, cover with clear film and set aside. Grate the remainder of the lemon rind and squeeze the lemon.

3 Put the grated rind in a large, non-metallic shallow dish and add the chopped sage, salt and pepper. Stir in 15ml/1 tbsp of the lemon juice, reserving the remainder, and about 15ml/ 1 tbsp of the oil, then add the turkey, turn to coat and leave to marinate for 30 minutes.

4 Place the breadcrumbs in another shallow dish. Dip the turkey escalopes in the crumbs, coating them on both sides.

5 In a heavy frying pan, heat 30ml/2 tbsp of the oil over a high heat, add the escalopes and cook for 2–3 minutes, turning once, until golden. Transfer to warmed plates and keep warm.

6 Wipe out the pan, add the remaining oil, the lemon julienne strips and the capers, and heat through, stirring. Spoon a little sauce over the turkey, garnish with sage leaves and lemon wedges, and serve.

Turkey with Wine & Grapes

Good stock and wine provide the flavour in this velvety sauce.

Serves 3
450g/1lb turkey breast portions, thinly sliced
45ml/3 tbsp plain (all-purpose flour
45–60ml/3–4 tbsp oil
120ml/4fl oz/ ½ cup white wine or sherry
120ml/4fl oz/ ½ cup Chicken Stock
150g/5oz white grapes
salt and freshly ground black pepper
fresh flat leaf parsley, to garnish
boiled new potatoes or rice, to serve

1 Put the turkey slices between two sheets of clear film (plastic wrap) and flatten them with a rolling pin or meat mallet. Spread out the flour on a plate and season with salt and pepper. Toss each turkey slice in it so that both sides are thoroughly coated and shake off any excess.

2 Heat the oil in a large frying pan and sauté the turkey slices for about 3 minutes on each side. Pour in the wine or sherry and boil rapidly to reduce it slightly.

3 Stir in the chicken stock, lower the heat and cook for another few minutes until the turkey is cooked through.

4 Halve and seed the grapes, and stir them into the sauce. Adjust the seasoning to taste.

5 Transfer to a warmed serving platter and serve, garnished with flat leaf parsley, accompanied by new potatoes or rice.

Cook's Tip
For a dark sauce you could use red wine and black grapes, and also add 115g/4oz/scant 2 cups sliced chestnut mushrooms. Sauté them in the oil before you cook the turkey in Step 2.

Anita Wong's Duck

A Chinese recipe, which would be served at celebrations, such as weddings where it denotes marital harmony.

Serves 4–6
60ml/4 tbsp vegetable oil
2 garlic cloves, chopped
2.25kg/5–5¼ lb duck, with giblets (if making your own stock)
2.5cm/1in piece fresh root ginger, thinly sliced

45ml/3 tbsp bean paste
30ml/2 tbsp light soy sauce
15ml/1 tbsp dark soy sauce
15ml/1 tbsp sugar
2.5ml/½ tsp Chinese five-spice powder
3 pieces star anise
450ml/¾ pint/scant 2 cups duck stock (see Cook's Tip)
salt
shredded spring onions (scallions), to garnish

1 Heat the oil in a large pan. Fry the garlic without browning, then add the duck. Turn frequently until the outside is slightly brown all over. Transfer to a plate.

2 Add the ginger to the pan, then stir in the bean paste. Cook for 1 minute, then add both soy sauces, the sugar and the five-spice powder. Return the duck to the pan and fry, turning, until the outside is coated. Add the star anise and stock, and season to taste. Cover tightly and simmer gently for 2–2½ hours or until the duck is tender. Skim off the excess fat. Leave the bird in the sauce to cool.

3 Cut the duck into serving portions and pour over the sauce. Garnish with shredded spring onions and serve cold.

Cook's Tip
To make stock, put the duck giblets in a pan with a small onion and a piece of bruised fresh root ginger. Cover with 600ml/ 1 pint/2½ cups water, bring to the boil and then simmer, covered, for 20 minutes. Strain and blot with kitchen paper to remove excess fat.

Pheasant with Apples

This luxurious dish bears the signature of Normandy: Calvados, the regional apple brandy, and rich cream.

Serves 2
2 pheasant breast fillets
25g/1oz/2 tbsp butter
1 onion, thinly sliced
1 eating apple, peeled and quartered

10ml/2 tsp sugar
60ml/4 tbsp Calvados
60ml/4 tbsp Chicken Stock
1.5ml/¼ tsp dried thyme
120ml/4fl oz/½ cup whipping cream
salt and freshly ground white pepper
sautéed potatoes, to serve

1 Score the thick end of each pheasant breast fillet.

2 In a heavy frying pan, melt half of the butter over a medium heat. Add the onion and cook for 8–10 minutes until golden, stirring occasionally. Transfer to a plate.

3 Cut each apple quarter crossways into thin slices. Melt half the remaining butter in the pan and add the apple. Sprinkle with the sugar and cook for 5–7 minutes until caramelized, turning occasionally. Transfer to the plate with the onion.

4 Wipe out the pan, add the remaining butter and increase the heat to medium-high. Add the pheasant breast fillets, skin side down, and cook for 3–4 minutes until golden. Turn and cook for a further 1–2 minutes until the juices run slightly pink when the thickest part of the meat is pierced with a knife or skewer. Transfer to a board and cover to keep warm.

5 Add the Calvados to the pan and boil until reduced by half. Add the stock and thyme, season and reduce by half again. Stir in the cream, bring to the boil and cook for 1 minute. Return the onion and apple slices to the pan, and cook for 1 minute.

6 Slice the pheasant breasts diagonally and arrange on warmed plates. Spoon over a little sauce with the onion and apples.

Duck with a Walnut & Pomegranate Sauce

This is an extremely exotic sweet-and-sour dish which originally came from Persia.

Serves 4
60ml/4 tbsp olive oil
2 onions, very thinly sliced
2.5ml/ ½ tsp ground turmeric
400g14oz/3½ cups walnuts,
    coarsely chopped
1 litre/1¾ pints/4 cups duck or
    Chicken Stock
6 pomegranates
30ml/2 tbsp caster
    (superfine) sugar
60ml/4 tbsp lemon juice
4 duck breast fillets, about
    225g/8oz each
salt and freshly ground
    black pepper

1 Heat half the oil in a frying pan. Add the onions and turmeric, and cook gently until soft. Transfer to a pan, add the walnuts and stock, then season with salt and pepper. Stir, bring to the boil and simmer, uncovered, for 20 minutes.

2 Cut the pomegranates in half and scoop out the seeds into a bowl. Reserve the seeds of one pomegranate. Transfer the remaining seeds to a blender or food processor and process to break them up. Strain through a sieve, to extract the juice, and stir in the sugar and lemon juice.

3 Score the skin of the duck breast fillets in a lattice fashion. Heat the remaining oil in a frying pan and place the duck in it, skin side down. Cook gently for 10 minutes, pouring off the fat from time to time, until the skin is dark golden and crisp. Turn over the fillets and cook for a further 3–4 minutes. Transfer to a plate and leave to rest.

4 Deglaze the frying pan with the pomegranate juice mixture, stirring with a wooden spoon, then add the walnut and stock mixture and simmer for 15 minutes until slightly thickened.

5 Slice the duck breast fillets, drizzle with a little sauce and serve, garnished with the reserved pomegranate seeds. Serve the remaining sauce separately.

Chicken Liver Risotto

The combination of chicken livers, bacon, parsley and thyme gives this risotto a rich flavour. Serve it as an appetizer for four or a lunch for two or three.

Serves 2–4
175g/6oz chicken livers
about 15ml/1 tbsp olive oil
about 25g/1oz/2 tbsp butter
3 rindless streaky (fatty) bacon
    rashers (strips), finely chopped
2 shallots, finely chopped
1 garlic clove, crushed
1 celery stick, thinly sliced
275g/10oz/1½ cups risotto rice
175ml/6fl oz/ ¾ cup dry
    white wine
900ml–1 litre/1½–1¾ pints/
    3¾–4 cups simmering
    Chicken Stock
5ml/1 tsp chopped fresh thyme
15ml/1 tbsp chopped
    fresh parsley
salt and freshly ground
    black pepper
fresh parsley and thyme sprigs,
    to garnish

1 Clean the chicken livers, removing any fat or membrane. Rinse, pat dry with kitchen paper and cut into small pieces.

2 Heat the oil and butter in a frying pan and fry the bacon for 2–3 minutes. Add the shallots, garlic and sliced celery, and fry for 3–4 minutes over a low heat until the vegetables are softened.

3 Increase the heat and add the livers. Stir-fry for a few minutes until they are brown all over, but still slightly pink in the centre.

4 Add the rice. Cook, stirring, for a few minutes, then pour over the wine. Bring to the boil, stirring frequently, taking care not to break up the livers. When all the wine has been absorbed, add the hot stock, a ladleful at a time, stirring constantly. About halfway through the cooking, add the thyme and season with salt and pepper. Continue to add the stock, making sure that each quantity has been absorbed before adding more.

5 When the risotto is creamy and the rice is tender, stir in the parsley. Adust the seasoning. Remove the pan from the heat, cover and leave to rest for a few minutes before serving, garnished with parsley and thyme sprigs.

Mushroom Picker's Chicken Paella

A good paella is based on a few well-chosen ingredients. Here, chicken combines with mixed wild mushrooms and vegetables.

Serves 4

45ml/3 tbsp olive oil
1 medium onion, chopped
1 small fennel bulb, sliced
225g/8oz/generous 3 cups
  assorted wild and cultivated
  mushrooms, trimmed and sliced
1 garlic clove, crushed
3 chicken legs, chopped through
  the bone
350g/12oz/1²⁄₃ cups short-grain
  Spanish or Italian rice
900ml/1½ pints/3¾ cups
  Chicken Stock, boiling
pinch of saffron threads or
  1 sachet saffron powder
1 fresh thyme sprig
400g/14oz can butter (lima)
  beans, drained and rinsed
75g/3oz/¾ cup frozen peas

1 Heat the oil in a 35cm/14in paella pan or a large frying pan. Add the onion and fennel and fry over a gentle heat for 3–4 minutes.

2 Add the mushrooms and garlic and cook until the juices begin to run, then increase the heat to evaporate them. Push the vegetables to the side. Add the chicken and fry briefly.

3 Stir in the rice, add the stock, saffron, thyme, butter beans and peas. Bring to simmering point and cook gently for 15 minutes without stirring.

4 Remove the pan from the heat and cover the surface of the paella with a circle of greased greaseproof (waxed) paper. Cover the paper with a clean dishtowel and allow the paella to finish cooking in its own heat for about 5 minutes. Bring to the table, uncover and serve.

Cook's Tip
Suitable mushrooms for this dish include ceps, bay boletus. chanterelles, saffron milk-caps, hedgehog fungus, St George's, Caesar's and oyster mushrooms.

Seven-vegetable Couscous

In this glorious, magically numbered Moroccan dish, chicken is partnered with lamb, carrots, parsnips, turnips, onions, courgettes, tomatoes and green beans. You can substitute different vegetables if you wish.

Serves 6

30ml/2 tbsp sunflower or olive oil
450g/1lb lean lamb, cut into
  bitesize pieces
2 chicken breast quarters, halved
2 onions, chopped
350g/12oz carrots, cut
  into chunks
225g/8oz parsnips, cut
  into chunks
115g/4oz turnips, cut into cubes
6 tomatoes, peeled and chopped
900ml/1½ pints/3¾ cups
  Chicken Stock
good pinch of ground ginger
1 cinnamon stick
400g/14oz can chickpeas,
  drained
400g/14oz/2⅓ cups couscous
2 small courgettes (zucchini), cut
  into julienne strips
115g/4oz green beans, halved
  if necessary
50g/2oz/⅓ cup raisins
a little harissa or Tabasco sauce
salt and freshly ground
  black pepper

1 Heat half the oil in a large, heavy pan or flameproof casserole and add the lamb, in batches if necessary, and fry until evenly browned, stirring frequently. Transfer to a plate using a slotted spoon. Add the chicken pieces to the pan and cook, turning occasionally, until evenly browned. Using a slotted spoon, transfer to the plate with the lamb.

2 Heat the remaining oil and add the onions. Fry over a gentle heat for 2–3 minutes, stirring occasionally, until softened, but not coloured. Add the carrots, parsnips and turnips. Stir well, cover with a lid and sweat over a gentle heat for 5–6 minutes, stirring once or twice.

3 Add the tomatoes, and return the lamb and chicken to the pan. Pour in the chicken stock. Season with salt and pepper to taste and add the ground ginger and cinnamon stick. Bring to the boil and simmer gently for 35–45 minutes until the meat is nearly tender.

4 Skin the chickpeas by placing them in a bowl of cold water and rubbing them between your fingers. The skins will rise to the surface. Discard the skins and drain. Prepare the couscous according to the instructions on the packet.

5 Add the skinned chickpeas, courgettes, beans and raisins to the meat mixture, stir gently and continue cooking for about 10–15 minutes until the vegetables and meat are tender. Pile the couscous on to a large warmed serving platter, making a slight well in the centre.

6 Transfer the chicken to a plate, and remove the skin and bones, if you wish. Spoon three to four large spoonfuls of stock into a separate pan. Stir the chicken back into the stew, add harissa or Tabasco sauce to taste to the separate pan of stock and heat both gently. Remove and discard the cinnamon stick, spoon the stew over the couscous and serve. Hand the harissa sauce in a separate bowl.

Duck Risotto

This makes an excellent appetizer for six or could be served for half that number as a lunch or supper dish.

Serves 3–6
2 duck breast fillets
30ml/2 tbsp brandy
30ml/2 tbsp orange juice
15ml/1 tbsp olive oil (optional)
1 onion, finely chopped
1 garlic clove, crushed

275g/10oz/1½ cups risotto rice
1–1.2 litres/1¾–2 pints/4–5 cups simmering Chicken Stock
5ml/1 tsp chopped fresh thyme
5ml/1 tsp chopped fresh mint
10ml/2 tsp grated orange rind
40g/1½ oz/½ cup grated Parmesan cheese
salt and freshly ground black pepper
strips of thinly pared orange rind, to garnish

1 Score the fatty sides of the duck and rub with salt. Dry-fry, fat side down, in a heavy frying pan over a medium heat for 6–8 minutes to render the fat. Transfer to a plate, and pull away and discard the fat. Cut the flesh into 2cm/¾in slices.

2 Pour all but 15ml/1 tbsp of the rendered duck fat into a jug (pitcher), then reheat the fat in the pan. Fry the duck slices for 2–3 minutes over a medium-high heat until evenly browned.

3 Add the brandy, heat to simmering point and then ignite. When the flames have died down, add the orange juice and season. Remove from the heat and set aside.

4 In a pan, heat either 15ml/1 tbsp of the remaining duck fat or the olive oil. Fry the onion and garlic over a gentle heat until the onion is soft but not browned. Add the rice and cook, stirring constantly, until the grains are coated in oil.

5 Add the stock, a ladle at a time, waiting for each addition to be absorbed completely before adding the next. Just before adding the final ladleful, stir in the duck with the thyme and mint. Continue cooking until the risotto is creamy and the rice is tender. Add the grated orange rind and Parmesan. Adjust the seasoning, then remove from the heat, cover and leave to stand for a few minutes. Serve, garnished with the pared orange rind.

Peruvian Duck with Rice

This is a very rich dish, brightly coloured with tomatoes, squash and fresh herbs.

Serves 4–6
4 duck breast fillets
1 Spanish onion, chopped
2 garlic cloves, crushed
10ml/2 tsp grated fresh root ginger
4 tomatoes (peeled, if liked), chopped

225g/8oz kabocha or acorn squash, cut into 1cm/½ in cubes
275g/10oz/1½ cups long grain rice
750ml/1¼ pints/3 cups Chicken Stock
15ml/1 tbsp finely chopped fresh coriander (cilantro)
15ml/1 tbsp finely chopped fresh mint
salt and freshly ground black pepper

1 Heat a heavy frying pan or flameproof casserole. Using a sharp knife, score the fatty side of the duck breast fillets in a criss-cross pattern, rub the fat with a little salt, then dry-fry, skin side down, for 6–8 minutes to render some of the fat.

2 Pour all but 15ml/1 tbsp of the fat into a jar or cup, then fry the duck fillets, meat side down, in the fat remaining in the pan for 3–4 minutes until brown all over. Transfer to a board, slice thickly and set aside in a shallow dish. Deglaze the pan with a little water and pour this liquid over the duck.

3 Fry the onion and garlic in the same pan for 4–5 minutes until the onion is fairly soft, adding a little extra duck fat if necessary. Stir in the ginger, cook for 1–2 minutes more, then add the tomatoes and cook, stirring, for another 2 minutes. Add the squash, stir-fry for a few minutes, then cover and leave to steam for about 4 minutes.

4 Stir in the rice and cook, stirring, until it is well coated. Pour in the stock, return the slices of duck to the pan and season.

5 Bring to the boil, then lower the heat, cover and simmer for 30–35 minutes until the rice is tender. Stir in the coriander and mint, and serve.

CHICKEN ROASTS

Roast chicken always seems to be something of a treat, but you will be surprised by the number of different ways it can be roasted and just how special these are. Superb stuffings, flavoured with herbs and spices or fruit and vegetables impart a magical richness to what is fundamentally a very simple dish. Alternatively, coat the chicken with a paste or sauce before roasting to seal in the juices and add colour, texture and flavour. You can even encase the bird with salt for a marvellously tender and deliciously moist result. While it is traditional to roast a whole bird, don't overlook the mouthwatering recipes for roasted chicken portions and stuffed rolls. This chapter also features a superb collection of recipes for roasting game birds and other poultry. Thanksgiving, for example, would not be much of a special occasion without roast turkey and, if you want to rediscover the true flavour of Christmas, try a roast goose – if you can choose between the two marvellous recipes here. Roast pheasant is the ideal choice for a sophisticated dinner party, while if you have never tried wild duck, roasting is undoubtedly the best place to start. Traditional roasts and classic dishes, as well as exotic recipes from places as far apart as Morocco, Mexico and Croatia offer a cornucopia of wonderful main courses that will turn any meal into a special occasion and any celebration into a banquet.

Olive Oil Roasted Chicken with Mediterranean Vegetables

A feast of vegetables is roasted in the chicken juices until they are meltingly tender and succulent.

Serves 4
1.75kg/4lb chicken
150ml/ ¼ pint/ ⅔ cup extra virgin olive oil
½ lemon
few sprigs of fresh thyme

450g/1lb small new potatoes
1 aubergine (eggplant), cut into 2.5cm/1in cubes
1 red (bell) pepper, seeded and quartered
1 fennel bulb, trimmed and quartered
8 large garlic cloves, unpeeled
coarse salt and freshly ground black pepper

1 Preheat the oven to 200°C/400°F/Gas 6. Rub the chicken all over with some of the olive oil and season with pepper. Place the lemon half inside the bird, with one to two sprigs of thyme. Put the chicken, breast side down, in a large roasting pan. Roast for about 30 minutes.

2 Remove the chicken from the oven and season with salt. Turn the chicken right side up and baste with the juices from the pan. Surround the bird with the potatoes, roll them in the juices and return the pan to the oven to continue roasting.

3 After 30 minutes add the aubergine, red pepper, fennel and garlic. Drizzle with the remaining oil and season. Add any remaining thyme. Return to the oven and cook for 30–50 minutes more, turning the vegetables occasionally.

4 To find out if the chicken is cooked, push the tip of a sharp knife or skewer into the thickest part of the thigh: if the juices run clear, it is done. The vegetables should be tender and just beginning to brown.

5 Serve the chicken and vegetables from the pan, or transfer the vegetables to a serving dish, joint the chicken and place it on top. Serve the skimmed juices in a gravy boat.

Roast Chicken Stuffed with Forest Mushrooms

Use a free-range bird for this dish and let its flavour mingle with the aroma of woodland mushrooms.

Serves 4
25g/1oz/2 tbsp unsalted (sweet) butter, plus extra for basting and to finish the gravy
1 shallot, chopped
225g/8oz wild mushrooms, e.g. chanterelles, ceps, bay boletus, oyster, trimmed and chopped
40g/1½oz/ ¾ cup fresh white breadcrumbs

2 egg yolks
1.75kg/4lb chicken
½ celery stick, chopped
½ small carrot, chopped
75g/3oz potato, peeled and chopped
250ml/8fl oz/1 cup Chicken Stock, plus extra if required
10ml/2 tsp wine vinegar
salt and freshly ground black pepper
fresh parsley sprigs, to garnish
roast potatoes and carrots, to serve

1 Preheat the oven to 220°C/425°F/Gas 7. Melt the butter in a pan and gently fry the shallot. Add half of the mushrooms and cook for 2–3 minutes until the juices run. Remove from the heat and stir in the breadcrumbs, seasoning and egg yolks. Spoon the stuffing into the neck of the chicken, enclose and fasten the skin on the underside with a skewer.

2 Rub the chicken with some butter and season. Put the celery, carrot, potato and remaining mushrooms in a roasting pan. Place the chicken on top, add the stock and roast for 1¼ hours or until the juices run clear when the thickest part of the thigh is pierced with a knife or skewer.

3 Transfer the chicken to a carving board, then process the vegetables and mushrooms. Pour the mixture back into the pan and heat gently, adjusting the consistency with chicken stock if necessary. Taste and adjust the seasoning, then add the vinegar and a knob (pat) of butter, and stir briskly. Pour the sauce into a gravy boat. Serve the chicken with roast potatoes and carrots, garnished with parsley and accompanied by the sauce.

Moroccan Roast Chicken

Ideally this chicken should be cooked whole, Moroccan-style, on a spit over hot charcoal. However, it is still excellent roasted in a hot conventional oven and can be cooked whole, halved or in quarters.

Serves 4–6
1.75kg/4lb chicken
2 small shallots
1 garlic clove
1 fresh parsley sprig
1 fresh coriander (cilantro) sprig
5ml/1 tsp salt
7.5ml/1½ tsp paprika
pinch of cayenne pepper
5–7.5ml/1–1½ tsp ground cumin
about 40g/1½oz/3 tbsp butter
½–1 lemon (optional)
sprigs of fresh parsley or
    coriander (cilantro), to garnish

1 Remove the chicken giblets if necessary and rinse out the cavity with cold running water. Pat dry with kitchen paper. Unless cooking it whole, cut the chicken in half or into quarters using poultry shears or a sharp knife.

2 Place the shallots, garlic, herbs, salt and spices in a food processor or blender and process until the shallots are finely chopped. Add the butter and process to make a smooth paste.

3 Thoroughly rub the paste over the skin of the chicken and then allow it to stand for 1–2 hours.

4 Preheat the oven to 200°C/400°F/Gas 6 and place the chicken in a roasting pan. If using, quarter the lemon and place one or two quarters around the chicken pieces (or in the body cavity if the chicken is whole) and squeeze a little juice over the skin. Roast in the oven for 1–1¼ hours (2–2¼ hours for a whole bird) until the juices run clear when the thickest part of the thigh is pierced with a skewer or knife. Baste occasionally during cooking with the juices in the roasting pan. If the skin starts to brown too quickly, cover the chicken loosely with foil or greaseproof (waxed) paper.

5 Allow the chicken to stand for 10–15 minutes, covered in foil, before carving. Serve, garnished with parsley or coriander.

Chicken with 40 Cloves of Garlic

This recipe is not as alarming as it sounds. Long, slow cooking makes the garlic soft, fragrant and sweet, and the delicious flavour permeates the chicken meat.

Serves 4–6
½ lemon
fresh rosemary sprigs
1.5–1.75kg/3½–4lb chicken
4 or 5 whole garlic bulbs
60ml/4 tbsp olive oil
salt and freshly ground
    black pepper
steamed broad (fava) beans and
    spring onions (scallions),
    to serve

1 Preheat the oven to 190°C/375°F/Gas 5. Place the lemon half and the rosemary sprigs in the chicken. Separate three or four of the garlic bulbs into cloves and remove the papery husks, but do not peel. Slice the top off the remaining garlic bulb.

2 Heat the oil in a large, flameproof casserole. Add the chicken, turning it in the hot oil to coat the skin completely. Season with salt and pepper and add all the garlic.

3 Cover the casserole with a sheet of foil, then the lid, to seal in the steam and the flavour. Cook for 1–1¼ hours until the chicken juices run clear when the thickest part of the thigh is pierced with a skewer or knife.

4 Serve the chicken with the garlic, accompanied by steamed broad beans and spring onions.

Cook's Tip
Make sure that each guest receives an equal portion of garlic. The idea is to mash the garlic into the pan juices to make an aromatic sauce.

Chicken with Burnt Almond Stuffing

Breadcrumbs are often the basis of stuffings, but this Jewish dish uses crunchy vegetables and matzo meal.

Serves 4

30ml/2 tbsp oil
60ml/4 tbsp flaked (sliced) almonds
4 fat spring onions (scallions), sliced
2 carrots, chopped
2 celery sticks, chopped
300ml/ ½ pint/1 ¼ cups Chicken Stock
90ml/6 tbsp medium-ground matzo meal
4 chicken breast portions with skin
salt and freshly ground black pepper
fresh dill sprigs, to garnish
mixed salad, to serve

1 Preheat the oven to 190°C/375°F/Gas 5. Heat the oil in a frying pan and sauté the almonds until light brown. Remove with a slotted spoon and set aside. Add the vegetables to the pan and sauté over a medium heat for a few minutes.

2 Add the seasoning and pour in half of the stock. Cook over a high heat until the liquid is slightly reduced and the vegetables are just moist. Mix in the matzo meal and the sautéed almonds.

3 Ease the skin off the chicken breast portions on one side and press some of the stuffing underneath each. Press the skin back over the stuffing and slash the skin to stop it curling up. Arrange the breast portions in a roasting pan.

4 Roast the chicken breast portions, skin side up, for about 20–30 minutes or until the meat is tender and white. The skin should be crisp and brown.

5 Keep the chicken warm while you make the gravy. Pour the remaining stock into the roasting pan and, over a medium heat, stir in any chicken juices or remaining stuffing. Bring to the boil and then strain into a jug (pitcher). Serve with a mixed salad and garnish with fresh dill sprigs.

Chicken Roulé

Relatively simple to prepare, this recipe uses beef as a filling. It is rolled in chicken meat spread with a creamy garlic cheese that just melts in the mouth.

Serves 4

4 chicken breast fillets, about 115g/4oz each
115g/4oz minced (ground) beef
30ml/2 tbsp chopped fresh chives
225g/8oz/1 cup roulé cream cheese with garlic
30ml/2 tbsp clear honey
salt and freshly ground black pepper
cooked green beans and mushrooms, to serve

1 Preheat the oven to 190°C/375°F/Gas 5. Place the chicken between two pieces of clear film (plastic wrap). Beat with a meat mallet or rolling pin until 5mm/¼in thick and joined.

2 Place the minced beef in a large pan. Fry for 3 minutes, stirring constantly to break up the clumps, then add the fresh chives and seasoning. Remove from the heat and leave to cool.

3 Place the chicken on a board and spread with the roulé. Top with the minced beef mixture. Carefully roll up the chicken to form a sausage shape.

4 Brush with honey and place in a roasting pan. Cook for 1 hour in the oven. Remove from the pan and slice thinly. Serve with freshly cooked green beans and mushrooms.

Cook's Tip

Chives are one of the classic four fines herbes *and have a subtle oniony flavour. They are often better snipped with kitchen scissors, rather than chopped – and this is an easier method of preparing them too. The attractive, round pink flowers are also edible and make an interesting garnish.*

Chicken in a Tomato Coat

This roasted chicken keeps deliciously moist as it cooks in its red "jacket".

Serves 4–6
1.5–1.75kg/3½–4lb chicken
1 small onion
knob (pat) of butter
75ml/5 tbsp Fresh
  Tomato Sauce
30ml/2 tbsp chopped mixed fresh
  herbs, e.g. parsley, tarragon,
  sage, basil and marjoram, or
  10ml/2 tsp dried mixed herbs
small glass of dry white wine
2–3 small tomatoes, sliced
olive oil
a little cornflour (cornstarch)
salt and freshly ground
  black pepper

1 Preheat the oven to 190°C/375°F/Gas 5. Wash and wipe dry the chicken, and place in a roasting pan. Place the onion, the knob of butter and some seasoning inside the chicken.

2 Spread most of the tomato sauce over the chicken, and sprinkle with half the herbs and some seasoning. Pour the wine into the roasting pan.

3 Cover with foil, then roast for 1½ hours, basting occasionally. Remove the foil, spread with the remaining sauce and the sliced tomatoes, and drizzle with oil. Continue cooking for a further 20–30 minutes until the chicken juices run clear when the thickest part of the thigh is pierced with a skewer or knife.

4 Remove the chicken from the oven and leave to rest for 10–15 minutes. Sprinkle with the remaining herbs, then carve into portions. Serve with the juices from the roasting pan, thickened with a little cornflour.

> **Cook's Tip**
> *Whenever possible, buy sun-ripened tomatoes, which have a sweeter and more concentrated flavour than those grown under glass. Plum tomatoes are ideal for cooking, as they are much less watery than standard varieties.*

Cold Sliced Roast Chicken

Cooking the chestnut stuffing under the skin keeps the breast meat succulent and creates an attractive striped effect when the chicken is carved. An excellent dish for a buffet.

Serves 6–8
2 onions, cut in half
30–45ml/2–3 tbsp vegetable oil
65g/2½oz/1¼ cups fresh
  white breadcrumbs
200g/7oz/¾ cup unsweetened
  chestnut purée (paste)
2kg/4½lb chicken
salt and freshly ground
  black pepper
fresh flat leaf parsley, to garnish
lettuce leaves and potato salad,
  to serve

1 Chop one of the onions finely. Heat half of the vegetable oil in a small frying pan and sauté the chopped onion until golden. Stir in 120ml/4fl oz/½ cup boiling water, take the pan off the heat and leave to stand for 5 minutes to allow some of the liquid to be absorbed.

2 Mix the breadcrumbs and chestnut purée with the onion and any liquid in the pan. Season well. Leave to cool completely.

3 Preheat the oven to 220°C/425°F/Gas 7. Wipe the chicken well with kitchen paper, inside and out, and carefully slide your hand under the skin on the breast to ease it away from the meat. Press the stuffing underneath the skin all over the breast.

4 Brush a roasting pan with the remaining oil and put in the chicken, breast side down, with the remaining onion. Roast for 1 hour, basting occasionally and pouring away any excess fat.

5 Turn the chicken over and continue to roast for a further 15 minutes or until the juices run clear when the thickest part of the thigh is pierced with a skewer or knife. Cover the top with a strip of foil if it looks too brown.

6 When the chicken is cooked, leave it to cool before cutting downwards into slices. Garnish with flat leaf parsley, and serve with lettuce leaves and potato salad.

Poussins with Bulgur Wheat & Vermouth

These young birds are filled with a bulgur wheat and nut stuffing laced with vermouth, and served with a medley of roast vegetables finished with a vermouth glaze.

Serves 4
50g/2oz/ ⅓ cup bulgur wheat
150ml/ ¼ pint/ ⅔ cup dry
   white vermouth
60ml/4 tbsp olive oil
I large onion, finely chopped
2 carrots, finely chopped
75g/3oz/ ¾ cup pine
   nuts, chopped
5ml/1 tsp celery seeds
4 poussins
3 red onions, quartered
4 baby aubergines
   (eggplants), halved
4 patty pan squashes
12 baby carrots
45ml/3 tbsp corn syrup
salt and freshly ground
   black pepper

I Preheat the oven to 200°C/400°F/Gas 6. Put the bulgur wheat in a heatproof bowl, pour over half the vermouth and cover with boiling water. Set aside.

2 Heat half the oil in a large, shallow frying pan. Add the onion and carrots and fry for 10 minutes, then remove the pan from the heat and stir in the pine nuts, celery seeds and the well-drained bulgur wheat.

3 Stuff the poussins with the bulgur wheat mixture. Place them in a roasting pan, brush with oil and sprinkle with salt and pepper. Roast for 45–55 minutes until the juices run clear when the thickest part of the thigh is pierced with a skewer or knife.

4 Meanwhile, spread out the red onions, aubergines, patty pans and baby carrots in a single layer on a baking sheet.

5 Mix the corn syrup with the remaining vermouth and oil in a small bowl. Season with salt and pepper to taste. Brush the corn syrup mixture over the vegetables and roast for 35–45 minutes until golden. Cut each poussin in half and serve immediately with the roasted vegetables.

Poussins with Raisin-walnut Stuffing

This easy-to-prepare traditional American dish offers something different for a midweek supper.

Serves 4
250ml/8fl oz/1 cup port
90g/3½oz/ ⅔ cup raisins
15ml/1 tbsp walnut oil
75g/3oz/1 cup mushrooms,
   finely chopped
I large celery stick,
   finely chopped
I small onion, chopped
50g/2oz/1 cup fresh breadcrumbs
50g/2oz/ ½ cup chopped walnuts
15ml/1 tbsp each chopped fresh
   basil and parsley or 30ml/
   2 tbsp chopped fresh parsley
2.5ml/ ½ tsp dried thyme
75g/3oz/6 tbsp butter, melted
4 poussins
salt and freshly ground
   black pepper
salad and vegetables, to serve

I Preheat the oven to 180°C/350°F/Gas 4. In a small bowl, combine the port and raisins and leave to soak for 20 minutes.

2 Meanwhile, heat the oil in a non-stick frying pan. Add the mushrooms, celery and onion and cook over a low heat for 8–10 minutes until softened. Leave to cool slightly.

3 Drain the raisins, reserving the port. Combine the raisins, breadcrumbs, walnuts, basil (if using), parsley and thyme in a bowl. Stir in the onion mixture and 60ml/4 tbsp of the melted butter. Add salt and pepper to taste.

4 Fill the cavity of each bird with the stuffing mixture. Do not pack too tightly. Tie the legs together, looping the tail with string to enclose the stuffing securely.

5 Brush the birds with the remaining butter and place in a roasting pan just large enough to hold them comfortably. Pour over the reserved port. Roast, basting occasionally, for about 1 hour or until the juices run clear when the thickest part of the thigh is pierced with a skewer or knife. Serve immediately, pouring some of the pan juices over each bird. Accompany with salad and vegetables.

Roast Chicken with Celeriac

Celeriac mixed with chopped bacon, onion and herbs makes a moist and tasty stuffing.

Serves 4
1.5kg/3½lb chicken
15g/½oz/1 tbsp butter
celery leaves and parsley,
  to garnish

For the stuffing
450g/1lb celeriac, chopped
25g/1oz/2 tbsp butter
3 bacon rashers (strips), rinded
  and chopped

1 onion, finely chopped
leaves from 1 fresh thyme
  sprig, chopped
leaves from 1 small fresh tarragon
  sprig, chopped
30ml/2 tbsp chopped
  fresh parsley
75g/3oz/1½ cups fresh
  brown breadcrumbs
dash of Worcestershire sauce
1 egg, beaten
salt and freshly ground
  black pepper

1 To make the stuffing, cook the celeriac in boiling water until tender. Drain well and chop finely.

2 Heat the butter in a pan, and gently cook the bacon and onion until the onion is soft. Stir in the celeriac and herbs, and cook, stirring occasionally, for 2–3 minutes. Meanwhile, preheat the oven to 200°C/400°F/Gas 6.

3 Remove the pan from the heat and stir in the breadcrumbs, Worcestershire sauce, seasoning and sufficient egg to bind. Use to stuff the neck end of the chicken. Season the bird's skin, then rub with the butter.

4 Roast the chicken, basting occasionally with the juices, for 1¼–1½ hours until the juices run clear when the thickest part of the thigh is pierced with a skewer or knife.

5 Turn off the oven, prop the door open slightly and allow the chicken to rest for 10–15 minutes before carving and serving, garnished with celery leaves and parsley.

Roast Chicken with Herb & Orange Bread Stuffing

Tender roast chicken scented with orange and herbs, served with gravy.

Serves 4–6
2 onions
25g/1oz/2 tbsp butter, plus extra
150g/5oz/2½ cups soft
  white breadcrumbs
30ml/2 tbsp chopped fresh
  mixed herbs
grated rind of 1 orange

1.5kg/3½lb chicken with giblets
1 carrot, sliced
1 bay leaf
1 fresh thyme sprig
900ml/1½ pints/3¾ cups water
15ml/1 tbsp tomato purée (paste)
10ml/2 tsp cornflour (cornstarch),
  mixed to a thin paste with
  15ml/1 tbsp cold water
salt and freshly ground
  black pepper
chopped fresh thyme, to garnish

1 Preheat the oven to 200°C/400°F/Gas 6. Finely chop one of the onions. Melt the butter in a pan and add the chopped onion. Cook for 3–4 minutes until soft. Stir in the breadcrumbs, chopped mixed herbs and orange rind. Season well.

2 Reserve the giblets. Wash the neck end of the chicken and dry with kitchen paper. Spoon in the stuffing, then rub a little butter into the breast and season it well. Put the chicken into a roasting pan and cook in the oven for 20 minutes, then reduce the temperature to 180°C/350°F/Gas 4 and cook for a further 1 hour or until the juices run clear when the thickest part of the thigh is pierced with a knife or skewer.

3 Put the giblets, the remaining onion, the carrot, bay leaf, thyme and water into a large pan. Bring to the boil, then simmer while the chicken is roasting.

4 Place the chicken on a warmed serving platter and leave to rest. Skim the fat off the cooking juices, strain the juices and stock into a pan, and discard the giblets and vegetables. Simmer for about 5 minutes. Whisk in the tomato purée. Whisk the cornflour paste into the gravy and cook for 1 minute. Season and serve with the chicken, garnished with chopped thyme.

Whisky Chicken with Onion Marmalade

Whisky-flavoured roasted chicken portions are served with meltingly tender onions and green pepper.

Serves 4

25g/1oz/4 tbsp sesame
  seeds, crushed
2 garlic cloves, crushed
pinch of paprika
30ml/2 tbsp oil
30ml/2 tbsp whisky

30ml/2 tbsp clear honey
4 chicken portions
salt and freshly ground
  black pepper

For the onion marmalade

30ml/2 tbsp oil
2 large onions, thinly sliced
1 green (bell) pepper, seeded
  and sliced
150ml/ 1/4 pint/ 2/3 cup
  vegetable stock

1 Preheat the oven to 190°C/375°F/Gas 5. In a bowl, make a paste with the sesame seeds, garlic, paprika, oil, whisky and honey. Season and add a little water if the paste is too thick.

2 Make several cuts in the chicken portions and place them in an ovenproof dish. Spread the paste over. Roast for 40 minutes or until cooked through.

3 Meanwhile, to make the marmalade, heat the oil in a frying pan and fry the onions over a medium heat for 15 minutes. Add the green pepper and fry for 5 minutes more. Stir in the stock, season with salt and pepper, and cook gently, stirring occasionally, for about 20 minutes.

4 Transfer the chicken to warmed plates and serve with the warm onion marmalade.

Variation
Instead of making cuts in the chicken portions, ease the skin away from the flesh and push the paste underneath.

Poussins with Courgette & Apricot Stuffing

If possible, buy very small poussins for this recipe. If these are not available, buy slightly larger poussins and serve half per person.

Serves 4

4 small poussins
about 40g/1 1/2 oz/3 tbsp butter
5–10ml/1–2 tsp ground coriander
1 large red (bell) pepper, seeded
  and cut into strips
1 fresh red chilli, seeded and
  thinly sliced
15–30ml/1–2 tbsp olive oil
120ml/4fl oz/ 1/2 cup
  Chicken Stock

30ml/2 tbsp cornflour
  (cornstarch)
salt and freshly ground
  black pepper
fresh flat leaf parsley, to garnish

For the stuffing

550ml/18fl oz/2 1/2 cups
  vegetable or Chicken Stock
275g/10oz/1 2/3 cups couscous
2 small courgettes (zucchini)
8 ready-to-eat dried apricots
15ml/1 tbsp chopped fresh flat
  leaf parsley
15ml/1 tbsp chopped fresh
  coriander (cilantro)
juice of 1/2 lemon

1 To make the stuffing, bring the stock to the boil and pour it over the couscous in a large bowl. Stir once and then set aside for 10 minutes.

2 Meanwhile, trim the courgettes and then grate coarsely. Coarsely chop the apricots and add to the courgettes. Preheat the oven to 200°C/400°F/Gas 6.

3 When the couscous has swollen, fluff up with a fork and then spoon 90ml/6 tbsp into a separate bowl and add the courgettes and chopped apricots. Add the herbs, seasoning and lemon juice and stir to make a fairly loose stuffing. Set aside the remaining couscous for serving.

4 Spoon the apricot stuffing loosely into the body cavities of the poussins and secure with cooking string or wooden cocktail sticks (toothpicks). Place the birds in a roasting pan so that they fit comfortably, but not too closely. Rub the butter into the skins, and sprinkle with ground coriander and a little salt and pepper. Place the red pepper and chilli in the roasting pan around the poussins and spoon over the olive oil.

5 Roast in the oven for 20 minutes, then reduce the oven temperature to 180°C/350°F/Gas 4. Pour the stock around the poussins and baste them with the stock and red pepper/chilli mixture. Return the pan to the oven and cook for a further 30–35 minutes until the poussins are cooked through. Baste occasionally with the stock.

6 Transfer the poussins to a warmed serving plate. Steam the reserved couscous to reheat. Blend the cornflour with 45ml/ 3 tbsp cold water, stir into the stock and peppers in the roasting pan and heat gently on the hob (stovetop), stirring, until the sauce is slightly thickened. Adjust the seasoning.

7 Pour the sauce into a jug (pitcher). Garnish the birds with parsley and serve with the reserved couscous.

Chicken Baked in a Salt Crust

This unusual dish is extremely simple to make. Once it is cooked, you just break away the salt crust to reveal the wonderfully tender, golden-brown chicken within.

Serves 4

bunch of mixed fresh herbs, e.g. rosemary, thyme, marjoram and parsley
1.5kg/3½lb corn-fed chicken
about 1.5kg/3½lb/7 cups coarse sea salt
1 egg white
1–2 whole garlic bulbs, baked for 1 hour, to serve

1 Preheat the oven to 190°C/375°F/Gas 5. Stuff the herbs into the chicken cavity, then truss the chicken.

2 Mix together the sea salt and egg white until all the salt crystals are moistened. Select a roasting pan into which the chicken will fit neatly, then line it with a large double layer of foil. Spread a thick layer of moistened salt in the foil-lined pan and place the chicken on top. Cover with the remaining salt and press into a neat shape, over and around the chicken, making sure it is completely enclosed.

3 Bring the foil edges up and over the chicken to enclose it and bake in the oven for 1½ hours. Remove from the oven and leave to rest for 10 minutes.

4 Carefully lift the foil package from the container and open it. Break the salt crust to reveal the chicken inside. Brush any traces of salt from the bird, then serve with baked whole garlic bulbs. Each clove can be slipped from its skin and eaten with a bite of chicken.

Cook's Tip
Sea salt is available in the form of whole crystals and coarsely or finely ground. Coarsely ground salt works best here.

Roast Turkey

A classic roast, served with stuffing balls, chipolata sausages and gravy.

Serves 8

4.5kg/10lb turkey, with giblets (thawed overnight if frozen)
1 large onion, peeled and stuck with 6 whole cloves
50g/2oz/4 tbsp butter, softened
10 chipolata sausages
salt and freshly ground black pepper

For the stuffing
225g/8oz rindless streaky (fatty) bacon, chopped
1 large onion, finely chopped
450g/1lb pork sausage (bulk sausage) meat
25g/1oz/⅓ cup rolled oats
30ml/2 tbsp chopped fresh parsley
10ml/2 tsp dried mixed herbs
1 large egg, beaten
115g/4oz/½ cup dried apricots, finely chopped

For the gravy
25g/1oz/2 tbsp plain (all-purpose) flour
450ml/¾ pint/scant 2 cups giblet stock

1 Preheat the oven to 200°C/400°F/Gas 6. To make the stuffing, cook the bacon and onion gently in a pan until the bacon is crisp and the onion tender. Transfer to a large bowl and mix in all the remaining stuffing ingredients. Season to taste.

2 Stuff the neck end of the turkey, tuck the flap of skin under and secure with a small skewer. Reserve any remaining stuffing.

3 Put the whole onion, studded with cloves, in the body cavity of the turkey and tie the legs together. Weigh the stuffed bird and calculate the cooking time; allow 15 minutes per 450g/1lb plus 15 minutes over. Place the turkey in a large roasting pan.

4 Spread the turkey with the butter and season it with salt and pepper. Cover it loosely with foil and cook it for 30 minutes. Baste the turkey with the pan juices. Then lower the oven temperature to 180°C/350°F/Gas 4 and cook for the remainder of the calculated time (about 3½ hours for a 4.5kg/10lb bird). Baste it every 30 minutes or so. Remove the foil from the turkey for the last hour of cooking and baste it.

5 Using wet hands, shape the remaining stuffing into small balls or pack it into a greased ovenproof dish. Cook in the oven for 20 minutes or until golden brown and crisp.

6 About 20 minutes before the end of cooking, place the chipolatas in an ovenproof dish and put them into the oven.

7 The turkey is cooked if the juices run clear when the thickest part of the thigh is pierced with a skewer or knife. Transfer it to a serving plate, cover with foil and let it stand for 10–15 minutes before carving. To make the gravy, spoon off the fat from the roasting pan, leaving the meat juices. Blend in the flour and cook for 2 minutes. Gradually stir in the stock and bring to the boil. Check the seasoning and pour into a jug (pitcher) or gravy boat. Remove the skewer from the bird and pour any juices into the gravy. To serve, surround the turkey with the chipolata sausages and stuffing balls.

Turkey Zador with Mlinces

In this Croatian recipe for special occasions, the unusual *mlinces* are used to soak up the juices from a roast turkey.

Serves 10–12
3kg/6½ lb turkey
2 garlic cloves, halved
115g/4oz smoked bacon, finely chopped
30ml/2 tbsp chopped fresh rosemary

120ml/4fl oz/ ½ cup olive oil
250ml/8fl oz/1 cup dry white wine
fresh rosemary sprigs, to garnish
grilled (broiled) bacon, to serve

For the mlinces
350g/12oz/3 cups plain (all-purpose) flour, sifted
120–150ml/4–5fl oz/ ½– ⅔ cup warm water
30ml/2 tbsp oil
salt

1 Preheat the oven to 200°C/400°F/Gas 6. Dry the turkey well inside and out. Rub all over with the garlic cloves.

2 Toss the bacon and rosemary together, and use to stuff the turkey neck flap. Secure the skin with a cocktail stick (toothpick). Brush the bird with the oil. Place in a roasting pan and cover loosely with foil. Roast for 45–50 minutes. Remove the foil and reduce the oven temperature to 160°C/325°F/Gas 3. Baste the turkey with the juices and pour over the wine. Cook for 1 hour, basting occasionally. Reduce the temperature to 150°C/300°F/ Gas 2 and cook for a further 45 minutes, basting occasionally.

3 Meanwhile, to make the *mlinces*, sift the flour with a little salt into a bowl. Add the water and oil, and mix to a soft but pliable dough. Knead briefly and divide equally into four. Roll out thinly on a lightly floured surface into 40cm/16in circles. Sprinkle with salt. Bake on baking sheets alongside the turkey for 25 minutes until crisp. Crush into pieces about 6–10cm/2½–4in.

4 About 6–8 minutes before the end of the cooking time for the turkey, add the *mlinces* to the meat juices in the roasting pan alongside the bird. Leave the turkey to rest for about 10–15 minutes before carving, then serve, garnished with rosemary and accompanied by the *mlinces* and grilled bacon.

Vine-leaf Wrapped Turkey with Noilly Prat

Pretty vine-leaf parcels conceal turkey escalopes filled with a delicious wild rice and pine nut stuffing flavoured with Noilly Prat.

Serves 4
115g/4oz drained vine leaves in brine
4 turkey escalopes (scallops), about 115–175g/4–6oz each
300ml/ ½ pint/1¼ cups Chicken Stock

For the stuffing
30ml/2 tbsp sunflower oil
3 shallots, chopped
75g/3oz/ ¾ cup cooked wild rice
4 tomatoes, peeled and chopped
45ml/3 tbsp Noilly Prat
25g/1oz/ ¼ cup pine nuts, chopped
salt and freshly ground black pepper

1 Preheat the oven to 190°C/375°F/Gas 5. Rinse the vine leaves a few times in cold water and drain.

2 To make the stuffing, heat the oil in a frying pan. Add the shallots and fry gently until soft. Remove the pan from the heat and stir in the cooked rice, tomatoes, Noilly Prat and pine nuts. Season with salt and pepper to taste.

3 Put the turkey escalopes between sheets of clear film (plastic wrap) and flatten with a rolling pin or meat mallet. Top each escalope with one-quarter of the stuffing and roll the meat over the filling.

4 Overlap one-quarter of the vine leaves to make a rectangle. Centre a turkey roll on top, roll up and tie securely with raffia or string. Repeat with the remaining leaves and turkey rolls to make four parcels.

5 Pack the rolls snugly in an ovenproof dish, pour over the stock and roast for 40 minutes. Skim any surface fat from the stock and pour the stock into a jug (pitcher). Serve immediately with the turkey parcels.

Wild Duck Roasted with Morels & Madeira

Wild duck has a rich, flavour that combines well with stronger-tasting mushrooms.

Serves 4

2 x 1kg/2¼lb mallards (dressed and barded weight)
50g/2oz/4 tbsp unsalted (sweet) butter
75ml/5 tbsp Madeira or sherry
1 medium onion, halved and sliced
½ celery stick, chopped
1 small carrot, chopped
10 large dried morel mushrooms
225g/8oz/3 cups blewits, parasol and field (portabello) mushrooms, trimmed and sliced
600ml/1 pint/2½ cups Chicken Stock, boiling
1 fresh thyme sprig
10ml/2 tsp wine vinegar
salt and freshly ground black pepper
fresh parsley sprigs and carrot juliennes, to garnish
game chips, to serve

1 Preheat the oven to 190°C/375°F/Gas 5 and season the ducks with salt and pepper. Melt half of the butter in a heavy frying pan. Add the ducks and brown the birds evenly. Transfer them to a shallow dish.

2 Heat the sediment in the pan, pour in the Madeira or sherry and bring to the boil, stirring constantly and scraping the base to deglaze the pan. Pour this liquid over the birds and set the dish aside.

3 Heat the remaining butter in a large, flameproof casserole and add the onion, celery and carrot. Place the birds on top (reserve the Madeira or sherry) and cook in the oven for 40 minutes.

4 Tie all the mushrooms in a 45cm/18in square of muslin (cheesecloth). Add the stock, the Madeira or sherry from the frying pan, the thyme and the muslin bag to the casserole. Cover and return to the oven for 40 minutes.

5 Transfer the birds to a warmed serving platter, remove and discard the thyme and set the mushrooms aside. Process the braising liquid in a food processor or blender and pour it back into the casserole. Break open the muslin bag and stir the mushrooms into the sauce. Add the vinegar, season to taste and heat through gently.

6 Garnish the ducks with parsley and carrot. Serve with game chips and hand the Madeira or sherry sauce separately in a jug (pitcher) or gravy boat.

Cook's Tip
Mallard is the most popular wild duck, although widgeon and teal are good substitutes. A widgeon will serve 2, but allow 1 teal per person.

Duckling Jubilee

This East European dish partners roast duck with a lightly spiced apricot sauce.

Serves 4

2kg/4½lb duckling
60ml/4 tbsp chopped fresh parsley
1 lemon, quartered
3 carrots, sliced
2 celery sticks, sliced
1 onion, roughly chopped
salt and freshly ground black pepper
apricots and sage flowers, to garnish

For the sauce

425g/15oz can apricots in syrup
50g/2oz/¼ cup granulated sugar
10ml/2 tsp English (hot) mustard
60ml/4 tbsp apricot jam
15ml/1 tbsp lemon juice
10ml/2 tsp grated lemon rind
50ml/2fl oz/¼ cup orange juice
1.5ml/¼ tsp each ground ginger and ground coriander
60–75ml/4–5 tbsp brandy

1 Preheat the oven to 220°C/425°F/Gas 7. Clean the duck well and pat dry with kitchen paper. Season the skin liberally. Mix together the parsley, lemon, carrots, celery and onion in a bowl, then spoon this mixture into the cavity of the duck.

2 Cook the duck for 45 minutes on a rack set over a roasting pan Baste the duck occasionally with its juices. Remove the duck from the oven and prick the skin well. Return to the oven, reduce the temperature to 180°C/350°F/Gas 4 and cook for a further 1–1½ hours or until golden brown, tender and crisp.

3 Meanwhile, to make the sauce, put the apricots and their syrup, the sugar and mustard in a food processor or blender. Add the jam and process until smooth.

4 Pour the apricot mixture into a pan and stir in the lemon juice and rind, orange juice and spices. Bring to the boil, add the brandy and cook for a further 1–2 minutes. Remove from the heat and adjust the seasoning. Pour into a gravy boat.

5 Discard the fruit, vegetables and herbs from inside the duck and arrange the bird on a serving platter. Garnish with fresh apricots and sage flowers. Serve the sauce separately.

Roast Duckling with Honey

A sweet-and-sour orange sauce is the perfect foil for this rich-tasting Polish duck recipe, and frying the orange rind intensifies the flavour.

Serves 4
2.25kg/5lb duckling
2.5ml/ ½ tsp ground allspice
I orange
15ml/1 tbsp sunflower oil
30ml/2 tbsp plain (all-purpose) flour
150ml/ ¼ pint/ ⅔ cup duck or Chicken Stock
10ml/2 tsp red wine vinegar
15ml/1 tbsp clear honey
salt and freshly ground black pepper
watercress and thinly pared orange rind, to garnish

I Preheat the oven to 220°C/425°F/Gas 7. Using a fork, pierce the duckling all over, except the breast, so that the fat runs out during cooking.

2 Rub all over the skin of the duckling with ground allspice and sprinkle with salt and pepper to season, pressing into the surface of the bird.

3 Put the duckling on a rack over a roasting pan and cook for about 20 minutes. Then reduce the oven temperature to 190°C/375°F/Gas 5 and cook for a further 2 hours.

4 Meanwhile, thinly pare the rind from the orange and cut into very fine strips. Heat the oil in a pan and gently fry the orange rind for 2–3 minutes. Squeeze the juice from the orange and set aside.

5 Transfer the duckling to a warmed serving dish and keep warm. Drain off all but 30ml/2 tbsp fat from the pan, sprinkle in the flour and stir well. Stir in the stock, vinegar, honey, orange juice and rind. Bring to the boil, stirring constantly. Simmer gently for 2–3 minutes and season to taste with salt and pepper. Pour into a serving bowl or jug (pitcher).

6 Serve the duckling, garnished with watercress and thinly pared orange rind and accompanied by the sauce.

Roast Wild Duck with Juniper

Wild duck should be served slightly underdone or the meat will be very tough.

Serves 2
15ml/1 tbsp juniper berries, fresh if possible
I wild duck (preferably a mallard)
25g/1oz/2 tbsp butter, softened
45ml/3 tbsp gin
120ml/4fl oz/ ½ cup duck or Chicken Stock
120ml/4fl oz/ ½ cup whipping cream
salt and freshly ground black pepper
watercress, to garnish

I Preheat the oven to 230°C/450°F/Gas 8. Reserve a few juniper berries for garnishing and put the remainder in a heavy plastic bag. Crush coarsely with a rolling pin.

2 Wipe the duck with damp kitchen paper. Tie the legs with string, then spread the butter over the duck. Season and press the crushed juniper berries on to the skin.

3 Place the duck in a roasting pan and roast for 20–25 minutes, basting occasionally; it is ready if the juices run clear when the thickest part of the thigh is pierced with a knife. Pour the juices from the cavity into the roasting pan and transfer the duck to a carving board. Cover loosely with foil and leave to stand for 10–15 minutes.

4 Skim off as much fat as possible from the roasting pan, leaving as much of the juniper as possible, and place the pan over a medium-high heat. Add the gin and stir, scraping the sediment from the bottom and bring to the boil. Cook until the liquid has almost evaporated, then add the stock and boil to reduce by half. Add the cream and boil for 2 minutes or until the sauce thickens slightly. Strain into a small pan and keep warm.

5 Carve the legs from the duck and separate the thighs from the drumsticks. Remove the breasts and arrange the duck in a warmed serving dish. Pour a little sauce over, sprinkle with the reserved juniper berries and garnish with watercress. Hand the rest of the sauce separately in a jug (pitcher) or gravy boat.

Roasted Duckling on a Bed of Honeyed Potatoes

The rich flavour of duck combined with sweetened potatoes glazed with honey makes an excellent treat for a dinner party.

Serves 4
1 duckling
60ml/4 tbsp light soy sauce
150ml/ ¼ pint/ ⅔ cup orange juice
3 large floury potatoes, cut into chunks
30ml/2 tbsp clear honey
15ml/1 tbsp sesame seeds
salt and freshly ground black pepper

1 Preheat the oven to 200°C/400°F/Gas 6. Place the duckling, breast side up, in a roasting pan. Prick the skin well.

2 Mix the soy sauce and orange juice together and pour over the bird. Cook in the oven for 20 minutes.

3 Place the potato chunks in a bowl, stir in the honey and toss to mix well. Remove the duckling from the oven and spoon the potatoes all around and under the bird.

4 Roast for 35 minutes, then remove from the oven. Toss the potatoes in the duckling juices and turn the duckling over so that the underside will be cooked. Return to the oven and cook for a further 30 minutes.

5 Remove the duckling from the oven and carefully scoop off the excess fat, leaving the juices behind.

6 Sprinkle the sesame seeds over the potatoes, season and turn the duckling back over, breast side up, and cook for a further 10 minutes. Remove the duckling and potatoes from the oven and keep warm, allowing the bird to rest for 10–15 minutes.

7 Pour off the excess fat from the roasting pan and simmer the juices on the hob (stovetop) for a few minutes. Serve the juices with the carved duckling and potatoes.

Duck with Orange Sauce

This is the classic French recipe.

Serves 2–3
2kg/4½ lb duck
2 oranges
90g/3½ oz/ ½ cup caster (superfine) sugar
90ml/6 tbsp white wine vinegar
120ml/4fl oz/ ½ cup Grand Marnier or other orange liqueur
salt and freshly ground black pepper
watercress and orange slices, to garnish

1 Preheat the oven to 150°C/300°F/Gas 2. Trim off the excess fat and skin from the duck, and prick the skin all over with a fork. Season the duck inside and out and tie the legs with cooking string. Place the duck on a rack in a large roasting pan. Cover tightly with foil and cook in the oven for 1½ hours.

2 With a vegetable peeler, remove the orange rind in wide strips, then slice into thin strips. Squeeze the juice from the oranges.

3 Place the sugar and vinegar in a small, heavy pan and stir to dissolve the sugar. Boil over a high heat, without stirring, until the mixture is a rich caramel colour. Remove from the heat and carefully add the orange juice, pouring it down the side of the pan. Swirl the pan to blend, bring back to the boil, and add the orange rind and liqueur. Simmer for 2–3 minutes.

4 Remove the duck from the oven and pour off all the fat from the pan Raise the oven temperature to 200°C/400°F/Gas 6. Return the duck to the oven and continue to roast, uncovered, for 25–30 minutes, basting a few times with some of the sauce, until the duck is brown and the juices run clear when the thickest part of the thigh is pierced with a knife or skewer.

5 Pour the juices from the duck cavity into the pan and transfer the bird to a carving board. Cover with foil and rest for 10 minutes. Pour the roasting juices into the pan with the remaining caramel mixture, skim off the fat and simmer gently. Serve the duck, garnished with watercress and orange slices, and accompanied by the sauce.

Roast Goose with Apples

The apples are filled with a hazelnut, raisin and orange stuffing and roasted around the bird.

Serves 6
115g/4oz/scant 1 cup raisins
grated rind and juice of 1 orange
25g/1oz/2 tbsp butter
1 onion, finely chopped
75g/3oz/¾ cup hazelnuts, chopped
175g/6oz/3 cups fresh
   white breadcrumbs

15ml/1 tbsp clear honey
15ml/1 tbsp chopped
   fresh marjoram
30ml/2 tbsp chopped
   fresh parsley
6 red eating apples
15ml/1 tbsp lemon juice
4.5–5kg/10–11lb young goose
salt and freshly ground
   black pepper
fresh herbs, to garnish
orange wedges, red cabbage and
   green beans, to serve

1 Preheat the oven to 220°C/425°F/Gas 7. Put the raisins in a bowl and pour over the orange juice. Melt the butter in a frying pan and fry the onions for 5 minutes. Add the nuts and cook for 4–5 minutes or until beginning to brown. Add the onion and nuts to the raisins with 50g/2oz/1 cup of the breadcrumbs, the orange rind, honey, herbs and seasoning. Mix well.

2 Remove the apple cores to leave a 2cm/¾in hole. Make a shallow cut horizontally around the middle of each apple. Brush the cut and the cavity with the lemon juice. Pack the centre of each apple with nut and raisin stuffing, reserving the remainder.

3 Mix the remaining breadcrumbs into the leftover stuffing and place in the bird's cavity. Close with a small skewer. Place the goose in a roasting pan and prick the skin with a skewer. Roast for 30 minutes, then reduce the temperature to 180°C/350°F/Gas 4 and cook for a further 3 hours or until the juices run clear when the thickest part of the thigh is pierced with a skewer or knife. Pour off the excess fat from time to time.

4 Bake the apples around the goose for the last 30–40 minutes of its cooking time. Rest the goose for 10–15 minutes before carving. Garnish with fresh herbs and serve with the stuffed apples, orange wedges, red cabbage and green beans.

Roast Goose with Caramelized Apples & Port & Orange Gravy

Choose a young goose with a pliable breastbone.

Serves 8
4.5–5.5kg/10–12lb goose,
   with giblets
salt and freshly ground
   black pepper

For the apple and nut stuffing
225g/8oz/1 cup prunes
150ml/¼ pint/⅔ cup port
675g/1½lb cooking apples,
   peeled, cored and cubed
1 large onion, chopped
4 celery sticks, sliced
15ml/1 tbsp dried mixed herbs
finely grated rind of 1 orange

1 goose liver, chopped
450g/1lb pork sausage (bulk
   sausage) meat
115g/4oz/1 cup chopped pecans
   or walnuts
2 eggs

For the caramelized apples
50g/2oz/4 tbsp butter
60ml/4 tbsp redcurrant jelly
30ml/2 tbsp red wine vinegar
8 small eating apples, peeled
   and cored

For the gravy
30ml/2 tbsp plain (all-
   purpose) flour
600ml/1 pint/2½ cups giblet stock
juice of 1 orange

1 To make the stuffing, soak the prunes in the port the day before serving. Then stone (pit) and cut each into four pieces, reserving the port. Mix with all the remaining stuffing ingredients and season. Moisten with half the reserved port.

2 Preheat the oven to 200°C/400°F/Gas 6. Stuff the neck end of the goose, tucking the flap of skin under and securing it with a small skewer. Remove the excess fat from the cavity and pack it with the stuffing. Tie the legs together to hold them in place.

3 Weigh the stuffed goose and calculate the cooking time: allow 15 minutes per 450g/1lb. Put the bird on a rack in a roasting pan and rub the skin with salt. Prick the skin all over.

4 Roast the goose for 30 minutes. Reduce the oven temperature to 180°C/350°F/Gas 4 and roast for the remaining time. Pour off any fat. The goose is cooked if the juices run clear when the thickest part of the thigh is pierced with a skewer or knife. Pour a little cold water over the breast to crisp the skin.

5 Meanwhile, to make the caramelized apples, melt the butter with the redcurrant jelly and vinegar in a small roasting pan or shallow ovenproof dish. Put in the apples, baste them well and cook in the oven for 15–20 minutes. Baste halfway through the cooking time. Do not overcook them or they will collapse.

6 Lift the goose on to a serving dish and let it stand for 10–15 minutes before carving. Pour off the excess fat from the roasting pan, leaving any sediment in the bottom. To make the gravy, stir the flour into the sediment and cook gently until golden brown, then blend in the stock. Bring to the boil, add the remaining reserved port, the orange juice and seasoning. Simmer for 2–3 minutes. Strain into a jug (pitcher) or gravy boat. Surround the goose with the caramelized apples, spoon over the redcurrant glaze and serve with the gravy.

Roast Pheasant with Port

Pheasant in Green Pipian Sauce

Keep pheasant tender and moist by cooking it in foil.

Serves 4
oil, for brushing
2 hen pheasants, about
   675g/1½lb each
50g/2oz/4 tbsp unsalted (sweet)
   butter, softened
8 fresh thyme sprigs

2 bay leaves
6 streaky (fatty) bacon
   rashers (strips)
15ml/1 tbsp plain (all-
   purpose) flour
175ml/6fl oz/ ¾ cup Chicken
   Stock, plus more if needed
15ml/1 tbsp redcurrant jelly
45–60ml/3–4 tbsp port
freshly ground black pepper

1 Preheat the oven to 230°C/450°F/Gas 8. Line a large roasting pan with a sheet of strong foil large enough to enclose the pheasants. Lightly brush the foil with oil.

2 Wipe the pheasants with damp kitchen paper and remove any extra fat or skin. Using your fingertips, carefully loosen the skin of the breasts. Spread the butter between the skin and breast meat of each bird. Tie the legs securely with string, then lay the thyme sprigs and a bay leaf over the breast of each bird. Lay bacon rashers over the breasts, place the birds in the foil-lined pan and season with pepper. Bring together the long ends of the foil, fold over securely to enclose, then seal the ends.

3 Roast the birds for 20 minutes, then reduce the oven temperature to 190°C/375°F/Gas 5 and cook for a further 40 minutes. Uncover the birds and roast for 10–15 minutes more or until they are browned and the juices run clear when the thickest part of the thigh is pierced with a knife or skewer. Transfer the birds to a board and leave to stand, covered with clean foil, for 10–15 minutes before carving.

4 Pour the juices from the foil into the roasting pan and skim off any fat. Sprinkle in the flour and cook over a medium heat, stirring, until smooth. Whisk in the stock and redcurrant jelly, and bring to the boil. Simmer until the sauce thickens slightly, adding more stock if needed, then stir in the port and adjust the seasoning to taste. Strain and serve with the pheasants.

An unusual and delicious way of cooking pheasant, Mexican-style, that keeps it wonderfully moist.

Serves 4
2 pheasants
30ml/2 tbsp corn oil
175g/6oz/generous 1 cup pepitas
  (Mexican pumpkin seeds)
15ml/1 tbsp annatto seeds

1 onion, finely chopped
2 garlic cloves, chopped
275g/10oz can tomatillos
  (Mexican green tomatoes)
475ml/16fl oz/2 cups
  Chicken Stock
salt and freshly ground
  black pepper
fresh coriander (cilantro),
  to garnish

1 Preheat the oven to 180°C/350°F/Gas 4. Using a large, sharp knife or poultry shears, cut the pheasants in half lengthways and season well with salt and pepper. Heat the oil in a large frying pan and sauté the pheasant pieces until lightly browned on all sides. Lift out of the pan, drain and arrange, skin side up, in a single layer in a roasting pan. Set aside.

2 Grind the pepitas finely in a nut grinder or a food processor. Shake through a sieve into a bowl. Grind the annatto seeds, add them to the bowl and set aside.

3 Place the onion, garlic, tomatillos and their juice into a food processor and purée. Pour into a pan. Add the pepita mixture, stir in the stock and simmer over a very low heat for about 10 minutes. Do not let the mixture boil as it will separate. Remove from the heat and leave to cool.

4 Pour the sauce over the pheasant halves. Bake for 40 minutes or until tender, basting from time to time with the sauce. Garnish with coriander and serve.

Cook's Tip
Annatto is a typical ingredient in Yucatán. There is no substitute. Look for it in Caribbean and tropical markets.

CHICKEN SALADS

One of the great things about chicken is that it tastes as good cold or warm as it does hot, so it makes fabulous salads. Light and easily digested, it is the perfect choice when the sun has been shining and it's almost too hot and too much effort to eat anything at all. But there is more to a salad than a slice of chicken, a few salad leaves and a spoonful of mayonnaise – which is pleasant enough, but rather ordinary. Special occasion salads are just that – delicious dishes with marvellous melt-in-the-mouth combinations of vegetables, fruit and subtle dressings that make chicken the first choice for *al fresco* dining with friends. Just as chicken combines so successfully with a vast range of other ingredients in hot dishes, so it goes well with pasta or rice for substantial salads, or fruit, nuts, herbs and even lavender for something truly tempting and unusual. Warm salads have become increasingly popular over the last few years – whether made from an assembly of cold ingredients tossed with a freshly cooked dressing or from a mixture of salad leaves or vegetables with a topping of pan-fried chicken or grilled breast portions straight from the barbecue. Once again, entertaining is easy because salads can be prepared in advance and assembled just before serving, leaving you free to spend time with your guests and enjoy your special occasion meal without hassle.

Pan-fried Chicken Liver Salad

The hot dressing includes vin santo, a sweet dessert wine from Tuscany, but this is not essential – any dessert wine will do, or a sweet or cream sherry.

Serves 4
75g/3oz baby spinach leaves
75g/3oz lollo rosso leaves
75ml/5 tbsp olive oil
15ml/1 tbsp butter
225g/8oz chicken livers, trimmed
    and thinly sliced
45ml/3 tbsp vin santo
50–75g/2–3oz Parmesan cheese,
    shaved into curls
salt and freshly ground
    black pepper

1 Wash the spinach and lollo rosso and spin dry. Tear the leaves into a large bowl, season with salt and pepper to taste and toss gently to mix.

2 Heat 30ml/2 tbsp of the oil with the butter in a large, heavy frying pan. When foaming, add the chicken livers and toss over a medium to high heat for 5 minutes or until the livers are browned on the outside, but still pink in the centre. Remove from the heat.

3 Remove the livers from the pan using a slotted spoon, drain them on kitchen paper, then place on top of the salad.

4 Return the pan to a medium heat, add the remaining oil and the vin santo, and stir until sizzling.

5 Pour the hot dressing over the spinach and livers, and toss to coat. Transfer the salad to a serving bowl and sprinkle over the Parmesan shavings. Serve immediately.

Warm Chicken Salad with Shallots & Mangetouts

Succulent cooked chicken pieces are combined with vegetables in a lightly spiced chilli dressing.

Serves 6
50g/2oz mixed salad leaves
50g/2oz baby spinach leaves
50g/2oz watercress
30ml/2 tbsp chilli sauce
30ml/2 tbsp dry sherry
15ml/1 tbsp light soy sauce
15ml/1 tbsp tomato ketchup
10ml/2 tsp olive oil
8 shallots, finely chopped
1 garlic clove, crushed
350g/12oz skinless chicken
    breast fillets, cut into thin strips
1 red (bell) pepper, seeded
    and sliced
175g/6oz mangetouts (snow
    peas), trimmed
400g/14oz can baby corn,
    drained and halved
275g/10oz cooked brown rice
salt and freshly ground
    black pepper
fresh flat leaf parsley sprig,
    to garnish

1 Wash the salad leaves and spinach and spin dry. Arrange the salad leaves, tearing up any large ones, and the spinach on a serving dish. Add the watercress and toss to mix.

2 In a small bowl, mix together the chilli sauce, sherry, soy sauce and tomato ketchup. Set aside.

3 Heat the oil in a large, non-stick frying pan or wok. Add the shallots and garlic, and stir-fry over a medium heat for 1 minute.

4 Add the sliced chicken to the pan and stir-fry for a further 4–5 minutes until the chicken pieces are nearly cooked.

5 Add the red pepper, mangetouts, corn and cooked rice, and stir-fry for 2–3 minutes.

6 Pour in the chilli sauce mixture and stir-fry for 2–3 minutes until hot and bubbling. Season to taste. Spoon the chicken mixture over the salad leaves, toss together to mix and serve immediately, garnished with a sprig of flat leaf parsley.

Warm Chicken Salad with Sesame & Coriander Dressing

This salad needs to be served warm to make the most of the wonderful sesame, lemon and coriander flavourings.

Serves 6

4 medium skinless chicken breast
   fillets, skinned
225g/8oz mangetouts
   (snow peas)
2 heads decorative lettuce,
   e.g. lollo rosso or oakleaf
3 carrots, cut into
   small batons

175g/6oz/generous 2 cups button
   (white) mushrooms, sliced
6 bacon rashers (strips), fried
   and chopped
15ml/1 tbsp chopped fresh
   coriander (cilantro) leaves,
   to garnish

For the dressing

120ml/4fl oz/ 1/2 cup lemon juice
30ml/2 tbsp wholegrain mustard
250ml/8fl oz/1 cup olive oil
75ml/5 tbsp sesame oil
5ml/1 tsp coriander
   seeds, crushed

1 To make the dressing, mix all the ingredients together in a bowl, beating well to blend. Place the chicken breast fillets in a shallow dish and pour on half the dressing. Chill overnight, and chill the remaining dressing also.

2 Cook the mangetouts for 2 minutes in boiling water, then cool under cold running water to stop them cooking any further, so they remain crisp.

3 Wash and spin dry the lettuces. Tear the leaves into small pieces and place in a large bowl. Add the mangetouts, carrots, mushrooms and bacon, and toss to mix thoroughly. Divide among individual serving dishes.

4 Grill (broil) the chicken until cooked through, then slice on the diagonal into quite thin pieces. Divide among the bowls of salad and sprinkle some dressing over the top. Combine quickly, scatter fresh coriander over each bowl and serve.

Chicken Salad with Cranberry Dressing

The unusual fruity dressing lifts this deceptively simple salad to a higher plane.

Serves 4

4 chicken breast fillets, about
   675g/1 1/2lb total weight
300ml/ 1/2 pint/1 1/4 cups Chicken
   Stock or a mixture of stock and
   dry white wine
fresh herb sprigs
200g/7oz mixed salad leaves
50g/2oz/ 1/2 cup chopped walnuts
   or hazelnuts

For the dressing

30ml/2 tbsp olive oil
15ml/1 tbsp walnut or
   hazelnut oil
15ml/1 tbsp raspberry or red
   wine vinegar
30ml/2 tbsp cranberry relish
salt and freshly ground
   black pepper

1 Skin the chicken breast fillets. Pour the stock or stock and wine mixture into a large, shallow pan. Add the herbs and bring the liquid to simmering point. Add the chicken and poach for about 15 minutes until cooked through. Alternatively, leave the skin on the chicken fillets and grill (broil) or roast them until tender, then remove the skin.

2 Wash and spin dry the salad leaves and arrange them on 4 plates. Slice each chicken fillet neatly, keeping the slices together, then place each fillet on top of a portion of salad, fanning the slices out slightly.

3 To make the dressing, place all the ingredients in a screw-top jar and shake vigorously.

4 Spoon a little dressing over each salad and sprinkle with the chopped walnuts or hazelnuts. Serve immediately.

Lemon & Tarragon Chicken Salad

Warm cooked chicken is tossed with salad leaves as soon as it comes out of the pan.

Serves 4

4 skinless chicken breast fillets,
   cut into strips
4 rindless smoked bacon rashers
   (strips), chopped (optional)
15ml/1 tbsp oil
25ml/5 tsp chopped
   fresh tarragon
juice of 1 lemon
mixed salad leaves, washed
ready-made French dressing
salt and freshly ground
   black pepper

1 Cook the chicken and bacon, if using, in the oil with half the tarragon for about 5 minutes until lightly browned. Add the lemon juice, season to taste and cook for about 5 minutes more.
2 Meanwhile, put the salad leaves in a large bowl, add a little French dressing, and toss. Stir the remaining tarragon into the chicken and add to the salad bowl. Serve immediately.

Warm Chicken Salad with Hazelnut Dressing

This quickly prepared, warm salad combines pan-fried chicken and spinach with a light, nutty dressing.

Serves 4

45ml/3 tbsp olive oil
30ml/2 tbsp hazelnut oil
15ml/1 tbsp white wine vinegar
1 garlic clove, crushed
15ml/1 tbsp chopped fresh
  mixed herbs
225g/8oz baby spinach leaves
250g/9oz cherry tomatoes, halved
1 bunch spring onions
  (scallions), chopped
2 skinless chicken breast fillets,
  cut into pieces
salt and freshly ground
  black pepper

1 Place 30ml/2 tbsp of the olive oil, the hazelnut oil, vinegar, garlic and chopped herbs in a small bowl or jug (pitcher) and whisk together until thoroughly mixed. Set aside.

2 Wash and spin dry the spinach leaves and trim any long stalks. Place the spinach in a large serving bowl with the tomatoes and spring onions and toss together to mix.

3 Heat the remaining olive oil in a frying pan, add the chicken and stir-fry over a high heat for 7–10 minutes until the chicken is cooked, tender and lightly browned.

4 Scatter the cooked chicken pieces over the salad, give the dressing a quick whisk to blend, then drizzle it over the salad and gently toss all the ingredients together to mix. Season to taste with salt and pepper, and serve immediately.

Variation
You could substitute walnut oil for the hazelnut oil and chicory (Belgian endive) for the spinach leaves.

Peanut Chicken Salad in a Pineapple Boat

This beautiful dish would go down well as part of a celebration meal.

2 small ripe pineapples
225g/8oz cooked chicken breast
  portions, cut into bitesize pieces
2 celery sticks, diced
50g/2oz spring onions
  (scallions), chopped
225g/8oz seedless green grapes
40g/1½oz/6 tbsp salted peanuts,
  coarsely chopped

For the dressing
75g/3oz/6 tbsp smooth
  peanut butter
120ml/4fl oz/½ cup mayonnaise
30ml/2 tbsp cream or milk
1 garlic clove, finely chopped
5ml/1 tsp mild curry powder
15ml/1 tbsp apricot jam
salt and freshly ground
  black pepper
fresh mint sprigs, to garnish

1 Make four pineapple boats (see box) from the pineapples. Cut the flesh removed from the boats into bitesize pieces. Combine the pineapple flesh, cooked chicken, celery, spring onions and grapes in a bowl.

2 To make the dressing, put all the ingredients in another bowl and mix with a wooden spoon or whisk until evenly blended. Season with salt and pepper. (The dressing will be thick at this point, but will be thinned by the juices from the pineapple.)

3 Add the dressing to the pineapple and chicken mixture. Fold together gently but thoroughly.

4 Divide the chicken salad among the pineapple boats. Sprinkle the chopped peanuts over the top before serving, garnished with mint sprigs.

Making a Pineapple Boat

1 Trim off any browned ends from the green leaves of the crown. Trim the stalk end if necessary. Using a long, sharp knife, cut the pineapple lengthways in half, through the crown. Cut a thin slice from the underside of each "boat" so it has a flat surface and will not rock.
2 Using a small sharp knife, cut straight across the top and bottom of the central core in each pineapple half.

3 Cut lengthways at a slant on either side of the core. This will cut out the core in a V-shape.
4 Using a curved, serrated grapefruit knife, cut out and reserve the flesh from each half.

Orange Chicken Salad

Chicken & Fruit Salad

For this delicious dish the long grain rice is cooked with thinly pared strips of orange rind for a more intense flavour.

Serves 4
3 large seedless oranges
175g/6oz long grain rice
475ml/16fl oz/2 cups water
175ml/6fl oz/⅔ cup ready-made
  French dressing
10ml/2 tsp Dijon mustard

2.5ml/ ½ tsp caster
  (superfine) sugar
450g/1lb cooked chicken, diced
45ml/3 tbsp chopped fresh chives
75g/3oz cashew nuts, toasted
salt and freshly ground
  black pepper
cucumber slices and chives,
  to garnish

1 Thinly peel one orange, taking only the coloured part of the rind and leaving the white pith.

2 Combine the orange rind, rice and water in a pan. Add a pinch of salt. Bring to the boil, cover and cook over very low heat for 15–18 minutes or until the rice is tender and all the water has been absorbed.

3 Peel all the oranges and cut out the segments, reserving the juice. Add the orange juice to the French dressing, then add the Dijon mustard and sugar and whisk to combine well. Taste and add more salt and freshly ground black pepper if needed.

4 When the rice is cooked, remove it from the heat and cool slightly, uncovered. Discard the orange rind.

5 Turn the rice into a serving bowl and add half of the dressing. Toss well and leave to cool completely.

6 Add the cooked chicken, the chives, cashew nuts and orange segments to the rice with the remaining dressing. Toss gently. Serve at room temperature, garnished with cucumber slices and chives.

An ideal party dish as the chickens may be cooked in advance and the salad finished off on the day. Serve with warm garlic bread.

Serves 8
4 fresh tarragon or
  rosemary sprigs
2 × 1.75kg/3½lb chickens
65g/2½oz/5 tbsp softened butter
150ml/ ¼ pint/ ⅔ cup
  Chicken Stock
150ml/¼ pint/⅔ cup white wine
115g/4oz/1 cup walnut pieces

1 small cantaloupe melon
450g/1lb seedless grapes or
  pitted cherries
salt and freshly ground
  black pepper
mixed lettuce, to serve

For the dressing
30ml/2 tbsp tarragon vinegar
120ml/4fl oz/½ cup light olive oil
30ml/2 tbsp chopped mixed
  fresh herbs, e.g. parsley, mint
  and tarragon

1 Preheat the oven to 200°C/400°F/Gas 6. Put the sprigs of tarragon or rosemary inside the chickens and season. Tie the chickens in a neat shape with string. Spread them with 50g/2oz/4 tbsp of the butter, place in a roasting pan and add the stock. Cover loosely with foil and roast for about 1½ hours, basting twice, until browned and the juices run clear. Remove the chickens from the roasting pan and leave to cool.

2 Add the wine to the juices in the pan. Boil until syrupy. Strain and cool. Heat the remaining butter in a frying pan and fry the walnuts until lightly browned. Drain on kitchen paper and cool. Scoop the melon into balls. Joint the chickens.

3 To make the dressing, whisk the vinegar and oil together with a little salt and pepper. Remove all the fat from the cooled chicken juices and add these to the dressing with the herbs.

4 Wash and spin dry the lettuce and arrange on a serving platter. Put the chicken pieces on top and sprinkle over the grapes or cherries and the melon. Spoon over the dressing, sprinkle with the walnuts and serve.

Dijon Chicken Salad

An attractive and elegant dish to serve for lunch with herb and garlic bread.

Serves 4
4 skinless chicken breast fillets
mixed salad leaves, e.g. frisée and
oakleaf lettuce or radicchio,
to serve

For the marinade
30ml/2 tbsp Dijon mustard
3 garlic cloves, crushed
15ml/1 tbsp grated onion
60ml/4 tbsp white wine

For the mustard dressing
30ml/2 tbsp tarragon
wine vinegar
5ml/1 tsp Dijon mustard
5ml/1 tsp clear honey
90ml/6 tbsp olive oil
salt and freshly ground
black pepper

1 To make the marinade, mix all the ingredients together in a shallow glass or earthenware dish that is large enough to hold the chicken in a single layer.

2 Add the chicken to the marinade and turn to coat. Cover with clear film (plastic wrap) and chill overnight.

3 Preheat the oven to 190°C/375°F/Gas 5. Transfer the chicken and the marinade into an ovenproof dish, cover with foil and bake for about 35 minutes or until tender. Remove from the oven and leave to cool in the liquid.

4 To make the mustard dressing, put all the ingredients into a screw-top jar and shake vigorously to emulsify. (This can be made several days in advance and stored in the refrigerator.)

5 Slice the chicken thinly, fan out the slices and arrange on a serving dish with the salad leaves. Spoon over some of the mustard dressing and serve.

French Chicken Salad

A light first course for eight people or a substantial main course for four, this is served with large, crisp, garlic-flavoured croûtons.

Serves 8
1.5kg/3½lb free-range chicken
300ml/½ pint/1¼ cups white
wine and water, mixed
24 slices French bread, 5mm/
¼in thick
1 garlic clove, peeled
225g/8oz green beans
115g/4oz young spinach leaves
2 celery sticks, thinly sliced

2 spring onions (scallions),
thinly sliced
2 sun-dried tomatoes, chopped
fresh chives and parsley,
to garnish

For the vinaigrette
30ml/2 tbsp red wine vinegar
90ml/6 tbsp olive oil
15ml/1 tbsp wholegrain mustard
15ml/1 tbsp clear honey
30ml/2 tbsp chopped mixed fresh
herbs, e.g. parsley and chives
10ml/2 tsp finely chopped capers
salt and freshly ground
black pepper

1 Preheat the oven to 190°C/375°F/Gas 5. Put the chicken into a casserole with the wine and water. Roast for 1½ hours until tender. Remove from the oven and leave to cool in the liquid. Discard the skin and bones and cut the flesh into small pieces.

2 To make the vinaigrette, put all the ingredients into a screw-top jar and shake vigorously to emulsify.

3 Toast the French bread under the grill (broiler) or in the oven until dry and golden brown, then lightly rub with the peeled garlic clove.

4 Trim the green beans, cut into 5cm/2in lengths and cook in boiling water for a few minutes until just tender. Drain and rinse under cold running water.

5 Wash the spinach and spin dry. Remove the stalks and tear the leaves into small pieces. Arrange on serving platter with the celery, beans, spring onions, chicken and tomatoes. Spoon over the vinaigrette dressing. Arrange the toasted croûtons on top, garnish with chives and parsley and serve the salad immediately.

Chicken Salad with Lavender & Sweet Herbs

Lavender may seem like an odd salad ingredient, but its delightful scent has a natural affinity with orange, sweet garlic and other wild herbs. The inclusion of polenta makes this salad both filling and delicious.

Serves 4
4 chicken breast fillets
750ml/1½ pints/3¾ cups
 Chicken Stock
175g/6oz/1½ cups fine polenta
 or cornmeal
50g/2oz/4 tbsp butter
450g/1lb young spinach

175g/6oz lamb's lettuce
 (corn salad)
8 fresh lavender sprigs
8 small tomatoes, halved
salt and freshly ground
 black pepper

For the lavender marinade
6 fresh lavender flowers
10ml/2 tsp finely grated
 orange rind
2 garlic cloves, crushed
10ml/2 tsp clear honey
30ml/2 tbsp olive oil
10ml/2 tsp chopped fresh thyme
10ml/2 tsp chopped
 fresh marjoram

1 To make the marinade, strip the lavender flowers from the stems and combine with the orange rind, garlic, honey and a pinch of salt. Add the olive oil and herbs. Slash the chicken deeply, spread the mixture over the chicken and leave to marinate in a cool place for at least 20 minutes.

2 To make the polenta, bring the chicken stock to the boil in a heavy pan. Add the meal in a steady stream, stirring constantly for 2–3 minutes until thick. Turn the cooked polenta out into a wide 2.5cm/1in deep buttered tin (pan) and allow to cool.

3 Heat the grill (broiler) to a moderate temperature. (If using a barbecue, let the embers settle to a steady glow.) Cook the chicken for about 15 minutes, turning once.

4 Cut the polenta into 2.5cm/1in cubes using a wet knife. Heat the butter in a large frying pan and fry the polenta until golden, turning once.

5 Wash the salad leaves and spin dry, then divide among four large plates. Slice each chicken fillet and lay over the salad. Place the polenta among the salad, arrange the sprigs of lavender and tomatoes decoratively on top, season and serve.

> **Cook's Tip**
> Be sure to use culinary lavender, not that sold by the cosmetics industry as it will have been treated and will not be edible.

Maryland Salad

Barbecue-grilled chicken, corn cobs, bacon, banana and watercress combine here in a sensational salad.

Serves 4
4 chicken breast fillets
oil, for brushing
225g/8oz rindless
 unsmoked bacon
4 sweetcorn cobs
40g/1½oz/3 tbsp softened butter
4 ripe bananas, peeled
 and halved

4 firm tomatoes, halved
1 escarole or round
 (butterhead) lettuce
1 bunch watercress
salt and freshly ground
 black pepper

For the dressing
75ml/5 tbsp groundnut
 (peanut) oil
15ml/1 tbsp white wine vinegar
10ml/2 tsp maple syrup
10ml/2 tsp mild mustard

1 Season the chicken fillets, brush with oil and cook on the barbecue or grill (broil) for 15 minutes, turning once. Cook the bacon on the barbecue or grill for 8–10 minutes.

2 Bring a large pan of salted water to the boil. Shuck and trim the corn cobs or leave the husks on if you prefer. Boil for 20 minutes. For extra flavour, brush with butter and brown over the barbecue or under the grill (broiler).

3 Cook the bananas and tomatoes on a the barbecue or grill for 6–8 minutes: you can brush them both with butter, too, if you like.

4 To make the dressing, combine the oil, vinegar, maple syrup and mustard with 15ml/1 tbsp water in a screw-top jar and shake well to emulsify.

5 Wash the salad leaves and spin dry. Place in a large bowl, pour over the dressing and toss to coat thoroughly.

6 Distribute the salad leaves among four large plates. Slice the chicken and arrange over the leaves with the bacon, banana, corn and tomatoes. Serve immediately.

Coronation Chicken

A dish that never fails to please, this was invented for the coronation of Queen Elizabeth II.

Serves 8
$^1/_2$ lemon
2.25kg/5lb chicken
1 onion, quartered
1 carrot, quartered
bouquet garni
8 black peppercorns, crushed
salt
watercress sprigs, to garnish

For the sauce
15g/$^1/_2$oz/1 tbsp butter
1 small onion, chopped
15ml/1 tbsp curry paste
15ml/1 tbsp tomato purée (paste)
120ml/4fl oz/$^1/_2$ cup red wine
1 bay leaf
juice of $^1/_2$ lemon, or more
  to taste
10–15ml/2–3 tbsp apricot jam
300ml/$^1/_2$ pint/1$^1/_4$ cups
  mayonnaise
120ml/4fl oz/$^1/_2$ cup whipping
  cream, whipped
freshly ground black pepper

1 Put the lemon half in the chicken cavity, then place the chicken in a pan that it just fits. Add the vegetables, bouquet garni, peppercorns and salt.

2 Add sufficient water to come two-thirds of the way up the chicken, bring to the boil, then cover and cook gently for 1$^1/_2$ hours or until the chicken juices run clear.

3 Transfer the chicken to a bowl, pour over the cooking liquid and leave to cool. When cold, lift the chicken from the liquid, discard the skin and bones and chop into bitesize pieces.

4 To make the sauce, heat the butter in a pan and cook the onion until soft. Add the curry paste, tomato purée, wine, bay leaf and lemon juice, and cook for 10 minutes. Add the jam, heat gently, stirring until it is incorporated, then remove the pan from the heat. Strain the sauce and leave to cool.

5 Beat the cooled sauce into the mayonnaise. Fold in the whipped cream. Add salt and pepper to taste, plus a little more lemon juice if needed. Stir in the chicken and serve garnished with watercress.

Swiss Cheese, Chicken & Tongue Salad with Apple & Celery

The rich, sweet flavours of this salad marry well with the tart, peppery nature of watercress. A minted lemon dressing combines to freshen the overall effect. Serve with warm new potatoes.

Serves 4
2 skinless chicken breast fillets
$^1/_2$ chicken stock (bouillon) cube
225g/8oz sliced ox tongue or
  ham, 5mm/$^1/_4$in thick
225g/8oz Gruyère cheese
1 lollo rosso lettuce
1 round (butterhead) or Batavian
  endive lettuce

1 bunch watercress
2 green-skinned apples, cored
  and sliced
3 celery sticks, sliced
60ml/4 tbsp sesame
  seeds, toasted
salt, freshly ground black pepper
  and grated nutmeg

For the dressing
75ml/5 tbsp groundnut (peanut)
  or sunflower oil
5ml/1 tsp sesame oil
45ml/3 tbsp lemon juice
10ml/2 tsp chopped fresh mint
3 drops Tabasco sauce

1 Place the chicken fillets in a shallow pan, cover with 300ml/ $^1/_2$ pint/1$^1/_4$ cups water, add the half stock cube and bring to the boil. Put the lid on the pan and simmer for 15 minutes. Drain, reserving the stock for another occasion, then cool the chicken under cold running water.

2 To make the dressing, put all the ingredients into a screw-top jar and shake vigorously. Cut the chicken, tongue and cheese into strips. Moisten with a little dressing and set aside.

3 Wash and spin dry the salad leaves and place in a large bowl. Add the apple and celery. Pour in some dressing and toss to coat thoroughly.

4 Distribute the salad leaves among four large plates. Pile the chicken, tongue and cheese in the centre, and sprinkle with toasted sesame seeds. Season with salt, freshly ground black pepper and grated nutmeg, and serve.

Chicken & Broccoli Salad

Gorgonzola makes a tangy dressing that goes well with both chicken and broccoli. Serve this salad for lunch or a light supper.

Serves 4
175g/6oz broccoli, divided into
   small florets
225g/8oz/2 cups farfalle
2 large cooked chicken
   breast portions
salt and freshly ground
   black pepper
fresh sage leaves, to garnish

For the dressing
90g/3½oz Gorgonzola cheese
15ml/1 tbsp white wine vinegar
60ml/4 tbsp extra virgin olive oil
2.5–5ml/½–1 tsp finely chopped
   fresh sage

1 Cook the broccoli florets in a large pan of boiling salted water for 3 minutes. Remove with a slotted spoon and rinse under cold running water, then spread out on kitchen paper to drain and dry.

2 Add the farfalle to the broccoli cooking water, then bring back to the boil and cook according to the packet instructions until *al dente*. When it is cooked, drain the pasta in a colander, rinse well under cold running water until cold, then allow to drain and dry, shaking the colander occasionally.

3 Remove the skin from the cooked chicken breast portions and cut the meat into bitesize pieces.

4 To make the dressing, put the cheese in a large bowl and mash with a fork, then whisk in the wine vinegar, followed by the oil, chopped sage, and salt and pepper to taste.

5 Add the pasta, chicken and broccoli to the bowl. Toss well, then taste and adjust the seasoning as necessary. Serve garnished with sage leaves.

Chicken & Pasta Salad

This is a delicious way to use up leftover cooked chicken and makes a really filling meal.

Serves 4
225g/8oz/2 cups tri-coloured
   pasta twists
30ml/2 tbsp bottled pesto sauce
15ml/1 tbsp olive oil
1 beefsteak tomato
225g/8oz cooked green beans
12 pitted black olives
350g/12oz cooked chicken, cubed
salt and freshly ground
   black pepper
fresh basil, to garnish

1 Cook the pasta in plenty of boiling salted water according to the packet instructions until *al dente*. Drain, rinse in plenty of cold running water, then drain again.

2 Put the pasta into a large bowl and stir in the pesto sauce and olive oil, mixing well.

3 Peel the tomato: place it in boiling water for about 10 seconds and then into cold water to loosen the skin, which you can then slip off easily. Cut the tomato into small cubes. Cut the green beans into 4cm/1½in lengths.

4 Add the tomato and beans to the pasta with the olives and seasoning to taste. Add the cubed chicken. Toss gently together and transfer to a serving platter. Garnish with basil and serve.

Penne Salad with Chicken & Peppers

A rainbow-hued salad that tastes as good as it looks.

Serves 4
350g/12oz/3 cups penne
45ml/3 tbsp olive oil
225g/8oz/1½ cups cooked
   chicken, cut into bitesize pieces
1 small red (bell) pepper, seeded
   and diced
1 small yellow (bell) pepper,
   seeded and diced
50g/2oz/½ cup pitted
   green olives
4 spring onions
   (scallions), chopped
45ml/3 tbsp mayonnaise
5ml/1 tsp Worcestershire sauce
15ml/1 tbsp wine vinegar
salt and freshly ground
   black pepper

1 Cook the pasta in a large pan of boiling salted water according to the packet instructions until *al dente*.
2 Drain and rinse under cold water. Drain again well and turn into a large bowl.
3 Toss with the olive oil and allow to cool completely.
4 Combine all the remaining ingredients, then mix into the pasta and serve immediately.

Turkey, Rice & Apple Salad

A flavoursome, healthy and crunchy salad to use up leftover turkey and fruit during the holiday festivities.

Serves 8

225g/8oz/1¼ cups brown rice
50g/2oz/⅓ cup wild rice
2 red-skinned apples, quartered, cored and chopped
2 celery sticks, coarsely sliced

115g/4oz seedless grapes
45ml/3 tbsp lemon or orange juice
150ml/¼ pint/⅔ cup thick mayonnaise
350g/12oz cooked turkey, chopped
salt and freshly ground black pepper
frisée lettuce leaves, to serve

1 Cook the brown and wild rice together in plenty of boiling salted water for about 30 minutes or until tender. Rinse under cold running water and drain thoroughly.

2 Turn the rice into a large bowl and add the apples, celery and grapes. In another bowl, beat the lemon or orange juice into the mayonnaise, season with salt and pepper, and pour over the rice, mixing thoroughly.

3 Add the cooked turkey and mix well to coat completely with the mayonnaise.

4 Arrange the lettuce over the bottom and around the sides of a large serving dish. Spoon the turkey and rice mixture on top and serve immediately.

Cook's Tip

This is a good choice for a summer buffet party, but keep the salad in the refrigerator until ready to serve.

Wild Rice & Turkey Salad

An attractive fanned pear garnish complements this salad, which is tossed in a walnut oil dressing.

Serves 4

175g/6oz/scant 1 cup wild rice, boiled or steamed
2 celery sticks, thinly sliced
50g/2oz spring onions (scallions), chopped

115g/4oz/1½ cups small button (white) mushrooms, quartered
450g/1lb cooked turkey breast, diced
120ml/4fl oz/½ cup ready-made French dressing
5ml/1 tsp fresh thyme leaves
2 pears, peeled, halved and cored
25g/1oz/¼ cup walnut pieces, toasted
fresh thyme sprigs, to garnish

1 Combine the cooled cooked wild rice with the celery, spring onions, mushrooms and turkey in a bowl.

2 Add the dressing and thyme leaves to the salad, and toss together well to mix.

3 Thinly slice the pear halves lengthways without cutting through the stalk end and spread the slices like a fan.

4 Divide the salad among four plates. Arrange a fanned pear half alongside each salad and sprinkle with walnuts. Garnish with thyme sprigs and serve.

Cooking Wild Rice

Although called "rice", this is actually an aquatic grass. Its deliciously nutty flavour and firm, chewy texture make it a perfect complement to many meat and poultry dishes. It is also an excellent partner for vegetables such as courgettes (zucchini) and mushrooms. It can be cooked like white rice, by boiling or steaming, needing only about 20 minutes longer cooking.

Warm Duck Salad with Orange

The distinct, sharp flavour of radicchio, frisée lettuce and fresh oranges is a perfect foil for the rich taste of duck. Serve with steamed new potatoes for an elegant main course.

Serves 4
2 duck breast fillets
2 oranges
frisée lettuce, radicchio and lamb's
    lettuce (corn salad) leaves
30ml/2 tbsp medium-dry sherry
10–15ml/2–3 tsp dark soy sauce
salt

1 Rub the skin of the duck breast fillets with salt and then slash the skin several times with a sharp knife.

2 Heat a heavy, cast-iron frying pan and fry the duck breasts, skin side down at first, for 20–25 minutes, turning once, until the skin is well browned and the flesh is cooked through. Transfer to a plate to cool slightly and pour off the excess fat from the pan, leaving behind the meat juices.

3 Peel the oranges. Separate the oranges into segments and use a sharp knife to remove all the pith, working over a small bowl to catch the juice.

4 Wash and spin dry the salad leaves and arrange in a wide, shallow serving bowl.

5 Heat the cooking juices remaining in the pan and stir in 45ml/3 tbsp of the reserved orange juice. Bring to the boil over a medium heat, add the sherry and then just enough soy sauce to give a piquant, spicy flavour.

6 Cut the duck into thin slices and arrange over the salad with the orange segments. Pour over the warm dressing and serve the salad immediately.

Apricot Duck with Fresh Beansprout Salad

The duck stays moist when cooked on a barbecue.

Serves 4
4 plump duck breast portions,
    with skin
1 small red onion, thinly sliced
115g/4oz/ ½ cup ready-to-eat
    dried apricots
15ml/1 tbsp clear honey
5ml/1 tsp sesame oil
10ml/2 tsp ground star anise
salt and freshly ground
    black pepper

For the salad
½ head Chinese leaves, (Chinese
    cabbage) finely shredded
150g/5oz/3 cups beansprouts
2 spring onions
    (scallions), shredded

For the dressing
15ml/1 tbsp light soy sauce
15ml/1 tbsp groundnut
    (peanut) oil
5ml/1 tsp sesame oil
5ml/1 tsp clear honey

1 Place a duck breast portion, skin side down, on a board and cut a long slit down one side, cutting not quite through, to form a large pocket. Tuck some slices of onion and apricots inside the pocket and press the meat firmly back into shape. Secure with a metal skewer. Repeat with the other breast portions.

2 Mix together the honey and sesame oil, and brush over the duck. Sprinkle over the ground star anise and season with salt and pepper.

3 To make the salad, mix together the shredded Chinese leaves, beansprouts and spring onions in a bowl.

4 To make the dressing, put all the ingredients in a screw-top jar with salt and pepper to taste and shake vigorously. Toss into the salad, mixing well.

5 Cook the duck over a medium-hot barbecue for about 12–15 minutes, turning once, until golden brown on the outside and cooked through. Divide the salad among four plates, place a duck breast portion on top of each salad and serve.

Choosing a Chicken

When choosing a fresh chicken for cooking, it should have a plump breast and the skin should be creamy in colour. The tip of the breastbone should be pliable when pressed. A bird's dressed weight is taken after plucking and drawing, and may include the giblets (neck, gizzard, heart and liver). A frozen chicken must be thawed slowly in the refrigerator or a cool room before cooking. Never try to thaw it in hot water, as this will toughen the flesh.

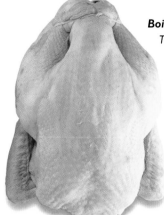

Boilers
These are about 12 months and over, and weigh 2–3kg/ 4¹/₂–6¹/₂ lb. They require long, slow cooking, around 2–3 hours, to make them tender.

Corn-fed Chickens
These are free-range birds and are generally more expensive. They usually weigh 1.2–1.5kg/ 2¹/₂–3¹/₂ lb.

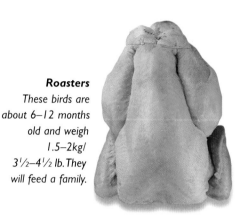

Roasters
These birds are about 6–12 months old and weigh 1.5–2kg/ 3¹/₂–4¹/₂ lb. They will feed a family.

Spring Chickens
These birds are about 3 months old and weigh 900g–1.2kg/ 2–2¹/₂ lb. They will serve 3–4 people.

Double Poussins
These are 8–10 weeks old and weigh 800–900g/1³/₄–2lb They will serve 2 people. Poussins are best roasted, grilled (broiled) or pot-roasted.

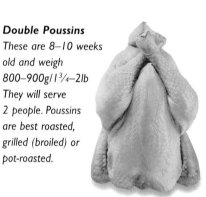

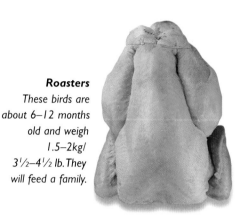

Poussins
These are 4–6 weeks old and weigh 450–500g/1–1¹/₄ lb. They are sufficient for one person.

Cuts of Chicken

Chicken pieces today are available pre-packaged in a variety of different ways. If you do not want to buy a whole bird, you can choose from the many selected cuts on the market. Most cooking methods are suitable for all cuts, but some are especially suited to specific cuts of meat. These are ideal for frying, grilling (broiling) and barbecuing.

Skinless Boneless Thigh
This makes tasks such as stuffing and rolling much quicker, as it is already skinned and jointed.

Liver
This makes a wonderful addition to pâtés or to salads.

Minced Chicken
This is not so strongly flavoured as minced (ground) beef, but may be used as a substitute.

Leg
The leg comprises the thigh and drumstick. Large pieces with bones, such as this, are suitable for slow-cooking, such as casseroling or poaching.

Wing
The wing does not supply much meat. It is often barbecued (grilled) or fried.

Drumstick
The drumstick is a firm favourite for barbecuing (grilling) or frying, either in batter or rolled in breadcrumbs.

Breast Portion
This comprises tender white meat and can be simply cooked in butter, as well as stuffed.

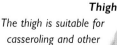

Thigh
The thigh is suitable for casseroling and other slow-cooking methods.

Techniques

Cutting up a Chicken

For recipes that call for chicken cuts, it is often cheaper to buy a whole chicken and cut it up yourself, particularly if you are cooking for a large number of people. It is important to have a portion of bone with the wing and breast joints, otherwise the flesh shrinks during cooking.

1 Hold the leg firmly with one hand. Using a sharp knife, cut the skin between the leg and breast.

2 Then press the leg down to expose the ball-and-socket joint, cut or break the joint apart and cut down towards the parson's nose (tail).

3 Turn the chicken over and loosen the "oyster" from the underside (this lies embedded alongside the backbone). Repeat with the other leg.

4 Now, with your finger, feel for the end of the breastbone, and, using a sharp knife, cut diagonally through the flesh to the rib cage.

5 Using strong kitchen scissors, cut through the rib cage and wishbone, separating the two wing joints.

6 Twist the wing tip and tuck it under the breast meat so that the cut is held flat. This will ensure that it has a good shape for cooking.

7 Using strong kitchen scissors, cut the breast meat from the carcass in a single piece. (All that remains of the carcass is half of the rib cage and the backbone.)

8 The legs can be cut in half through the joint to give a thigh joint and a drumstick. The breast can also be cut into two pieces through the breastbone.

Spatchcocking a Chicken

This is a good way to prepare chickens for grilling (broiling) or barbecuing, especially the smaller sizes of bird, such as poussins. By removing their backbones, poussins can be opened out and then flattened ready for even and fast cooking.

1 Using a very sharp pair of kitchen scissors, cut the poussin on either side of its backbone.

2 Flatten the bird with the palm of your hand or a rolling pin. Turn it over and cut away the fine rib cage, leaving the rest of the carcass intact to hold its shape. Thread thin skewers through the wings.

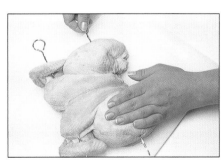

3 Then thread thin skewers through the legs to hold them in position and keep the bird flat. Brush liberally with melted butter. It will take 10–15 minutes on each side, depending on the heat.

Stuffing a Chicken

Stuffing helps to keep chickens moist during cooking, which is important because they have very little fat. The stuffing also helps to make the meal go further. There are many different flavours of stuffing that may be used to enhance the taste of chicken, without detracting from its own delicate flavour. Bread, rice or potatoes can be used as the basis to which other ingredients may be added. Fat is important in stuffing because it prevents it from becoming dry and crumbly.

1 Stuff only the small neck-end of the chicken and not the large cavity inside the carcass, as the heat from the oven will not penetrate all the way through the chicken. Any leftover stuffing should be made into small balls and fried separately or put into a shallow, buttered ovenproof dish, baked in the oven with the chicken and cut into squares for serving with the chicken.

2 Never pack the stuffing too tightly, as breadcrumbs will expand during cooking and this may cause the skin to burst open. The flap of neck skin should then be tucked under the chicken and secured with the wing tips or sewn into place with a needle and fine trussing thread. Remember to weigh the chicken after it has been stuffed to calculate the cooking time accurately.

Casseroling

This slow-cooking method is good for large cuts of chicken with bones, or more mature meat.

1 Heat some olive oil in a flameproof casserole and fry the chicken joints until they are browned on all sides.

2 Add stock, wine or a mixture of both to a depth of 2.5cm/1in. Add seasonings and herbs, cover and cook on the hob (stovetop) or in the oven for 1½ hours or until the chicken is tender.

3 Add a selection of lightly fried vegetables such as button (pearl) onions, mushrooms, carrots and small new potatoes about halfway through the cooking time.

Braising

This method can be used for whole chickens or pieces and is ideal for strongly flavoured meat.

1 Heat some olive oil in a flameproof casserole and lightly fry a whole bird or chicken pieces until golden on all sides.

2 Remove the chicken from the casserole and fry 450g/1lb diced vegetables, such as carrots, onions, celery and turnips, until soft.

3 Replace the chicken, cover with a tight lid and cook very slowly on the hob (stovetop) or in the oven, preheated to 160°C/325°F/Gas 3, until tender.

Carving a Chicken

It is best to allow the chicken to stand (or "rest") for 10–15 minutes before carving (while the gravy is being made). This allows the meat to relax, so the flesh will not tear while carving. Use a sharp carving knife and work on a plate that will catch any juices that can be added to the gravy. The leg can be cut into two for a thigh and a drumstick.

1 Hold the chicken firmly with a carving fork, between the breast and one of the legs, down to the backbone. Cut the skin around the opposite leg, press gently outwards to expose the ball-and-socket joint and cut through. Slip the knife under the back to remove the "oyster" with the leg.

2 With the knife at the top end of the breastbone, cut down parallel on one side of the wishbone to take a good slice of breast meat with the wing joint.

3 With the knife at the end of the breastbone, cut down the front of the carcass, removing the wishbone. Carve the remaining breast into slices.

Chicken Stock

A good chicken stock is called for in many dishes, so make a large quantity and freeze it in small batches.

1 onion
4 cloves
1 carrot
2 leeks
2 celery sticks
1 chicken carcass, cooked or raw
bouquet garni
8 black peppercorns
2.5ml/ ½ tsp salt

1 Peel the onion, cut into quarters and spike each quarter with a clove. Scrub and roughly chop the other vegetables.

2 Break up the chicken carcass into several pieces and place in a large pan with the remaining ingredients.

3 Cover with 1.75 litres/3 pints/7½ cups water. Bring to the boil, skim and simmer, partially covered, for 2 hours. Strain the stock and allow to cool. When cold, remove the hardened fat before using.

How to Make Gravy

After roasting, transfer the chicken to a serving dish and remove any trussing string. Cover loosely with foil and leave to rest in a warm place before carving. Meanwhile, spoon the fat from the juices left in the roasting pan. Stirring constantly, blend 15ml/ 1 tbsp plain (all-purpose) flour into the juices and cook gently on the hob (stovetop) until golden brown. Add 300ml/½ pint/1¼ cups chicken stock or vegetable cooking water and bring to the boil, to thicken. Season to taste. Strain into a jug or gravy boat.

Roasting Times for Poultry

Note: Birds should be weighed after stuffing.

Poussin	450–675g/1–1½lb	1–1¼ hours at 180°C/350°F/Gas 4
Chicken	1.2–1.3kg/2½–3lb	1–1¼ hours at 190°C/375°F/Gas 5
	1.5–1.75kg/3½–4lb	1¼–1¾ hours at 190°C/375°F/Gas 5
	2–2.25kg/4½–5lb	1½–2 hours at 190°C/375°F/Gas 5
	2.25–2.75kg/5–6lb	1¾–2½ hours at 190°C/375°F/Gas 5
Duck	1.3–2.25kg/3–5lb	1¾–2¼ hours at 200°C/400°F/Gas 6
Goose	3.6–4.5kg/8–10lb	2½–3 hours at 180°C/350°F/Gas 4
	4.5–5.4kg/10–12lb	3–3½ hours at 180°C/350°F/Gas 4
Turkey *(whole bird)*	2.75–3.6kg/6–8lb	3–3½ hours at 160°C/325°F/Gas 3
	3.6–5.4kg/8–12lb	3–4 hours at 160°C/325°F/Gas 3
	5.4–7.2kg/12–16lb	4–5 hours at 160°C/325°F/Gas 3
Turkey *(whole breast)*	1.75–2.75kg/4–6lb	1½–2¼ hours at 160°C/325°F/Gas 3
	2.75–3.6kg/6–8lb	2¼–3¼ hours at 160°C/325°F/Gas 3

Index

A

Almonds: chicken with burnt almond stuffing, 66
Anita Wong's duck, 58
Apples: pheasant with, 58
roast goose with, 76
roast goose with caramelized apples, 76
Apricots: apricot duck with fresh beansprout salad, 89
chicken & apricot filo pie, 27
curried apricot & chicken casserole, 30
duckling jubilee, 73
herbed chicken with apricot & pecan potato baskets, 36
poussins with courgette & apricot stuffing, 70
spiced chicken & apricot pie, 30

Asian duck consommé, 13
Asparagus: chicken with, 52
Aubergines: with sesame chicken, 21
Avocados: chicken & avocado mayonnaise, 18
lemon chicken with guacamole sauce, 46

B

Bacon: chicken, bacon & walnut terrine, 16
chicken, leek & bacon casserole, 38

Badacsonyi wine, chicken in, 29
Beef: chicken roulé, 66
steamboat, 37
Bell peppers, see Peppers
Bisteeya, 29
Blueberries, stir-fried duck with, 49
Boilers, 90
Bouchée, chicken, 28
Braising, 92
Bread: roast chicken with herb & orange bread stuffing, 69
Breast portions, 90
Broccoli: chicken & broccoli salad, 87
chicken & ham with green vegetables, 39
Bulgur wheat, poussins with vermouth &, 68
Butter, clarified, 14

C

Canapés, spicy chicken, 18
Cannelloni: rolled stuffed cannelloni, 42
Capers, turkey escalopes with, 57
Carving chicken, 93
Casseroles & stews, 92
Celeriac, roast chicken with, 69
Cheese: chicken Cordon Bleu, 53
chicken roulé, 66
chicken with prosciutto & cheese, 41
lasagne, 42
Parmesan chicken bake, 43
Swiss cheese, chicken & tongue salad, 86
Chestnuts: cold sliced roast chicken, 67
duck & chestnut casserole, 40
duck with chestnut sauce, 48
Chianti, chicken with, 33
Chickpeas: chicken kdra with chickpeas & almonds, 34

Lebanese-style chicken soup, 10
Cigars, chicken, 21
Cold sliced roast chicken, 67
Cooking techniques, 92
Coq au vin, 31
Cordon Bleu chicken, 53
Corn-fed chickens, 90
Coronation chicken, 86
Courgettes: poussins with courgette & apricot stuffing, 70
Couscous: poussins with courgette & apricot stuffing, 70
seven-vegetable, 60
Cranberries: chicken salad with cranberry dressing, 81
Cream sauce, stuffed chicken breast fillets with, 35
Croquettes, chicken, 22
Croûte, chicken en, 27
Curries: coronation chicken, 86
curried apricot & chicken casserole, 30
curry mayonnaise, 18
Cuts of chicken, 90
Cutting up a chicken, 91

D

Dijon chicken salad, 84
Drumsticks, 90
Drunken chicken, 37
Duck: Anita Wong's duck, 58
apricot duck, 89
Asian duck consommé, 13
duck & chestnut casserole, 40

duck with a walnut & pomegranate sauce, 59
duck risotto, 61
duck stew with olives, 40
duckling jubilee, 73
Peruvian duck with rice, 61
roast duckling with honey, 74
roast wild duck with juniper, 74
roasted duckling on a bed of honeyed potatoes, 75
roasting times, 93
stir-fried duck with blueberries, 49
warm duck salad with orange, 89
wild duck roasted with morels & Madeira, 73
with chestnut sauce, 48
with orange sauce, 75
with peppercorns, 55

E

Eggplant, see Aubergines

F

Figs: chicken casserole with spiced figs, 33
turkey with fig, orange & mint marmalade, 56
Fish: steamboat, 37
French chicken salad, 84
Fricassées: chicken fricassée forestier, 31
old-fashioned chicken fricassée, 32
Fruit: chicken & fruit salad, 83

G

Garlic: chicken with 40 cloves of garlic, 65

Goose: roast goose with
apples, 76
roast goose with
caramelized apples, 76
roasting times, 93
Goujons, chicken, 22
Grapes: chicken with, 54
turkey with wine &, 57
Gravy, 93
Guacamole sauce, lemon
chicken with, 46

H
Ham: chicken & ham with
green vegetables, 39
Hazelnut dressing, warm
chicken salad with, 82
Honey: roast duckling
with, 74
roasted duckling on a
bed of honeyed
potatoes, 75

K
Kiev, chicken, 50
Kotopitta, 28

L
Lamb: seven-vegetable
couscous, 60
Lasagne, 42
Lavender: chicken salad
with sweet herbs &, 85
lavender chicken, 35
Lebanese-style chicken
soup, 10
Leeks: chicken, leek & bacon
casserole, 38
Legs, 90
Lemon: chicken with
preserved lemon &
olives, 34
lemon & tarragon chicken
salad, 81

lemon chicken with
guacamole sauce, 46
Lentils: turkey & lentil
soup, 13
Liver, 90
chicken liver mousse, 15
chicken liver pâté, 14
chicken liver pâté with
Marsala, 14
chicken liver risotto, 59
chicken livers in
sherry, 19
pan-fried chicken liver
salad, 80
polenta with, 19
Lockshen, chicken soup
with, 12

M
Mangetouts: warm chicken
salad with shallots &, 80
Marsala cream sauce, turkey
with, 56
Maryland salad, 85
Matzo kleis balls, chicken
soup with, 12
Mayonnaise: chicken &
avocado mayonnaise, 18
curry mayonnaise, 18
Mexican chicken
soup, 10
Minced chicken, 90
Minestrone, rich, 11
Minty yogurt
chicken, 46
Morels, chicken with, 51
Moroccan roast
chicken, 65
Mousse, chicken liver, 15
Mushrooms: chicken &
mushroom terrine, 16
chicken fricassée
forestier, 31
chicken in Badacsonyi
wine, 29

chicken with morels, 51
chicken with wild
mushrooms &
vermouth, 55
coq au vin, 31
mushroom picker's
chicken paella, 60
roast chicken stuffed with
forest mushrooms, 64
wild duck roasted with
morels & Madeira, 73

O
Old-fashioned chicken
fricassée, 32
Old-fashioned chicken
pie, 26
Olive oil roasted chicken
with Mediterranean
vegetables, 64
Olives: chicken with
preserved lemon &, 34
chicken with white wine,
garlic &, 52
duck stew with, 40
Onions: whisky chicken with
onion marmalade, 70
Orange: duck with orange
sauce, 75
orange chicken salad, 83
warm duck salad
with, 89

P
Paella: mushroom picker's
chicken, 60
Pan-fried chicken liver
salad, 80
Parmesan chicken
bake, 43
Pasta: basic dough, 23
chicken & pasta salad, 87
chicken stellette soup, 10
pasta bonbons, 23
Pâtés: chicken liver, 14
chicken liver with
Marsala, 14
chicken & pistachio, 15
Peanut butter: peanut
chicken salad in a
pineapple boat, 82
Penne: penne salad with
chicken & peppers, 87
Peppercorns, duck with, 55

Peppers, penne salad with
chicken &, 87
Persian chicken with walnut
sauce, 41
Peruvian duck with rice, 61
Pheasant: in green pipian
sauce, 77
pheasant with apples, 58
roast pheasant with
port, 77
Pies: bisteeya, 29
chicken & apricot filo
pie, 27
chicken bouchée, 28
chicken cigars, 21
chicken en croûte, 27
kotopitta, 28
old-fashioned chicken
pie, 26
spiced chicken & apricot
pie, 30
traditional chicken pie, 26
Pineapple: peanut chicken
salad in a pineapple
boat, 82

Pistachio: chicken &
pistachio pâté, 15
Polenta with chicken livers, 19
Pork: chicken & pork
terrine, 17
steamboat, 37
Potatoes: herbed chicken
with apricot & pecan
potato baskets, 36
roasted duckling on a
bed of honeyed
potatoes, 75
Potted chicken, 16
Poussins, 90
baby chickens with lime
& chilli, 48
baked poussins, 43
pan-fried marinated
poussin, 51

poussins with
citrus glaze, 47
spatchcocked
poussins, 47
roasting times, 93
with bulgur wheat &
vermouth, 68
with courgette & apricot
stuffing, 70
with raisin-walnut
stuffing, 68
Prawns: chicken
Marengo, 50
steamboat, 37
Prosciutto, chicken with
cheese &, 41
Prunes: turkey with sage,
brandy &, 49
Pumpkin seeds: pheasant
in green pipian
sauce, 77

R
Rice: mushroom picker's
chicken paella, 60
orange chicken salad, 83
Peruvian duck with
rice, 61
stuffed chicken rolls, 38
turkey, rice & apple
salad, 88
see also risotto
Risotto: chicken liver, 59
duck, 61
Roasting times, 93
Roasters, 90
Roulades, chicken, 20
Roulé, chicken, 66

S
Salads: apricot duck with
fresh beansprout
salad, 89
chicken & broccoli
salad, 87

chicken & fruit salad, 83
chicken & pasta salad, 87
chicken salad with
cranberry dressing, 81
chicken salad
with sweet herbs &
lavender, 85
Dijon chicken salad, 84
French chicken salad, 84
lemon & tarragon
chicken salad, 81
Maryland salad, 85
orange chicken salad, 83
pan-fried chicken liver
salad, 80
peanut chicken salad in a
pineapple boat, 82
penne salad with chicken
& peppers, 87
Swiss cheese, chicken &
tongue salad, 86
turkey, rice & apple
salad, 88
warm chicken salad with
hazelnut dressing, 82
warm chicken salad with
sesame & coriander
dressing, 81
warm chicken salad with
shallots &
mangetouts, 80
warm duck salad with
orange, 89
wild rice & turkey
salad, 88
Salt crust, chicken baked
in a, 71
Sauces: fresh tomato, 19
gravy, 93
Sesame & coriander
dressing, warm chicken
salad with, 81
Seven-vegetable
couscous, 60
Shallots, chicken with, 32
Shrimps, see Prawns
Sloe gin, chicken with
juniper &, 36
Sour cream dip, turkey
sticks with, 23
Soy sauce: soy-braised
chicken, 39
Snowpeas, see Mangetouts
Spatchcocking a chicken, 91

Spinach: chicken
roulades, 20
Spring chickens, 90
Spring rolls, mini, 20
Steamboat, 37
Stellette soup, chicken, 10
Stock, 93
Stuffed chicken rolls, 38
Stuffings, 92
Sweetcorn: Maryland
salad, 85
Swiss cheese, chicken &
tongue salad, 86

T
Tarragon chicken, 54
Techniques, 91–93
Terrines: chicken &
mushroom, 16
chicken & pork, 17
chicken, bacon &
walnut, 16
turkey, juniper & green
peppercorn, 17
Thighs, 90
Tomatoes: chicken in a
tomato coat, 67
chicken Marengo, 50
fresh tomato sauce, 19
Tongue: Swiss cheese,
chicken & tongue
salad, 86
Traditional chicken
pie, 26
Turkey: roast turkey, 71
roasting times, 93
turkey & lentil soup, 13
turkey escalopes with
capers, 57
turkey, juniper & green
peppercorn
terrine, 17
turkey, rice & apple
salad, 88
turkey sticks with sour
cream dip, 23
turkey with wine
& grapes, 57
turkey zador with
mlinces, 72
vine-leaf wrapped turkey
with Noilly Prat, 72
wild rice & turkey
salad, 88

with fig, orange & mint
marmalade, 56
with Marsala cream
sauce, 56
with sage, prunes &
brandy, 49

V
Vegetables: Mediterranean
vegetables, 64
rich minestrone, 11
seven-vegetable
couscous, 60
Vermicelli: chicken soup
with, 11
chicken soup with
lockshen, 12

Vine-leaf wrapped turkey
with Noilly Prat, 72
Vinegar: chicken with red
wine vinegar, 53

W
Walnuts: chicken, bacon &
walnut terrine, 16
duck with a walnut &
pomegranate sauce, 59
Persian chicken with
walnut sauce, 41
Whisky chicken with onion
marmalade, 70
Wild rice & turkey salad, 88
Wings, 90

Y
Yogurt: minty yogurt
chicken, 46

Z
Zucchini, see Courgettes